Coleridge, Lamb, Hazlitt, and the Reader of Drama

The Play Scene from "Hamlet" (1842), a painting by Daniel Maclise,
courtesy of the Tate Gallery, London.

Coleridge, Lamb, Hazlitt,

and the

Reader of Drama

Janet Ruth Heller

University of Missouri Press
Columbia and London

Copyright © 1990 by
The Curators of the University of Missouri
University of Missouri Press, Columbia, Missouri 65201
Printed and bound in the United States of America
All rights reserved
5 4 3 2 1   94 93 92 91 90

Library of Congress Cataloging-in-Publication Data

Heller, Janet Ruth.
    Coleridge, Lamb, Hazlitt, and the Reader of Drama / Janet
Ruth Heller.
        p.   cm.
    Bibliography: p.
    ISBN 0-8262-0718-9 (alk. paper)
    1. Dramatic criticism—Great Britain—History—19th century.
2. English drama—History and criticism. I. Title.
PN1707.H45   1989
822'.709—dc20   89-4841
                                                               CIP

Designer: Kristie Lee
Typesetter: Connell-Zeko Type & Graphics
Printer: Thomson-Shore, Inc.
Binder: Thomson-Shore, Inc.
Type face: Palatino

To all the friends and relatives who
encouraged me while I worked on this book.

Contents

Acknowledgments

I am grateful to Stuart M. Tave and Elizabeth K. Helsinger, who have painstakingly read and commented on all the drafts of these chapters. I am also grateful to Michael Krischer, Susan Noakes, Perry Gethner, Diana Postlethwaite, and Allon Fisher, who have offered suggestions for further reading, for clarifying my argument, and for eliminating digressions.

The staffs of the Rare Book Room and the Interlibrary Loan Department at the University of Chicago and Northern Illinois University have been extremely helpful in obtaining eighteenth- and nineteenth-century books. I am indebted to the staff at the Newberry Library and to my typist, Joan Allman. Editor Wendy Warnken, Managing Editor Jane Lago, and Associate Director Susan McGregor Denny of the University of Missouri Press have been extremely helpful in shepherding my manuscript through the process of publication.

I am also grateful to Oliver Evans and William Irwin of Nazareth College for giving me the opportunity to revise my book during the fall of 1988.

The moral support of friends and family members was invaluable as I traced the history of the bias against spectacle in Great Britain. I would especially like to thank my husband, Michael Krischer; my parents, Joan Pereles Heller and William C. Heller, Jr.; and my grandmother, Ruth Rosenberg Pereles (may her memory be a blessing).

Portions of Chapter 1 of this book appeared in 1982 as an article in *The Eighteenth Century*. Earlier versions of Chapter 4 and Chapter 5 were published in 1983 and 1987 in *The Charles Lamb Bulletin*.

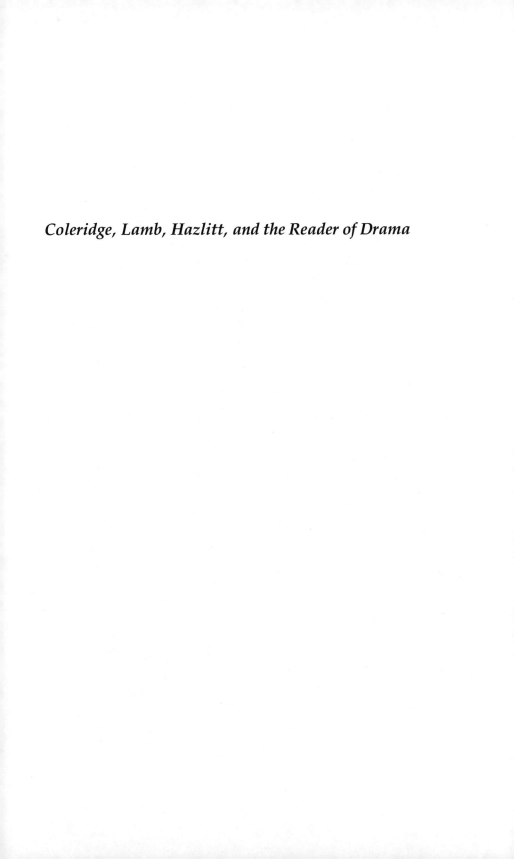

Coleridge, Lamb, Hazlitt, and the Reader of Drama

Introduction

Whenever S. T. Coleridge saw a performance of Shakespeare's tragedies, he felt "pain, disgust, and indignation." The proper place for these dramas was "in the heart and in the closet." Charles Lamb experienced the same emotions when King Lear appeared on stage: "the Lear of Shakspeare cannot be acted. . . . The play is beyond all art." Similarly, William Hazlitt wrote in one review, "The reader of the plays of Shakespear is almost always disappointed in seeing them acted; and, for our own parts, we should never go to see them acted, if we could help it."[1]

Most twentieth-century critics are dismayed by this vehement condemnation of stage spectacle. They view Lamb, Coleridge, and Hazlitt as eccentric and explain that the oversized theaters and stylized acting of the last century provoked the romantics' bias. For example, J. R. de J. Jackson argues that Coleridge's "statements of antipathy to the stage are only relevant to the peculiar conditions of the early nineteenth century." Similarly, Joan Coldwell contends, "Lamb bases a weak argument on the experience of unfortunate productions." Jonas Barish goes even further, condemning the "romantic incomprehension of the stage."[2]

While it is true that the cavernous theaters and stylized acting of the era handicapped performances, the commentary of the romantics goes far beyond technical matters of stage movement and scenery. Writers such as Lamb, Coleridge, and Hazlitt argue that the experience of reading drama, especially tragedy, stimulates the imagination more than witnessing a performance, regardless of the quality of the representation. Furthermore, the romantics' objections to performance were not new or eccentric in the 1800s, and these scholars and theatergoers were not writing in ignorance of the stage. *Coleridge, Lamb, Hazlitt, and the Reader of Drama* is a reevaluation of romantic drama criticism that puts their writings in the context of literary history of ideas.

In this book, I will use the term *romantic* to refer to early nineteenth-century British writers, including Coleridge, Lamb, Hazlitt, and Shelley. This label will not be used to mean the manifestations of passionate love. Because the above writers did not use *romantic* to refer to themselves and because it is a convenient label rather than a precise category, I have chosen not to capitalize this word.

In Chapter 1, I trace the history of the bias against stage spectacle, focusing on British writers of the eighteenth century, who frequently debated the issue. My basic contention is that the romantics were influenced by an established and intellectually justifiable tradition in drama criticism. Some of the bias against performance arose from misinterpretations of Aristotle's *Poetics*. In this work, Aristotle maintains that spectacle is the least important aspect of a performed tragedy and that hearing an oral recitation of a play is an equally meaningful experience. However, later commentators argue that spectacle degrades the literary text.

Horace's condemnation in the *Epistles* of those who demand a visually sumptuous representation was also influential. He was among the first to argue that readers make a better audience for good drama than spectators do. Many Renaissance and seventeenth-century dramatists in England also viewed the reading public as more sophisticated and better able to appreciate the virtues of their plays than the theater audience. The prefaces of Ben Jonson and John Dryden often attack stage spectacle.

Some contemporary British clergymen objected to the theater because they believed that licentious drama would encourage immorality. For example, Jeremy Collier condemned many plays as lewd, blasphemous, and devoid of poetic justice.

During the Restoration, managers of public theaters increased the size of the theaters and began to emphasize elaborate spectacles to attract larger audiences. Both of these trends continued in the eighteenth and nineteenth centuries. Reacting to the new spectacles, literary critics and playwrights such as Richard Flecknoe, Joseph Addison, Oliver Goldsmith, and Richard Brinsley Sheridan condemned productions that emphasized scenery, costumes, and music more than literary substance. To such writers, pantomimes represented the ultimate degradation of the stage because the elaborate spectacles and the action, which included acrobatic stunts, violence, and defecation, were often more important than the language of the skit. Some pantomimes were even silent. Critics preferred sophisticated poetry, witty dialogue, and psychological probing of the main characters.

Drama critics also attacked the taste of the theater audience and blamed certain groups of spectators, especially the lower and middle classes, for the overuse of scenery, acrobatics, low comedy, and extraneous pageants. Publishers began to market "poetic plays" designed solely for readers. Many writers agreed with Henry Fielding that these closet dramas were wittier and more meaningful than staged plays.

Eighteenth- and nineteenth-century idolatry of Shakespeare's artistry added to the hostility toward performances. Critics insisted that Shakespeare deserved a reverent close reading, and they scorned the shortened, rearranged, adulterated, and spectacular acting versions of his plays. Commentators also worried about the tendency of a famous actor's performance to eclipse a good playwright's use of language and wit. Thomas Rymer, Goldsmith, and Sheridan contended that the power of star actors would threaten literary excellence.

Like their predecessors, the romantics emphasized the dangers of spectacle and the primacy of language and of readers. This continuity has often been overlooked by later writers. Instead of viewing Coleridge and his contemporaries as isolated extremists, the twentieth-century scholar should place the romantics' essays in their historical context to assess objectively their contributions to drama criticism.

In Chapter 2, I examine the relationship between the romantics' assault on the senses and their bias against stage spectacle. Again, their allegedly eccentric position has classical roots. Plato argues in the *Phaedo* that sense perception confuses and pollutes the soul, while philosophical reasoning purifies the soul and enables it to attain true wisdom by means of intellectual principles. Anyone who relies on the five senses to reveal the truth cannot apprehend philosophic concepts, which are not palpable and require mental agility. Later writers like Francis Bacon and Joseph Addison value literature and other imaginative experiences that subordinate external appearances to ideas and that help people transcend their senses and their egos. The German philosophers Immanuel Kant and Friedrich Schiller also seek ways to bridge the gap between the senses and the intellect. Schiller contends that an aesthetic education enables a person to proceed from mere passive sensation to active logical and moral thought. Kant especially values contemplation of the sublime because it evokes a mental faculty capable of transcending the senses.

The British romantics, except for Shelley and Keats, retain Plato's distrust of the senses and continue Kant and Schiller's attempts to explain how one can move from reliance on the senses to analytic thought and morality. Coleridge, Lamb, and Hazlitt believe that great literature helps people to transcend their senses because it engages the intellect by means of well-chosen images and significant unifying ideas. In contrast, bad literature presents an overly detailed "copy" of nature that appeals only to the senses. Performances of good dramas, especially tragedies, demean the text because the words and ideas are lost in a profusion of spectacle that assaults the senses and deadens the mind. However, the act of reading plays allows the "abstraction," the distance from sense perception, needed for the unhampered activity of the imagination. The romantics view themselves as teachers and friends of the reading public who can help contemporaries overcome their addiction to the five senses and teach them to think more dynamically.

Chapters 3, 4, and 5 are devoted to the drama criticism of Coleridge, Hazlitt, and Lamb. These authors portray the reader as an active participant in the process of interpreting literature, and they compare the reader's imaginative powers to those of great writers. The romantics feel that performance frustrates the audience by making it passive. Detailed analyses of selected texts illustrate the romantics' interest in their own reading public and their attempts to broaden the reader's imaginative and analytic powers.

Coleridge, especially, sees himself as an educator, and his essays about education are closely related to his lectures on Shakespeare. Coleridge insists that students should thoroughly understand underlying concepts rather than simply memorize facts. True learning enables a student to apply basic principles creatively to new situations. Unlike John Locke, who believed that teachers should appeal to the senses of children by using concrete objects, Coleridge argues that appeals to the senses are wrongheaded because they frustrate the development of abstract thought. Students will never be capable of abstraction if they think that knowledge must be palpable. In general, Coleridge worries that his contemporaries' overreliance on sense impressions has made most people mentally lazy and unwilling to analyze ideas independently.

He values the study of language and literature because these disciplines develop a person's capacity to contemplate abstract ideas and develop one's sympathy for other people, thus fostering human nobility. Just as good students must actively try to apply the intellectual principles that they are learning, good readers must exert themselves to understand the complex works of great writers like Shakespeare.

Coleridge is especially interested in how Shakespeare's opening scenes (1) embody the play's central idea, (2) move the reader from normal consciousness to an imaginative state, and (3) persuade the reader to participate in the dramatic illusion. For these reasons, Coleridge devotes a large percentage of his lectures on drama to an examination of Shakespeare's first acts.

Coleridge designs his own writings to change his readers and students by activating their minds. He uses questions in his lectures and essays to focus the audience's attention on important critical issues or dramatic problems. Instead of presenting detailed explications of literary texts, Coleridge tries to illustrate basic principles and relies on his audience to reflect on the matter and to draw additional conclusions. This emphasis on principles is designed to wean the public from overreliance on the senses. Coleridge's insistence on the creative application of basic principles instead of the memorization of isolated facts anticipates the work of twentieth-century educators such as Alfred North Whitehead and Jerome S. Bruner.

Critics have alleged that Hazlitt's essays are disorganized and overly subjective. However, when one examines books like *Characters of Shakespear's Plays,* it is clear that Hazlitt uses his personal responses to dramas and a special rhetorical structure to help the reader identify with tragic heroes and to arouse the reader's enthusiasm and sympathetic imagination. His favorite tragedies include *Hamlet* and *Othello,* which deeply involve the reader in the protagonists' sufferings and evoke the imagination, because these dramas allow the reader to escape selfishness and egotism. He finds that Shakespeare's poetic imagery and complex characterization are lost when the plays are staged: theaters reduce drama to the level of pantomime.

Chapter 5 relates Lamb's literary criticism to the work of reader-response critics such as Stanley Fish, Walter Slatoff, and Wolfgang Iser. Like these twentieth-century critics, Lamb is interested in the demands that poets and novelists make on the reading public. Lamb's exploration of the unwritten contract between authors and readers stresses the mutual respect and the creative effort that both parties must bring to literature. Unlike most twentieth-century commentators, who view drama as solely a performing art, Lamb examines the reactions of readers to plays. For example, in "On the Tragedies of Shakspeare, Considered with Reference to their Fitness for Stage Representation," he contrasts the reader's imaginative freedom when reading drama to the more superficial and limited response of the spectator. Lamb's argument that the theater overwhelms the senses with specific pictorial images and obscures the intellectual meaning of tragedies anticipates the film criticism of Siegfried Kracauer and Seymour Chatman.

Many nineteenth-century writers besides Coleridge, Lamb, and Hazlitt manifest the ambivalence toward spectacle that runs through British drama criticism. The final chapter examines the works of Percy

B. Shelley, G. H. Lewes, Henry James, Matthew Arnold, John Ruskin, G. B. Shaw, Oscar Wilde, and W. B. Yeats, among others. Victorian writers both praise and attack advances in stage technology and lighting that make increasingly realistic sets possible. These critics also discuss the public's demand for historically correct scenery and costumes. In general, writers such as Lewes, Shaw, Wilde, and Yeats have more faith than the romantics in the ability of "beautiful" and well-designed scenery and properties to stimulate the audience's aesthetic taste and receptivity to literature. Furthermore, these later critics directly challenge the bias against spectacle and the belief that Shakespeare's best work suffers on stage. They contend that drama should involve the whole man or woman, mind and senses, and that performance is useful in achieving this total engagement.

1. The Bias against Spectacle in Tragedy
The History of an Idea

Classical Sources

The writings of Plato and Aristotle contain many concepts that directly or indirectly apply to the staging of drama. Greek writers were studied at the best seventeenth- and eighteenth-century British schools, and works such as the *Poetics* were sometimes dissected.[1] Englishmen who did not know Greek could read the classics in translation: for example, English versions of the *Poetics* had been available since 1623. In the following discussion, I will use Floyer Sydenham and Thomas Taylor's translation of *The Works of Plato* (1804) because Coleridge refers to it in his *Notebooks*, and I will use Thomas Twining's 1789 translation of the *Poetics*, which became standard.

Plato's *Phaedo* is especially important to literary critics concerned with dramatic spectacle because it emphasizes that the human soul can never be wise or pure until it disassociates itself from the body. The five senses obstruct the formation of accurate and clear ideas by tempting a person to think that all knowledge is palpable. An individual who comes to believe this "is accustomed to hate, dread and avoid, that which is dark and invisible to the eyes of sense." In other words, anyone overly dependent on the senses is incapable of conceiving abstract ideas. Socrates argues that his soul may ironically become "blinded through beholding things with the eyes of my body, and through endeavouring to apprehend them by means of the several senses." Only by examining "reasons" logically and philosophically can one arrive at the truth. Thus, a true philosopher's goal is "separating himself from the body as much as possible, and . . . converting himself to his soul."[2]

This argument has obvious implications for the debate about the place of spectacle in drama. The wise and philosophic citizen will avoid performances because they appeal to the senses and will prefer reading drama because it allows one to formulate more profound and abstract ideas. Later writers also use Plato's syllogisms to combat the public's tendency to honor good actors more than great writers. Cicero, in defending the poet Archias's right to Roman citizenship, assumes that his audience agrees that the mind and soul transcend the body. Cicero points out that if cities routinely grant citizenship to mere actors, who are skillful in maneuvering their bodies, how much more reason there is to give this honor to a poet like Archias, who manifests "the divine enthusiasm of genius, and the glowing energy of the soul." In a 1720 essay, John Dennis cites Cicero's *Pro Archia* to support his argument that actors are far below other artists in the hierarchy of greatness. According to Dennis, actors are just "the Apes of a Poet's Meaning."[3]

In the *Poetics*, Aristotle analyzes and ranks the different aspects of tragedy. He views spectacle as a very minor component and deprecates its effect on an audience.

> The DECORATION has, also, a great effect, but, of all the parts, is most foreign to the art. For the power of Tragedy is felt without representation, and actors; and the beauty of the decorations depends more on the art of the mechanic, than on that of the Poet.

Apparently, the Greek philosopher is reacting to contemporary schemes for ranking literary genres. The epic,

> it is urged, addresses itself to hearers of the better sort, to whom the addition of gesture is superfluous: but Tragedy is for *the people*; and being, therefore, the most vulgar kind of imitation, is evidently the inferior.

Aristotle considers this distinction specious. In a good tragedy,

> the fable should be so constructed, that, without the assistance of the sight, its incidents may excite horror and commiseration in those, who *hear* them only: an effect, which every one, who hears the fable of the *Oedipus*, must experience.[4]

Aristotle never argues that Sophocles's tragedies should not be performed. Basically, he contends that reading a play and seeing it performed are similar experiences, both of which appeal to "hearers of the better sort." For example, in part 5, Aristotle insists, "Tragedy, as well as the Epic, is capable of producing its effect, even without action; we can judge of it perfectly by *reading*."[5] The Greek critic probably uses the word "reading" to mean an oral recitation, which was the mode of studying drama in contemporary academies.

However, most later critics took "reading" quite literally and removed Aristotle's commentary from its context in the *Poetics*, forgetting that his remarks were originally made to defend the primacy of tragedy over epic poetry. (His observations on unity of place and time met a similar fate: they were interpreted as rules by commentators like Giraldi Cintio and Castelvetro.) In the hands of British writers, Aristotle's arguments were transformed into a formidable weapon for attacking the common spectator's experience of tragedy. These later critics used the Greeks' distinction between those who need "the addition of gesture" and those who do not to differentiate between the experiences of spectators and readers of drama.

Note that Aristotle does not discuss whether *comedy* is equally effective when read. This is one reason that later critics give more latitude to comedy than to tragedy on stage. The distinction is clear in essays like Samuel Johnson's Preface to *The Plays of William Shakespeare* (1765). Johnson writes,

> Familiar comedy is often more powerful on the theatre than in the page; imperial tragedy is always less. The humour of *Petruchio* may be heightened by grimace; but what voice or what gesture can hope to add dignity or force to the soliloquy of *Cato*.[6]

Another classical document that influenced drama criticism was Horace's *Epistles*, especially the first epistle in his second book. Horace complains about the poor taste of the "unlearned, and foolish" spectators who

> in the midst of the play call for either a bear or boxers; for in these the mob delight. Nay, even all the pleasure of our knights now is transferred from the ear to the uncertain eyes and their vain amusements. . . . You would think the grove of Garganus, or the Tuscan sea, was roaring; with so great noise are viewed the shews, and contrivances, and foreign riches! with which the actor being daub'd o'er, as soon as he appears upon the stage, *each* right hand encounters with the left. Has he said anything yet? Nothing at all. What then pleases *the people so much*? The cloth resembling *the colour of* violets, with the dye of Tarentum.

Horace lists other crowd-pleasing spectacles, such as elephants, captive kings, squadrons of horsemen, and model ships. For obvious reasons, many writers would "rather trust themselves with a reader."[7] Horace associates extravagant spectacles with the "eyes" of the audience, while the "ears" are used to take in nobler messages. This dichotomy resembles that of the ancient Greeks mentioned in the *Poetics*, who distinguish between the populace and "hearers of the better sort" who do not need visual stimuli to appreciate literature.

Renaissance and Restoration Prefaces

Renaissance dramatists were very aware of the issue of spectacle because the invention of the printing press allowed them to choose whether to stage their plays or to direct them specifically to the reading public—or to do both. While some Renaissance authors like Heywood and Marston begrudgingly allowed their dramatic works to be printed, often in order to foil piraters, other playwrights like Fletcher, Jonson, and Webster welcomed the opportunity to gain a new and potentially more sophisticated audience. The prefaces to the published works of these latter playwrights indicate that they considered the literate layman a "hearer of the better sort." In fact, John Webster calls the theater audience "uncapable" and "ignorant asses" in his preface to *The White Divel* (1612).[8]

Despite Ben Jonson's success as a playwright and author of court masques, he frequently complains about the abuse of stage spectacle. Jonson pretends to defend spectacle in "An Expostulation with Inigo Jones," but he undermines this position with irony and sarcasm. In this essay in poetic form, Jonson refers to the architect as "skenoplos" (stage mechanic), the term used by Aristotle in *Poetics,* part 2. In 1616, Jonson warns readers of *The Alchemist* to beware of poor dramas, despite their appeal for mere spectators. He contends in the preface,

> Thou wert never more fair in the way to be coz'ned (than in this Age) in *Poetry,* especially in Plays: wherein, now, the Concupiscence of Dances, and Antiques so reigneth, [that] to run away from Nature, and be afraid of her, is the only point of art that tickles the *Spectators.* . . . For they commend Writers, as they do Fencers, or Wrestlers; who if they come in robustuously, and put for it with a great deal of violence, are receiv'd for the braver fellows.[9]

In other essays, the playwright reverts to the classical distinction between sophisticated spectators with "quick ears" (that is, aware of the subtleties of language) and spectators who want gross visual entertainment. "The Prologue for the Court" from the 1631 folio of *The Staple of News* emphasizes the distance between intellectuals and groundlings. Jonson offers his play "as a *Rite,* / To *Scholars,* that can judge, and fair report / The sense they hear, above the vulgar sort / Of Nutcrackers, that only come for sight."[10]

By the end of the seventeenth century, prefaces of dramas had become an important vehicle for literary criticism and debates. This indicates that playwrights appreciated the potential of the genre to influence the taste of their reading public. John Dryden used his prefaces to address central concerns, such as the relationship between the ancients and the moderns, the place of verbal wit in comedy, Shakespeare's dramatic style (in contrast to that of Fletcher and Jonson), and the rules for writing drama.

Dryden knew Dacier's French edition of the *Poetics* as well as the Greek text. The influence of Horace is also likely in many of the English critic's remarks. In the Dedication for *The Spanish Friar* (1681), Dryden writes,

> A judicious reader will discover, in his closet, that trashy stuff, whose glittering deceived him in the action. I have often heard the stationer sighing in his shop, and wishing for those hands to take off his melancholy bargain which clapped its performance on the stage. In a play-house, everything contributes to impose upon the judgment; the lights, the scenes, the habits, and, above all, the grace of action, which is commonly the best where there is the most need of it, surprise the audience, and cast a mist upon their understandings.

Dryden returns to the subject in the concluding paragraphs of his dedication. Here, he speaks of his own desires as an author.

> But, as 'tis my interest to please my audience, so 'tis my ambition to be read: that I am sure is the most lasting and the nobler design: for the propriety of thoughts and words, which are the hidden beauties of a play, are but confusedly judged in the vehemence of action: all things are there beheld as in a hasty motion, where the objects only glide before the eye and disappear. [11]

Again we find spectacle associated with the eye and contrasted with the more cerebral delights of reading. According to Dryden, the stage impedes the audience's ability to understand the ideas and to appreciate the language of drama.

Religious Objections to the Stage

British clergymen objected to the stage because they viewed it as a corrupter of morality. They traced their position back to the second, third, and tenth sections of *The Republic*, where Plato bans most poets from his ideal state and accuses them of appealing to the lowest mental faculties and emotions, portraying heroes and gods engaged in unethical conduct, and violating the principles of poetic justice by rewarding some evil characters and making some good characters suffer. In addition, the British clergy recalled that early Christians had avoided dramas and other public spectacles in order to distance themselves from idolatrous Greek and Roman practices. Alarmed by the popularity of drama, Renaissance authors like John Reynolds and William Prynne published diatribes against the stage.

During the Puritan dominance of England, plays were banned by an act of Parliament (1642–1660). However, drama flourished at regional fairs and was performed surreptitiously in the cities. Occasionally, special permission to stage a play could be obtained from the authorities, especially if the work was not called a drama. For example, in 1656, Sir William D'Avenant received official approval for a production of the "opera" *The Siege of Rhodes.*

With the Restoration of the monarchy, most restrictions were repealed, and playwrights began to make up for lost ground. New pamphlets protested the "licentious" new dramas. The most influential of these pamphlets was Jeremy Collier's *A Short View of the Immorality and Profaneness of the English Stage: Together with The Sense of Antiquity Upon this Argument* (1698). Collier cites classical writers, including Seneca, Aristotle, and Horace, out of context to support his argument. He also quotes from various Church Fathers and canon laws. In general, he contends that the plays of writers such as Dryden, Wycherley, Vanbrugh, and Congreve "make Lewdness a Diversion" and are a particularly bad influence on young people.[12] Specifically, contemporary dramas were said to contain blasphemy, mockery of the clergy (see Collier's chapter 3), and violations of poetic justice (see chapter 4). Many playwrights, including Congreve, Vanbrugh, Dennis, and Farquhar, wrote replies to Collier's pamphlet in order to vigorously defend the stage.

Although literary critics were influenced by Collier and other attacks on the stage, these religious objections are really an assault on certain kinds of literature, especially comedy of manners, not spectacle per se. In my study, I will concentrate on aesthetic justifications for the opposition to staging tragedies.[13]

Stage Technology and Spectacle

In contrast to the simple staging of the Renaissance public theaters, the Restoration theaters emphasized elaborate spectacles to attract larger audiences, and this trend was continued in the eighteenth and nineteenth centuries. To accommodate more people, managers progressively enlarged the London theaters. In 1674, Drury Lane could seat about 700 spectators. After several expansions, it could hold over 2,000 people by 1762. Rebuilt in 1794, Drury Lane could accommodate 3,600 playgoers (see figures 1 and 2). The new large auditoriums made it difficult for many members of the audience to see the actors and to hear the dialogue. Because so many spectators were far from the stage, actors were forced to speak more loudly and to exaggerate their gestures and their movements. Another solution to this problem was to introduce the latest technological marvels to change scenes, to make ghosts fly, and otherwise to entertain even those spectators in the back rows. The development of "drops," painted scenes on rollers, gave designers more time to rearrange the set while a scene took place in front of the drop. This encouraged the adoption of more three-dimensional, built-up sets that included usable stairways and bridges. Judicious use of lighting accented the new sets, and various inventions allowed managers to control the intensity and the color of the stage lighting. Designers like Philip James de Loutherbourg whirled colored silk screens in front of lights to create special effects, such as simulated clouds and storms. Theaters competed with one another to produce increasingly ornate shows, replete with real animals (including the descendants of Horace's elephants), dancers, acrobats, processions, earthquakes, volcanoes, cascades, towns on fire, and sea fights with battleships.[14]

The public theaters were also influenced by the court masques, which featured elaborate spectacles. Stephen Orgel contends in *The Illusion of Power* that Inigo Jones's spectacles were an integral part of the masques' glorification of royal power and the transforming power of art.[15]

Spectacular effects were tacked on to dramas in the standard repertory, like Shakespeare's *Henry V, Henry VIII, King John*, and *Romeo and Juliet*, and Rowe's *Jane Shore*. Playwrights began to include specific stage directions indicating where such displays should be inserted. Allardyce Nicoll cites full pages of these directions in his *History of English Drama*.[16] The demands of spectacle also influenced the length and placement of scenes, often to the detriment of plot and structure.

Literary critics were well aware of these changes, and they frequently debated the proper place of spectacle in drama. Most commentators condemned productions that emphasized scenery, cos-

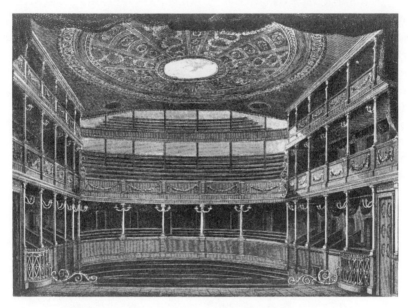

1. *Drury Lane Theatre in 1792, a drawing by William Capon,*
courtesy of the University of Bristol Theatre Collection.

2. *Drury Lane Theatre after being enlarged in 1794, a print*
published by Richard Philips in 1804, courtesy of the
University of Bristol Theatre Collection.

tumes, and music rather than literary substance. Over and over, writers in different eras echo the classical distinction between drama that merely appeals to the eyes and drama that pleases the ears. In "A Short Discourse of the English Stage" (1664), Richard Flecknoe contrasts the "plain and simple" theaters of the Renaissance with the extravagant new seventeenth-century stages:

> ours now for cost and ornament are arriv'd to the heighth of Magnificence; but that which makes our Stage the better makes our Playes the worse perhaps, they striving now to make them more for sight than hearing, whence that solid joy of the interior is lost, and that benefit which men formerly receiv'd from Playes, from which they seldom or never went away but far better and wiser then they came.

Yet a few paragraphs later, Flecknoe extols the virtues of the new technology. The scenes and machines

> are excellent helps of imagination, most grateful deceptions of sight, and graceful and becoming Ornaments of the Stage, transporting you easily without lassitude from one place to another, or rather by a kind of delightful Magick, whilst you sit still, does bring the place to you.[17]

This ambivalent response is typical of many commentators. Though dramatic spectacles have magical properties, they frustrate "that solid joy of the interior."

Many eighteenth- and nineteenth-century writers set up a dichotomy between "wit" and "spectacle." Wit refers to clever dialogue, while spectacle refers to machinery, costumes, lighting, sound effects, and low-comedy routines. Though Richard Steele wrote plays for the stage, he worried about the tendency of the theaters to substitute "Activity for Wit." In his Prologue for *The Funeral, or Grief A-la-Mode* (1701), he scolds his contemporaries for consuming "intemp'rate Meals" full of "Gay Lights, and Dresses, long extended Scenes, / Daemons and Angels moving in Machines." Such dramas "Dazle now the Eye" but neglect "the Heart" and the emotions. Steele emphasizes that spectacles require only skillful stage carpenters, not good writers or actors.[18] Later critics would develop Steele's metaphor and portray the theaters as bad restaurants.

Joseph Addison devoted several *Spectator* essays to the topic of spectacle. In number 5 (6 March 1711), he objects to the "inconsistency" of using real birds, fountains, and horses on stage.

> A little Skill in Criticism would inform us that Shadows and Realities ought not to be mix'd together in the same Piece; and that the Scenes, which are designed as the Representations of Nature, should be filled with Resemblances, and not with the Things themselves.

In number 44 (20 April 1711), he lists various stage devices that can save a playwright the trouble of evoking passion through dialogue and character development. While Addison strongly objects to these tricks in serious drama, he allows "greater Latitude for comick than tragick Artifices." The critic cites Aristotle and Horace as authorities in *Spectator* number 42 (18 April 1711). Addison's epigraph quotes from the epistle of Horace discussed above, lines 202 through 207, and Addison begins his essay by paraphrasing part 2, section 13, of the *Poetics*:

> Aristotle has observ'd, that ordinary Writers in Tragedy endeavour to raise Terrour and Pity in their Audience, not by proper Sentiments and Expressions, but by the Dresses and Decorations of the Stage. There is something of this Kind very ridiculous in the *English* Theatre.[19]

Henry Fielding also objected to the overdone pageantry of contemporary stage productions, as is evident in his *Champion* essays. Fielding's persona, Captain Hercules Vinegar, pokes fun at one manager's predilection for "prospects of hell" in many performances. In a letter to Captain Vinegar, "Vander Bruin" complains that most eighteenth-century theaters present exhibitions that are "very little better than raree-shows, and which a sensible lad of eighteen would be ashamed to frequent."[20]

In letter 79 (1760) of *The Citizen of the World*, Oliver Goldsmith condemns the rivalry between Covent Garden and Drury Lane Theatre over superficial matters such as child actors, fancy costumes, sound effects, dances, waterfalls, and tightrope walkers. The major problem with such spectacle is that it deadens the minds of the audience. "If I enter the house with any sentiments in my head, I am sure to have none going away, the whole mind being filled with a dead march, a funeral procession, a cat-call, a jigg, or a tempest." Goldsmith compares the eighteenth-century plays to "opium" that fills the heart with "a rapture of insensibility, and can dismiss the mind from all the fatigue of thinking."[21]

Similarly, in *The Critic* (1781), Richard Brinsley Sheridan makes fun of authors who rely on stage effects and spectacle instead of on dialogue and character development. Puff, the playwright, tells his friends, "This scene goes entirely for what we call SITUATION and STAGE EFFECT, by which the greatest applause may be obtained, without the assistance of language, sentiment or character." In the ridiculous scene, two nieces, their lover, and their uncles all draw swords or daggers on one another. Puff concludes his tragedy with typical eighteenth-century histrionics and spectacles: a heroine gone mad, a sea battle, drums, trumpets, cannon, and a procession.[22]

Even philosophers like Adam Smith criticized the abuse of spectacle. In *Essays on Philosophical Subjects* (published in 1795), Smith argues,

> By endeavouring to extend the effects of scenery beyond what the nature of the thing will admit of, it has been much abused; and in the common, as well as in the musical drama, many imitations have been attempted, which after the first and second time we have seen them, necessarily appear ridiculous. . . . Such imitations resemble those of painted Statuary; they may surprize at first, but they disgust ever after, and appear evidently such simple and easy tricks as are fit only for the amusement of children and their nurses at a puppet-show.[23]

Coleridge later expanded this comparison between true art, which suggests ideas, and false art, which attempts to copy nature.

The Popularity of Pantomime, Melodrama, and Opera

Entertainment genres that involved much pageantry flourished in eighteenth- and nineteenth-century England: pantomimes, melodramas, and operas were box-office hits and often had long runs. Theaters stressed their new sets, costumes, and mechanical wonders in advertisements. Transformation scenes were especially popular; these included Jupiter's metamorphosis into a bull and dragons that dropped demons from their claws. Because of the importance of spectacle, talented scene designers and costumers were paid top salaries.[24]

Many of the pantomimes were based on the improvised skits, songs, and dialogues of the commedia dell'arte, which appealed to all social classes because erudition was not required to understand the dramas. Giacomo Oreglia observes that in the commedia, "the action often has more significance than the words and sometimes involves the most daring and perilous acrobatics." Similarly, Evert Sprinchorn likens the commedia to "a circus with a plot." Harlequin, a comic servant, was an especially popular character due to his acrobatic skill.

He would often leap through special trap doors in the side or back walls of the theater and disappear. Harlequin also amused the audience by tightrope walking, climbing walls, falling from balconies, imitating animals or objects, walking on stilts, dancing, and tumbling. One famous Harlequin, Visentini, could somersault backward without spilling a glass of wine. Many routines (*lazzi*) of the commedia involve violence and cruelty: masters and servants frequently trip or beat one another. The physical needs and problems of humans are stressed in skits that emphasize eating, sex, enemas, defecation, impotence, vomiting, and nudity.[25]

Although the early commedias had simple scenery, later plays depend on stage properties and spectacles. Many of the props create magical effects and amusing tricks, including books that burst into flames, fruit that disappears, tables piled with food that move away from starving characters, false limbs, and guns that do not fire properly. Allardyce Nicoll argues that when the commedia established itself in Paris and other centers outside of Italy, spectacle was introduced to attract audiences that were unfamiliar with the Italian language, the typical plots, and the conventions of commedia troupes. The language barrier also tempted the actors to add more silent pantomime to their productions. Commedia spectacles featured temples, forests, setting moons, and naval battles.[26]

In Great Britain, pantomimes were often presented after tragedies like *Hamlet* to provide variety, regardless of any dissonance between the main feature and the afterpiece. Nicholas Rowe was already worrying in 1700 that the latter would displace the former: "Must *Shakespear, Fletcher,* and laborious *Ben* / Be left for *Scaramouch* and *Harlequin*?"[27]

In 1717, John Rich, who owned Lincoln's Inn Fields Theatre, introduced pantomimes in London that adapted the French harlequinades. Richard Bevis points out that

> Rich's pantomimes were basically operettas, in which relatively serious scenes, often telling stories from classical mythology, alternated with the silent farce of Harlequin and Columbine, featuring ingenious transformations and frequently spoofing the mythical plot.

Rich himself portrayed Harlequin in numerous productions, which were so successful that rival theaters copied the idea. According to Leo Hughes, *Harlequin Doctor Faustus* appeared as an added feature in thirty-six of ninety-two bills at Drury Lane between 23 November 1723 and 28 March 1724.[28]

In addition to pantomimes, managers added dances, comic monologues, fireworks, songs, musical interludes, acrobatic displays, mimicry of people and animals, boxing, fencing, and other entertainments to make the public's three- to six-hour evening visit to the theater even more varied. These features were often inserted *between* the acts of the mainpiece.[29]

In a 1727 dedication, Rich defends pantomime and "those various Embellishments of Machinery, Painting, Dances" because they insure financial success for theaters. Similarly, David Garrick, who managed Drury Lane later in the century, argues that actors must accommodate themselves to public taste or starve, despite their natural preference for Lear and Hamlet over Harlequin.[30] In Garrick's popular pantomime *Harlequin's Invasion* (1759), Harlequin tries to invade Shakespeare's territory but is defeated.

The commedia's emphasis on clowning, acrobatics, songs, dances, and spectacle alienated many literary critics, who preferred sophisticated poetry, witty dialogue, and psychological probing of the main characters. In an epilogue for a production of *The Silent Woman* at Oxford in 1673, Dryden urges the audience to reject the Italian commedia, which has replaced "wit and humors" with "lewd grimace," and to spurn plays that feature animals, thunder, lightning, and "machines." He hopes that the scholars in Oxford will reinstate good British plays, like those by Jonson and Fletcher. Similarly, Pope has little sympathy for the arguments of managers like Rich. In *The Dunciad* (1729), Pope satirizes the farces and afterpieces that were popular in the 1720s, including *Harlequin Doctor Faustus, The Necromancer,* and Lewis Theobald's *Rape of Prosperpine: with the Birth and Adventures of Harlequin.* Pope ridicules Rich's stunts as Harlequin, especially the trick of hatching from a huge egg, and Rich's stage effects at Lincoln's Inn Fields, especially his storms, stars, suns, fires, and fake snow and hail. The Goddess of Dullness tells her followers that bad playwrights who cannot match Shakespeare or Jonson can always use "the wond'rous pow'r of Noise" to arouse theater audiences. Pope concludes that poorly written spectacles cause the audience's taste to degenerate: even magistrates and peers "from each show rise duller than the last." He comments in his notes that the farcical afterpieces of Theobald and others "get acted at the end of the best Tragedies, to spoil the digestion of the audience."[31] Pope's food metaphor, like that of Steele, reduces theaters to the status of bad restaurants.

Even artists like Hogarth satirized stage spectacle and the commedia. In *A Just View of the British Stage* (1724), the heads of statues representing comedy and tragedy are covered by posters announcing two pantomimes, *Harlequin Doctor Faustus* and *Harlequin Shepherd*.[32] The rehearsal in progress features a scene of Newgate Prison with a flying monster, a dog, puppets, Scaramouch, and an annoyed ghost of Ben Jonson emerging from a trapdoor. Sheets of plays by Shakespeare and Congreve are being used as toilet paper. Obviously, Hogarth implies that outrageous spectacle and farce have replaced meaningful tragedy and comedy.

In the essay entitled "On the present State of our Theatres" (1760), Goldsmith criticizes the managers of Drury Lane and Covent Garden for competing for attention with vapid pantomimes while neglecting theater classics and good new plays. The first paragraph of the essay is especially sarcastic.

> Our theatres seem now to aim at glorious opposition; harlequin is set against harlequin, one dancing-master opposes another; the scene shifters, the singers, and even the drummers figure at each house by turns, and it is to be hoped soon that mere actors will thus become useless. The audience now sit uneasy at the sprightly sallies of Vanburgh [sic], or Congreve, and with impatience desire only to see the Invasion or the Fair [two afterpieces]. These are the scenes that charm; to see the stage crowded with figures, to hear trumpets, crackers, and tempests, these are what lift our souls into greatness.

Thus, the stage has become "a scene for absurdity" instead of "a fine school for instruction."[33]

Thomas Twining also waxes sarcastic on the topic of pantomime. He imagines Aristotle rolling in his grave when he discovers that eighteenth-century Britain elevates spectacle over all other elements of drama and that "the carpenter takes the lead of the Poet." For Twining, the ultimate absurdity is that pantomime is "a species of drama *without words*."[34]

Pantomimic effects were influencing traditional British comedies and tragedies. By the late eighteenth century, the success of pantomimes derived from the commedia pressured dramatists to add more action, intrigue, stage business, and spectacle to their plays. This made dramas "increasingly unsuited for reading," according to Richard Bevis. In some scenes, facial expressions and gestures replaced impassioned speeches: the audience had to deduce the meaning without verbal clues. Sheridan exposes this trend in act 3 of *The Critic*. Puff takes about fifty words to explain the meaning of a character's shaking his head.[35]

Ridicule of the commedia was not confined to England. For example, Carlo Goldoni portrays the antics of Harlequin as unfit for educated people. In *Pamela fanciulla* (1750), Goldoni's adaptation of Samuel Richardson's *Pamela*, Bonfil scolds young Sir John Arnold, who has been praising Harlequin and the commedia:

> You will not make me believe that in Italy any men of learning or wit can laugh at such nonsense. . . . There is a noble ridicule founded in smart repartees, witty conceits, sprightly humour and pleasantry. There is a low ridicule founded in scurrility and buffoonery.

Bonfil recommends that Sir John obtain more education in order to understand good literature and true culture.[36]

The persistence of pantomime in England is clear in a sonnet by Tennyson, "To W. C. Macready," published in 1851. Tennyson attacks the superficiality of the genre, which he terms "brainless pantomime, / And those gilt gauds men-children swarm to see."[37] Like his predecessors, Tennyson views pantomime as a simplistic and juvenile form of entertainment.

New musicals and songs added to existing dramas were so popular that by 1700 both Covent Garden and Drury Lane Theatre had their own resident composers. The composers were listed in playbills, along with the names of the designers of scenery and costumes. The importance of music and dance is clear in Matthew Gregory Lewis's 1798 recipe for dramatic success: "That his Play must succeed, may the Bard safely boast, / Who opens the piece with a Song by a Ghost; / But in popular plaudits unbounded he revels, / If he follows the Song with a Dance by two Devils."[38] Obviously, Lewis, who wrote *The Castle Spectre* and other successful Gothic dramas, saw through the self-conscious theatricality of the genre.

Besides satirizing the overuse of music in regular dramas, many British critics opposed the performance of opera entirely. British nationalism is clearly behind some of the satire of Italian opera and French dancing masters: the words "foreign" and "effeminate" often appear in such attacks. However, critics are also concerned about the opera's assault on the senses. John Dennis devotes to the subject a work entitled "An Essay on the Opera's after the Italian Manner, Which Are About to Be Establish'd on the English Stage: With Some Reflections on the Damage Which They May Bring to the Publick" (1706). Dennis does not rule out *all* use of music in plays; rather, he insists that music must be made

> subordinate to some nobler Art, and subservient to Reason; but if it presumes . . . to set up for it self, and to grow independent, as it does in our late Operas, it becomes a mere sensual Delight, utterly incapable of informing the Understanding, or reforming the Will.

Ultimately, habitual doses of opera will "so far debauch the Minds of Men, as to make them incapable of those reasonable Diversions, which have got the just Possession of the Stage." Similarly, Steele condemns the audience at the opera *Pyrrhus and Demetrius* for accepting "shallow satisfaction of the eyes and ears only." Pope is even more severe in the 1743 editions of *The Dunciad*, where he depicts Italian opera as a "Harlot" dressed in patchwork, supported by "singing Peers." The patchwork represents the lack of form in operas, and the peers represent the British nobility, who should know better than to sustain the opera. In the burlesque *The Author's Farce* (1730), Henry Fielding also makes fun of contemporary operas. Luckless speaks for the playwright when he observes, "Signior Opera is created archpoet to the Goddess of Nonsense." On another occasion, Luckless pronounces an opera "a puppet-show" and complains, "What have been all the playhouses a long while but puppet-shows?"[39]

The Influence of Audience Taste

Note how frequently critics like Adam Smith and Henry Fielding compare the stage to a "puppet-show" in its appeal to childlike, poorly educated people. We find many writers attacking different segments of the theater audience and blaming them for the overuse of spectacle. An early example is Thomas Shadwell's censure of both the groundlings and the gentry in his Preface to *The Humorists, A Comedy* (1671).

> The rabble of little people are more pleas'd with *Jack Puddings* being soundly kick'd, or having a Custard handsomely thrown in his face, than with all the wit in Plays; and the higher sort of Rabble (as there may be a rabble of very fine people in this illiterate age) are more pleased with the extravagant and unnatural actions, the trifles and fripperies of a Play, or the trappings and ornaments of Nonsense, than with all the wit in the world.[40]

Throughout this essay, Shadwell cites Horace's *Epistle* 2.1 in the Latin version, reminding the reader that very little has changed since ancient times.

In Sir John Vanbrugh's satirical play *The Relapse* (1696), Lord Foppington reveals much about upper-class behavior at theaters. Foppington explains to Amanda that a beau must sleep late in order "to look wholesome, lest he make so nauseous a figure in the side-box, the ladies should be compelled to turn their eyes upon the play."[41]

In *The Drama's Patrons,* Leo Hughes dissects the eighteenth-century London audience. He describes the noisy footmen in the gallery, the upper-class fops and fine ladies who exhibited themselves onstage and in the boxes, and the prostitutes and their quarrelsome admirers. William Hogarth's print *The Laughing Audience* (1733) shows the reactions of different social classes—and a scowling drama critic—to a comedy (see figure 3). In order to make a profit, managers allowed overcrowding in the theaters. This exacerbated the tendency of some playgoers to distract others with side conversations and practical jokes. There were also noisy struggles for the best seats. Sometimes theatergoers came prepared to hiss or brought catcalls to disrupt a play. More unruly patrons threw oranges, peas, apples, potatoes, and bottles at the actors.[42] It is no wonder that writers condemned these antics.

Charles Beecher Hogan argues that the fully illuminated theaters of the eighteenth and early nineteenth century, which were not darkened for performances, created a rapport between the spectators and the actors. Members of the audience felt comfortable shouting praise or criticism from their seats. The lighting also allowed restless spectators to move around and to quarrel.[43] In Edward Dayes's *Interior of Drury Lane Theatre,* the entire audience is watching a fight among spectators instead of watching the play (see figure 4).

All this tumult, which continued through the early nineteenth century, tended to diminish the dignity of the theater in the eyes of many literary critics. Their comments reveal some snobbery and elitism. However, the theater managers needed the bourgeois and lower-class crowds to fill their auditoriums and had no intention to limit ticket sales by discouraging the attendance of unsophisticated spectators.

John Dennis blames the poor taste of the nouveaux riches, who frequented the theater to be fashionable, for the prevalence of "Tumbling and Vaulting and Ladder Dancing" on the stage. Part of Dennis's hostility stems from his disappointment when his own dramas failed

3. *The Laughing Audience* (1733), *an engraving by William Hogarth,*
courtesy of the British Museum, London.

in performance. In "A Large Account of the Taste in Poetry" (1702), he
argues that common audiences are not the best judges. He puts his
faith in "those who have taste," "the knowing few."[44]

Pope complains that "the Pit" has corrupted the taste of the nobility. In his free rendering of *The First Epistle of the Second Book of Horace*
(1737), he updates Horace's satire of the typical audience and its short
attention span.

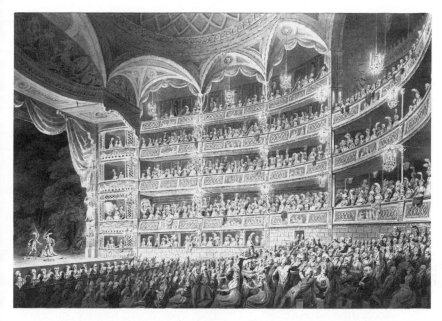

4. *Interior of Drury Lane Theater* (1795), *a watercolor by Edward Dayes, courtesy of the Henry E. Huntington Library and Art Gallery, San Marino, California.*

There still remains to mortify a Wit,
The many-headed Monster of the Pit;
A sense-less, worth-less, and unhonour'd crowd;
Who to disturb their betters mighty proud,
Clatt'ring their sticks, before ten lines are spoke,
Call for the Farce, the Bear, or the Black-joke [a popular ballad].
What dear delight to Britons Farce affords!
Ever the taste of Mobs, but now of Lords;
(Taste, that eternal wanderer, which flies
From heads to ears, and now from ears to eyes.)

Pope proceeds to make fun of his countrymen's fondness for pageants and elaborate costumes.[45]

At the same time that the theater audience was expanding, the reading public was also growing. Better and more general education reached many members of the British working class, and new, inexpensive printing methods made books and periodicals more affordable. However, the fact that there were *more* readers does not mean that they all were equally capable of understanding what they read. Vanbrugh satirizes the public's reading in *The Relapse*. Lord Foppington's attitude toward reading is as superficial as his attitude toward the theater. He enjoys looking at his gilded and neatly arranged library shelves, but he informs Amanda, "I never think of what I read" because he finds thinking "the greatest fatigue in the world." Satires like this one influenced the romantics: Lamb quotes part of Foppington's speech as an epigraph for the 1822 essay entitled "Detached Thoughts on Books and Reading."[46]

Besides the reprints of popular plays for the general public, publishers also marketed "poetic plays" for readers only. Fielding's Bookweight in *The Author's Farce* explains the difference between an "acting play" and a "reading play." The former "is entirely supported by the merit of the actor; in which case, it signifies very little whether there be any sense in it or no. Now, your reading play is of a different stamp, and must have wit and meaning in it." In 1780, William Hodson compared the two dramatic species in his essay "Observations on Tragedy." According to Hodson, "The Poet who composes for the closet . . . addresses himself only to the judicious." In contrast, "The Dramatic Poet . . . writes for the Public (a mixed audience of different dispositions . . .)." A stage play appeals "to the passions," while the closet play appeals "to the judgment."[47]

Not all critics agree with Bookweight and Hodson that stage and closet drama are composed according to different principles. Critics like Francis Gentleman hedge by finding most plays of Shakespeare suitable both for the closet and for the stage. *The Monthly Review* of March 1780 attacks Hodson's arguments and contends, "Plays are avowedly written to be acted." The journalist cites Aristotle as support.[48] Of course, this claim exposes the *Monthly Review* writer's misunderstanding of Aristotle's position.

The vast new audiences of readers and theatergoers created a demand for both new literature and new literary criticism to guide their tastes. Writers were glad to comply with both demands; however, they rebuked the public almost as often as they flattered it. Literary critics were divided on the issue of whether theater could benefit the middle and working classes. Richard Steele championed the stage, defending it as a force for refining the morals and manners of the uncouth. Though Steele protests the *abuse* of spectacle, his *Tatler* essays consistently defend the importance of performing dramas in general (numbers 3 and 8 are good examples). He also emphasizes the advantages of performance in his Preface to *The Conscious Lovers*:

> it must be remember'd a Play is to be Seen, and is made to be Represented with the Advantage of Action, nor can appear but with half the Spirit, without it; for the greatest Effect of a Play in reading is to excite the Reader to go see it; and when he does so, it is then a Play has the Effect of Example and Precept.

John Dennis cites the above passage in "Remarks on a Play, Call'd, *The Conscious Lovers, a Comedy*" (1723). He strongly disagrees with Steele about the relative merits of reading and seeing plays. Dennis reminds his contemporaries that Milton's *Samson Agonistes* and Dryden's *State of Innocence* "were never design'd to be seen." Furthermore, a true genius writes for "all Countries, and to all Ages," instead of directing his drama to a mere theater audience. Dennis concludes,

> If he who reads a Play is qualified to read and to judge, he reads it with a truer and juster Spirit than can be supplied by any Company of Actors. If such a Reader happens at any Time to be better pleased with the Representation of a Play than the reading it, 'tis an infallible Sign, that such a Play is a very wretched Performance.[49]

One must bear in mind that Dennis is attacking a more successful rival here. However, Steele and Dennis are representative of the divergent points of view of their era. The former has great hopes for the new audiences; the latter worries that middle-class taste will debase the dramatic art.

Idolatry of Shakespeare

The eighteenth century witnessed a resurgence of interest in Shakespeare and a growing animosity toward the stage versions of his plays. In contrast to earlier critics like Thomas Rymer and Voltaire, who denigrated the bard for neglecting the three unities and violating decorum, late eighteenth-century writers stressed his conscious artistry, his poetic genius, and his skillful characterizations. Robert Witbeck Babcock chronicles this drastic change in *The Genesis of Shakespeare Idolatry, 1766–1799*.[50] Ultimately, Shakespeare was deified by many critics, who insisted that he deserved a reverent close reading.

Under the guise of preserving the unities and tragic decorum, many scenes in Shakespeare's plays had been deleted, condensed, or shifted to different acts. For example, Garrick removed the comic scenes in *Hamlet* and *Macbeth*. Shakespeare's plays were also altered to make them easier for actors: the "prompters' books" shortened various speeches or translated them into contemporary English. In addition, managers shortened stock dramas from five acts to three acts to provide more time for pantomimes, afterpieces, and new spectacles that exhibited the theaters' machinery. During the Restoration, *The Tempest* was transformed into a musical or dramatic opera replete with sinking ships and flying spirits. Hazelton Spencer blames the emphasis on spectacle for "the most violent mangling" of Shakespeare's texts. For example, the witches in D'Avenant's version of *Macbeth* (1674) become "vaudevillians" who sing, dance, and "cavort on the 'machines.'" Similarly, Charles Gildon's adaptation of *Measure for Measure* (1700) adds an irrelevant masque with dancers and ascending and descending spirits. Influenced by the many scene changes for popular pantomimes, Drury Lane's production of *Macbeth* in April 1794 featured fourteen different, elaborate scene changes. Some managers went as far as converting *Macbeth, Faust,* and other serious dramas into pantomimes.[51]

At the same time, adapters added new scenes from popular contemporary plays on related subjects or interpolated snatches of several Shakespearean plays, as Colley Cibber did in his *King Richard III* (1700). Characters were also changed to fit the mold of heroic tragedy, with its conventional conflicts between love and honor. In many cases, the "improved" versions were so popular that they drove the originals off the stage.[52]

Literary critics' hatred for these butchered editions increased their resistance to stage spectacle. The romantics condemn misrepresentations of Shakespeare's plays with a vehemence approaching Collier's protests against blasphemy. For example, Hazlitt terms Dryden's adaptation of *The Tempest* as performed at Covent Garden in 1815 a "travestie" and a "caricature" of the original play. Because the comedy is so "disfigured," Hazlitt nearly vows to banish himself from the theater audience.[53] In a letter to *The Spectator* in 1828, Lamb mocks the practice of adding love affairs that distract the audience from the themes of Shakespeare's tragedies. He is especially horrified by the Cordelia/Edgar intrigue in Nahum Tate's *The History of King Lear* (1681) and the Timon/Evandra affair in Thomas Shadwell's *The History of Timon of Athens, the Man Hater* (1678). Lamb suggests sarcastically that the improvers should add a mistress for Reuben or Issachar to the Genesis account of Joseph and his brothers (*Works of Lamb,* 1:321–22). Note that Lamb compares the artistry of Shakespeare to that of the Bible in its validity and human interest.

Acting Styles and Famous Actors

Commentators also reacted to innovations in acting techniques, and the best actors generated reams of reviews. For example, after the death of Thomas Betterton, Steele devoted *Tatler* number 167 (1710) to a general evaluation of the actor's roles. The critic was especially impressed by Betterton's portrayal of Othello in the handkerchief scene. Steele uses the player's skill to support his theory that performance can bring a drama to life.

> Whoever reads in his closet this admirable scene, will find that he cannot, except he has as warm an imagination as Shakespeare himself, find any but dry, incoherent, and broken sentences: but a reader that has seen Betterton act it, observes there could not be a word added; that longer speeches had been unnatural, nay impossible, in Othello's circumstances.[54]

In this case, Betterton's expression of Othello's trauma gives the spectator new insight into the tragedy.

Perhaps the most famous actor of the eighteenth century was David Garrick. While earlier acting was based on the tradition of imitating one's predecessors, Garrick helped to introduce greater freedom of interpretation and a new, less rhetorical style, which contemporaries termed "natural." Fielding praises his acting hyperbolically in the essay introducing book 7 of *Tom Jones* (1749): "I regard [him] in tragedy to be the greatest genius the world hath ever produced." Later in the novel, Fielding describes Garrick's portrayal of Hamlet as convincingly natural. Tom Jones and Mrs. Miller admire the actor's unconventional style; in contrast, country bumpkin Partridge prefers the self-conscious rhetoric of the actor who plays Claudius. Partridge is also impressed by the theater building, the musicians, and "the fineness of the dresses." In other words, the bumpkin focuses on the spectacle, while the more sophisticated viewers concentrate on the innovative acting of Garrick. Francis Gentleman proclaims Garrick Shakespeare's "greatest and best commentator, who not only presents his beauties to the imagination, but brings them home feelingly to the heart."[55]

However, other critics worried about the tendency of an actor's performance to eclipse the playwright's use of language and wit. Aristotle had lamented in his *Rhetoric* that, because of the public's infatuation with fine delivery of speeches, "in drama the actors now count for more than the poets."[56] This problem remained a critical concern centuries after Aristotle's death.

Thomas Rymer worried that acting and spectacle could blur the distinction between good plays and terrible ones. In *The Tragedies of the Last Age* (1677), he praises Hart's acting but fears that the player will mislead the auditors:

> their *eyes* are prepossest and charm'd by his *action,* before ought of the *Poets* can approach their *ears;* and to the most wretched of *Characters,* he gives a lustre and brillant which dazles the *sight,* that the *deformities* in the Poetry cannot be perceiv'd.
>
> Therefore a distinction is to be made between what *pleases naturally* in it self, and what *pleases* upon the account of *Machines, Actors, Dances* and circumstances which are meerly *accidental* to the *Tragedy.*[57]

Rymer refers to Aristotle's *Poetics* as support for his argument.

Goldsmith also anticipates the romantics in questioning the priorities of a theater in which actors receive more attention than poets do. He complains in *The Citizen of the World,* "The actors [sic] business is not so much to adapt himself to the poet, as the poet's to adapt himself to the actor."[58] This hierarchy endangers literary excellence.

In *The Critic,* Sheridan satirizes the tendency of powerful star actors to render a drama meaningless by eliminating key passages. His extreme example illustrates Goldsmith's observation. Puff, the playwright, is annoyed that the actors have cut the second scene of his tragedy, leaving out important background information. Sneer, the theater critic, points out that the drama's pronouns no longer have antecedents. Puff vows to restore all cut passages when he publishes the play.[59]

Toward the end of the eighteenth century, the "grand style" advocated by Mrs. Siddons and John Kemble gained ascendancy. Contemporary descriptions of their acting stress its classical grace and dignity. Henry James Pye, who became poet laureate, argues that Great Britain's theater excels that of ancient Greece in its "language and apparatus." He cites the acting of Garrick and Siddons as examples: "And perhaps it may admit a doubt, whether even Aristotle, if he had seen a

Garrick in Lear, or a Siddons in Isabella, would have . . . asserted that a tragedy attained its end by reading as well as in representation." However, Pye goes on to qualify his praise of acting. He repeats Aristotle's dictum, "Tragedy also as well as the epopee may attain its end without representation, for we can judge of its merit by reading only" (Pye's 1792 translation). Pye comments,

> This is strictly true; and perhaps there are few good tragedies in which the effect is not in general, at least as forcible in the closet as on the stage, even in the modern theatre. In the strongly impassioned parts, where every other consideration of effect is lost in feeling, we are wonderfully moved by the natural efforts of a Garrick and a Siddons; but this is independent of the stage effect, and would be as strong in a room as on the stage. But the appearance of scene-shifters, the panting dead bodies, and other circumstances of the same nature that must necessarily attend the representation, rather weaken than encrease the force of the illusion; and the exception just made can extend only to few performers. There are not many actors who are able to give us in the representation, the ideas we form of the characters of Shakespear from reading his plays.[60]

I have chosen to quote this passage at length because it summarizes many of the topics mentioned in this chapter: the influence of Aristotle, the new emphasis on Shakespeare's skill in characterization, the popularity of the best actors, and the distracting effects of spectacle. Also, Pye's previous statement, which I have cited above, is quoted by various twentieth-century critics out of context. When considered jointly with this second passage, the text reveals a writer struggling with his ambivalent feelings about the stage. A few paragraphs later, Pye qualifies himself again: "It is not every play that justifies the observation which is the subject of this note."[61]

Conclusion

Pye's ambivalence toward spectacle is typical of many British commentators. Even successful playwrights such as Jonson, Dryden, Fielding, Goldsmith, and Lewis express doubts about the stage and the taste of the theater audience. Like the seventeenth-century author, Richard Flecknoe, most of these writers are fascinated by the "delightful Magick" of the stage, but they wince when extravagant spectacles displace "that solid joy of the interior" that results from a stimulated imagination.

A reevaluation of the drama criticism of Coleridge, Lamb, and Hazlitt seems in order. Their bias against spectacle has been misinterpreted as being directed solely against the limitations of early nineteenth-century theaters. However, a careful reading of their essays reveals a kinship with earlier commentaries. Like their predecessors, the romantics emphasize the primacy of readers and the need for individuals to become imaginatively involved when reading drama. They would agree with Flecknoe that spectacle impedes this imaginative participation. Instead of viewing Coleridge and his contemporaries as isolated extremists, a twentieth-century scholar should place the romantics' essays in their historical context to objectively assess their contributions to a long-standing critical controversy.

2. *The Romantics' Critique of Appeals to the Senses in the Arts*

Many scholars have argued that what distinguishes romantic art and literature from that of the eighteenth century is a departure from "abstraction" and a new emphasis on the concrete and on sense perception. For example, Walter Jackson Bate maintains in *Criticism: The Major Texts* that Hazlitt's writings reveal a "distrust of abstraction" and a "confidence in concrete nature." In *A History of Modern Criticism: 1750–1950*, René Wellek also portrays Hazlitt as hostile to abstraction: "He demanded particularity and distrusted abstraction and system." The most emphatic statements about this alleged romantic hostility toward abstraction can be found in the studies of Roy Park, *Hazlitt and the Spirit of the Age: Abstraction and Critical Theory* (1971) and *Lamb as Critic* (1980). Park stresses Hazlitt's "criticism of all forms of abstraction." Similarly, Park contends that Lamb uses "abstract" as an antonym for the "poetic, imaginative, even religious." Park concludes in *Lamb as Critic* that the romantics see good literature and abstraction as opposites: "The Romantic abandonment of abstraction for poetry . . . is so widespread that it is, perhaps, the most important feature of the age."[1]

While it is true that the romantics condemn *over*generalization, Park's sweeping conclusion overlooks the many *positive* connotations that the term "abstraction" has in early nineteenth-century aesthetic criticism, especially in the drama and art criticism of S. T. Coleridge, A. W. Schlegel, Charles Lamb, and William Hazlitt. In this chapter, I will examine the roots of the romantic concept of "abstraction" and demonstrate that the romantics believe that both great artists and good reader/spectators need a certain degree of abstraction from the senses.

The roots of nineteenth-century writers' distrust of the senses and overly concrete art can be found in the aesthetic theory of Plato and Aristotle. In the *Phaedo*, Plato had argued that sense perception confuses and pollutes the soul, while philosophical reasoning purifies the soul and enables it to attain true wisdom by means of intellectual principles. Anyone who relies on the five senses to reveal the truth cannot apprehend philosophic concepts, which are not palpable and require mental agility.[2]

Similarly, Aristotle distinguishes between the negative effects of strong stimulation of the senses and the positive effects of strong stimulation of the intellect.

> After strong stimulation of a sense we are less able to exercise it than before, as e.g. in the case of a loud sound we cannot hear easily immediately after . . . but in the case of mind[,] thought about an object that is highly intelligible renders it more and not less able afterwards to think objects that are less intelligible: the reason is that while the faculty of sensation is dependent upon the body, mind is separable from it.[3]

The romantics agree with Plato that overreliance on the senses is the main obstacle to clear and analytic thinking, and they agree with Aristotle that the mastery of intellectual concepts leads to a greater capacity for more difficult reasoning.

Developing the same dichotomy, Francis Bacon argues in *The Advancement of Learning* (1605) that literature aids people by subordinating external appearances to ideas. Literature partakes of the divine "because it doth raise and erect the mind, by submitting the shows of things to the desires of the mind." Hazlitt cites this passage in his *Lectures on the English Poets*.[4]

By the late 1600s, dramatists were debating about when plays should appeal to the senses and when plays should appeal to the imagination. John Dryden wrestles with this issue in "Of Dramatic Poesy: An Essay" (1668), where he discusses whether portraying violence in a theater violates decorum. In the essay, Lisideius defends the French practice of having duels, battles, and deaths in a drama take place offstage. He argues that the playwright's choosing a character to describe and narrate these violent actions is more powerful than having fights and deaths enacted before the audience. Spectators can easily perceive that onstage violence is fake, so the dramatic illusion is shattered. For this reason, audiences tend to laugh during death scenes. Lisideius maintains,

> "The words of a good writer, which describe it lively, will make a deeper impression of belief in us than all the actor can persuade us to, when he seems to fall dead before us; as a poet in the description of a beautiful garden, or a meadow, will please our imagination more than the place itself can please our sight."[5]

Other writers emphasize the power of language to convey complicated ideas by arousing the imagination. For example, Joseph Addison insists in his *Spectator* essays about the "Pleasures of the Imagination"

(1712) that words can be more evocative than real objects. He begins with a statement similar to Dryden's observation.

> Words, when well chosen, have so great a Force in them, that a Description often gives us more lively Ideas than the Sight of Things themselves. The Reader finds a Scene drawn in stronger Colours, and painted more to the Life in his Imagination, by the help of Words, than by an actual Survey of the Scene which they describe. . . . The Reason, probably, may be, because in the Survey of any Object we have only so much of it painted on the Imagination, as comes in at the Eye; but in its Description, the Poet gives us as free a View of it as he pleases, and discovers to us several Parts, that either we did not attend to, or that lay out of our Sight when we first beheld it. As we look on any Object, our Idea of it is, perhaps, made up of two or three simple Ideas; but when the Poet represents it, he may either give us a more complex Idea of it, or only raise in us such Ideas as are most apt to affect the Imagination.[6]

Like earlier writers, Addison wants to free the public from dependence on the sense of sight. Thus, he argues that literature may reveal more truth than sense perception and that literature can relate ideas to one another in a way that powerfully stimulates the mind and the imagination. From Addison's perspective, literature mediates between the real world and the human imagination.

Like Addison, Edmund Burke emphasizes the intellectual stimulation provided by words. However, Burke differs from many earlier writers on this subject because he also stresses the power of language to evoke strong emotion in the reader or listener. His explanation of how words arouse sympathy anticipates the literary criticism of the romantics.

In *A Philosophical Enquiry into the Origin of our Ideas of the Sublime and Beautiful* (1757), Burke disagrees with contemporary critics who assert that the greatest poetry is pictorial and presents clear images. While painting is the best medium for "clear ideas" and "exact description," poetry and rhetoric appeal more powerfully to human sympathy with their relatively "obscure ideas." Obscure ideas are sublime and strongly affect our emotions because they evoke "infinity," while clear ideas are bounded and thus "little." Burke uses Milton's description of Satan in *Paradise Lost* (1.589–99) as an example of the sublime in literature. Here, Milton compares Satan to so *many* other images—a tower, an archangel, the sun seen through fog, and a solar eclipse—

that the reader cannot form a clear picture of Satan. Burke comments, "The mind is hurried out of itself, by a croud of great and confused images; which affect because they are crouded and confused." Burke also cites Job 4:13–17, in which Eliphaz describes his dream about a mysterious spirit. The passage is solemn and frightening because of the obscure images, which Burke contrasts to overly clear and "ludicrous" paintings of hell. Burke's art criticism in this passage resembles that of Coleridge and Lamb, who also object to overly minute details in paintings.[7]

According to Burke, poetry relies very little "for its effect on the power of raising sensible images." Literature's obscurity and independence of the senses make it far more evocative than painting. In fact, Burke contends, "Eloquence and poetry are . . . much more capable of making deep and lively impressions than any other arts, and even than nature itself in very many cases."[8] This last statement is an especially emphatic refutation of pictorial poetic theory.

German philosophers like Immanuel Kant and Friedrich Schiller reexamine the classical distinction between sense perception and cognition. They seek ways to bridge the gap between the senses and the intellect. In *On the Aesthetic Education of Man* (1795), Schiller contends that an aesthetic education enables a person to proceed from mere passive sensation to active logical and moral thought. Similarly, Kant argues in *The Critique of Judgement* (1790) that students of the fine arts need to learn both aesthetic concepts and moral ideas. Unifying concepts make good art universally appreciated, while art that appeals solely to the senses has only "private validity." According to Kant, the fine arts are "advancing the culture of the mental powers in the interests of social communication." Like Burke, Kant especially values the sublime because it evokes a mental faculty capable of "transcending every standard of sense." Furthermore, the sublime stimulates "a mental *movement*," in contrast to one's passive reception of sense impressions and merely beautiful images.[9] This emphasis on intellectual activity and the need for aesthetic education also influenced the romantics.

Alarmed by the excesses of the French Revolution, Schiller insists that a thorough liberal education is necessary before people are ready for the responsibilities of citizenship. He stresses the relationship among true freedom, the development of taste, and an appreciation for beauty. A person governed by the senses cannot be free because intellectual and moral development is stunted. However, the ability to appreciate beauty gives an individual "the freedom to be what he

ought to be." Before a person has attained aesthetic and moral awareness, he cannot sympathize with other people because he is too egocentric. Like Kant, Schiller believes that appreciation of beauty "unites
[members of a] society, because it relates to what is common to them
all."[10]

Schiller and Goethe apply these principles to literature in their
essay "On Epic and Dramatic Poetry" (1797). In a comparison of the
epic and dramatic genres, the authors maintain that the epic appeals
"only to the imagination," while the performed drama appeals to the
senses. At a play,

> The senses of spectators and listeners must be constantly stimu-
> lated. They must not rise to a contemplative frame of mind, but
> must follow eagerly; their imagination must be completely sup-
> pressed; no demands must be made upon it; and even what is
> narrated must be vividly brought before their vision, as it were, in
> terms of action.[11]

In this return to a topic raised by Aristotle in the *Poetics*, Schiller and
Goethe disagree with the Greek philosopher's contention that tragic
drama is superior to the epic. While Aristotle considered spectacle a
minor aspect of drama, the German writers insist that spectacle dominates any performance, to the detriment of the audience's imagination.

The British romantics, except for Shelley and Keats, retain the
ancient Greeks' distrust of the senses and continue Kant and Schiller's
attempts to explain how one can move from reliance on the senses to
analytic thought and morality. Like Goethe and Schiller, the romantics
apply the mind/body dichotomy to their discussions of drama.

Although William Blake did not write drama criticism, his ambivalence about the senses links him to the other romantics. With the
exception of "The Marriage of Heaven and Hell," his writings condemn the senses and the body as obstructions to spiritual knowledge
and growth. In a poem mailed to Thomas Butts on 22 November 1802,
Blake distinguishes between four different kinds of vision: the highest
form is fourfold vision, which is spiritual, while the lowest form is
single vision, which is mere sense perception. Blake insists in another
poem, "The Everlasting Gospel" (written circa 1818), that one can
"Believe a Lie / When you see with, not thro', the Eye." After finishing
the epic *Milton* in 1803, Blake writes to Butts, "Allegory address'd to
the Intellectual powers, while it is altogether hidden from the Cor-
poreal Understanding, is my Definition of the most Sublime Poetry; it

is also somewhat in the same manner defin'd by Plato." In his marginal annotations to Reynolds's *Discourses*, Blake argues that the great writer does not copy nature but rather draws on forms in the imagination.[12]

Blake admired William Wordsworth's translation of the sonnet by Michelangelo that includes the following four Platonic lines:

> Heaven-born, the Soul a heavenward course must hold;
> Beyond the visible world she soars to seek
> (For what delights the sense is false and weak)
> Ideal form, the universal mould.

Wordsworth recalls in *The Prelude* a time in his life when the sense of sight dominated him to a degree that was dangerous for his intellectual and moral development. He argues that the eye is "the most despotic of our senses." For this reason, he worries about his contemporaries' obsession with illustrations. While language is an integral part of human nobility, Wordsworth insists in "Illustrated Books and Newspapers" (a sonnet written in 1845 and published in 1850) that illustrations manifest the childish taste of his era. He returns to Horace's eye/ear dichotomy:

> Avaunt this vile abuse of pictured page!
> Must eyes be all in all, the tongue and ear
> Nothing? Heaven keep us from a lower stage![13]

Coleridge agrees with Schiller that aesthetic taste can mediate between the mind and the senses. "TASTE is the intermediate faculty which connects the active with the passive powers of our nature, the intellect with the senses." In "On Poesy or Art" (1818), Coleridge argues that poetry is the "primary art" because it is the least dependent on the senses. Poetry derives its "materials . . . from the mind, and all its products are for the mind. . . . It elevates the mind by making its feelings the object of its reflexion."[14]

The romantics' critique of the senses is central to the distinction made by Coleridge, Lamb, and Hazlitt between an imitation and a copy. In Discourse Three (1770), Sir Joshua Reynolds had argued that by copying nature, one can never produce great art because a copy "can never raise and enlarge the conceptions, or warm the heart of the spectator." A copy appeals to "the superficial sense of the spectator," but great art exhibits a "grandeur of . . . ideas" that engages the imagination. Capturing every minute detail is less important than embodying an idea: "It is not the eye, it is the mind, which the painter of genius desires to address."[15] Coleridge adapts Reynolds's and Burke's concepts in his lectures, where he compares overly detailed poems and paintings that appeal to the senses with what he considers great literature, which embodies significant unifying ideas in a few well-chosen images. Coleridge contrasts the works of geniuses like Shakespeare, Dante, and Milton to overly descriptive "modern poems, where all is so dutchified . . . by the most minute touches, that the reader naturally asks why words, and not painting, are used" (*SC*, 2:134). Works of art which are "imitations" are superior to works of art which are "copies" of nature because the former challenge the reader or beholder to decipher them, while the latter are obvious to the senses and do not engage the intellect. Coleridge compares our tepid response to "a glass reflection" or a "waxen image" (copies) to our "delight" with a painting on canvas of the same object. The two-dimensional, flat surface makes it impossible to copy a three-dimensional object (*SC*, 2:80; 1:200, n. 1; *BL*, 2:255–56, 259). The imitation provides "*intellectual pleasure*" (*SC*, 2:78) by exciting the reader or the spectator to decode its meaning. Poetry challenges the reader even more than painting challenges a viewer because poetry is more independent of the senses. Instead of appealing to mere visual perception, good literature appeals to the imagination by using as few details as possible to convey an image. "The power of poetry is, by a single word perhaps, to instil that energy into the mind, which compels the imagination to produce the picture" (*SC*, 2:174). Coleridge cites the first scenes of *The Tempest* as examples.

In general, Coleridge believes that Shakespeare designed his dramas as "more a delight and employment for the intellect, than [an] amusement for the senses." Nineteenth-century theaters emphasize realistic sets and plays, but realism mangles Shakespeare's works because he did not intend them to produce "strong excitement of the senses" (*SC*, 2:85–86).

Hazlitt agrees with Coleridge that literature, which stimulates the mind, is the best form of art. For this reason, Hazlitt dislikes opera, where the words are lost in a profusion of music, dancing, and scenery. Like John Dennis, Hazlitt views opera as the most dangerous kind of theater: both men argue that opera overwhelms the spectators by assaulting the senses. Hazlitt complains in "On the Opera" (1818),

> The multitude and variety of objects distracts the attention. . . .
> The powers of the mind are exhausted, without being invigorated.
> . . . The mind is made 'the fool of the senses,' and cheated of itself.
> . . . It is a species of intellectual prostitution; for we can no more

receive pleasure from all our faculties at once than we can be in love with a number of mistresses at the same time. (*Works of Hazlitt*, 20:92–94)

This notion that the mind needs to concentrate on words and ideas and is distracted by a combination of the visual and performing arts is a keystone of romantic drama criticism.

Whenever the British romantics discuss literature and education, they stress the need to free people from egotism and absorption in the senses. An important term that they repeat in these discussions is "abstraction." This concept has caused some confusion in twentieth-century analyses of romantic texts because the meaning of the word has changed. Aristotle and Plato had used "abstraction" to mean a "departure from the immediate data of sense." This term had positive connotations for the Greeks, who used it to indicate the ability to separate the essential aspects of something from the superficial aspects. For example, Aristotle defines a mathematician as one who

investigates abstractions (for before beginning his investigation he strips off all the sensible qualities, e.g. weight and lightness, hardness and its contrary, and also heat and cold and the other sensible contraries, and leaves only the quantitative and continuous . . .).[16]

The romantics also view this ability as positive and important. In *Remarks on the Systems of Hartley and Helvetius* (1805), Hazlitt includes abstraction among the operations that are "essential, or honourable to the human mind" (*Works of Hazlitt*, 1:66–67). Coleridge goes even further in his *Logic*, where he insists that a good education teaches students "that power of abstraction" which is the ability "to abstract from all the accidents of sense," the ability to generalize valid principles from the jumble of sensory perceptions. Very few people have minds capable of true abstraction. Most individuals are thus subject to "the tyranny of appearances." Coleridge believes that this power of abstraction is attained only by those who (1) can perceive similarities among superficially different things and (2) can reflect consciously on the acts of their intellect. Without abstraction, self-knowledge and profound knowledge of one's world are impossible.[17]

When Coleridge and other early nineteenth-century writers discuss abstraction, they associate it with the process of establishing an intellectual "distance" between a person and something that he or she is trying to understand and evaluate. In an 1811 lecture, Coleridge argues that

> both poetry and religion throw the object of deepest interest to a distance from us, and thereby not only aid our imagination, but in a most important manner subserve the interest of our virtues; for that man is indeed a slave, who is a slave to his own senses, and whose mind and imagination cannot carry him beyond the distance which his hand can touch, or even his eye can reach. (*SC*, 2:147)

Similarly, in examining the topic "Why Distant Objects Please," Hazlitt argues that separation in space and time allows us to transcend sense perceptions to consider distant objects from the perspective of the fancy. Distance enables us to rise above our ordinary concerns to attain something higher (*Works of Hazlitt*, 8:255). This distance can also be achieved by generating a central concept that unifies disparate facts and sensations. Hazlitt discusses this process in his essay "On Depth and Superficiality" (1826). He defines depth as

> tracing any number of particular effects to a general principle, or . . . distinguishing an unknown cause from the individual and varying circumstances with which it is implicated, and under which it lurks unsuspected. It is in fact resolving the concrete into the abstract. (12:355)

Skill in abstraction is essential to any good artist or writer. Coleridge gives an example of how artists can use abstraction in "On Poesy or Art": a painting of a person should be dominated by a unifying concept rather than by perfect verisimilitude. "Hence a good portrait is the abstract of the personal" (*BL*, 2:259).

Spectators and readers also need some abstraction in order to appreciate drama fully. The romantics often praise the act of reading plays because it allows more distance and abstraction than viewing a performance does. According to Lamb, stage spectacle frustrates "that vantage-ground of abstraction" required for the unhampered operation of the imagination. Similarly, Hazlitt finds that small London theaters have ruined "abstraction" by placing the audience too close to the actors (*Works of Hazlitt*, 18:297). A. W. Schlegel also argues that one needs aesthetic distance from a play. He criticizes the practice of seating spectators on the stage in France because "all theatrical effect requires a certain distance, and when viewed too closely appears ludicrous."[18] Abstraction is valuable when it frees the mind from the senses and thus allows a wide variety of imaginative responses.

Park's analysis of Lamb and Hazlitt's view of abstraction is really more true of other writers like John Keats and W. B. Yeats, who value sensation and are suspicious of generalizations. Keats celebrates "a Life of Sensations" more than abstract thought and philosophy. Likewise, Yeats uses the terms "abstract" and "abstraction" to describe the alienation of much cerebral art from the "beauty" that arises from sensations.

> Art bids us touch and taste and hear and see the world, and shrinks from what Blake calls mathematic form, from every abstract thing, from all that is of the brain only, from all that is not a fountain jetting from the entire hopes, memories, and sensations of the body.[19]

The very title of this essay, "The Thinking of the Body" (1906), emphasizes Yeats's departure from earlier aesthetics. I will return to this distinction in Chapter 6 of this book.

In the following chapters, I will examine how Coleridge, Hazlitt, and Lamb apply their critique of the senses to literary analysis. These romantics insist that the best artists, authors, and audiences all must exercise abstraction to produce and understand masterpieces. In fact, Coleridge, Lamb, and Hazlitt design their own literary criticism to train readers to concentrate on the essential elements, such as theme and characterization. By teaching their readers to disregard "copies" and elaborate spectacles, the romantics hope to foster more active and creative involvement with art.

3. Coleridge's Emphasis on the Importance of "Abstraction" in Education, Reading Drama, and Self-Realization

Scattered throughout Coleridge's lectures and writings are many comments on the subject of education. Few critics have discussed the relationship between these comments about teaching and learning and his ideas about literature.[1] In the second edition of *Shakespearean Criticism* (1960), T. M. Raysor omits two lectures that Coleridge presented on education as part of his Bristol Lectures in 1813 and 1814, as well as scattered notes on education in Coleridge's other manuscripts. Raysor comments, "The two lectures on education have no connection with Shakespearean criticism."[2] In this chapter, I hope to demonstrate that these apparent digressions are closely related to Coleridge's approach to literature, especially to his insistence that Shakespeare's plays must be read, not performed, to be fully appreciated. I will focus on Coleridge's *Shakespearean Criticism*, much of which was prepared for public lectures to adults. I will also draw on his other prose works, including *Biographia Literaria*, *The Friend*, *Aids to Reflection*, *Lay Sermons*, *Logic*, *Miscellaneous Criticism*, *On the Constitution of the Church and State*, *The Notebooks*, and the *Collected Letters*. In addition, "The Rime of the Ancient Mariner" and other poems will be used to demonstrate Coleridge's concern with the interaction between writers and their audience.

Teaching and Learning

Education was important to nineteenth-century idealists like Coleridge because it allowed people to transcend their animal nature and to perfect themselves by means of self-realization. The goal of education and self-realization was "to raise *everyone's* consciousness so that everyone could become a vehicle of the divine purpose." Northrop Frye views "the attaining of an expanded consciousness, the sense of identity with God and nature" as a primary theme of the British romantics. Thus, for the idealists there is no gap between individual good and common good, because as individuals increase their knowledge and self-awareness, they help to spiritualize their society.[3]

Coleridge became interested in the reform of education in part because of his dissatisfaction with his own schooling. He reports in *Biographia Literaria* that he still has nightmares about the "severities" of his teacher at Christ's Hospital, Reverend James Bowyer (*BL*, 1:6). During his 1808 lectures, Coleridge declares "that even now his life is embittered by the recollection of ignominious punishments he suffered when a child," and he denounces the practice of "cramming" students (*SC*, 2:12–13). In "Frost at Midnight," he is haunted by the memory of "the stern preceptor's face" and the school where he was "pent 'mid cloisters dim." He envisions a better education for his baby son, who will learn from wandering freely in nature.[4]

These images from "Frost at Midnight" are clearly influenced by Jean Jacques Rousseau's *Émile* (1762). Rousseau insists that conventional methods of education constrain the child's physical, mental, and spiritual development and discourage self-reliance. Rousseau recommends that young children not be taught from books but rather learn from observing their environment. A child learns best when "Nature, not man, is his schoolmaster" and when the child can be "carrying out his own ideas, not those of other people."[5]

However, Coleridge advocates that parents and teachers take an active role in shaping a child's education when he or she is ready to learn to read. Leaving children to learn in a purely natural way is like leaving a garden to grow weeds and flowers at random (*SC*, 2:11, 291–92).

Coleridge insists that students should thoroughly understand basic concepts, instead of memorizing facts. This mastery of abstract ideas is central to real learning.

> To understand what I know . . . is the end of all . . . science, . . . and the aim of all liberal Education as far as the Intellect is concerned. The very word implies it—for the mind is *educed*, drawn forth, or developed, in exact proportion as the consciousness is extended.

He laments that young men of his era are "expensively be-schoolmastered" but not well educated. Using a military metaphor, Coleridge argues that such students "have received arms and ammunition, instead of skill, strength, and courage." He prefers what he considers "the method dictated by nature herself": that is, "all true and living knowledge [must] proceed from within; . . . it may be trained, supported, fed, excited, but can never be infused or impressed." This organic view of learning is parallel to his idea of organic form in literature and to his perspective on self-realization.[6]

Besides supervising the education of his sons, Coleridge tutored some children of friends. The letters to James Gillman, Jr., one of his students, are a good source for Coleridge's ideas about education. In an 1826 letter, Coleridge reminds young Gillman about the etymology of the term *"liberal* education." Like Schiller, Coleridge emphasizes that a good education frees people to use their minds creatively and to arrive at original ideas.

> And what is a liberal Education? That which *draws* forth and trains up the germ of free-agency in the Individual—Educatio, quae *liberum* facit: and the man, who has mastered all the conditions of *freedom,* is *Homo Liberalis. . . .* He alone is *free* & entitled to the name of a Gentleman, who knows himself and walks in the light of his own consciousness. (Italics are Coleridge's.)

Thus, a liberal education should include only those subjects that are "a Mean of acquainting the Learner with the nature and laws of his own Mind." A good education avoids "merely mechanical" knowledge but emphasizes learning capable of

> re-acting on the mind . . . —all knowlege [*sic*], I say, that enlightens and liberalizes, is a form and a means of Self-knowlege, whether it be grammar, or geometry, logical or classical. For such knowlege must be founded on *Principles:* and those Principles can be found only in the Laws of the Mind itself.

Coleridge compares learning isolated facts to "the Dots in Frog-spawn" or "a Lumber-garret"; in contrast, ideas associated by principles and laws eventually will "become the mind itself and are living and constituent parts of it."[7]

Over and over in his other writings, Coleridge emphasizes the main points discussed in this letter: (1) the purpose of liberal education is to produce men who are truly free; (2) freedom results from self-knowledge; (3) students should be taught subjects like logic, psychology, and literature, which give learners insight into the principles of creative human minds; (4) ideas carefully linked by principles will add to the student's own mental powers and enable him to apply the principle to new fields. A good education thus results in self-realization.

In his lectures on Shakespeare and Milton, Coleridge derides contemporary systems of education that instruct people without really teaching them how to think. He advises, "Let it be our first duty to teach thinking, and then what to think about." Coleridge goes on to compare true intellectual effort to the agility of a chamois hunter bounding across the Alps. Just as a man aspiring to become a chamois hunter would need "vigour and elasticity" before he could learn to leap skillfully, anyone who desires mental ability must strive "in every possible way to cultivate and improve the thinking powers: the mind as much requires exercise as the body" (SC, 2:60).[8]

Coleridge's concern with educational reform was natural in an era when many new schools were established in Great Britain, especially schools for the indigent. In A Lay Sermon, he praises "the unprecedented zeal and activity in the education of the poor" during the early nineteenth century. In a footnote, he also lauds the new interest of the middle and upper classes in the education of their children, as witnessed by the many volumes published in the 1800s for parents who wanted to instruct their children at home. Furthermore, the distribution of Bibles and the new emphasis placed on reading them pleased Coleridge.[9]

He repeatedly defends the concept of universal education because the responsibilities of citizenship in a free country require learning. Education develops "the potential divinity in every man," regardless of his social class. In The Statesman's Manual, Coleridge warns his educated and influential readers to reject the false belief that peace

> may be re-established by excluding the people from all knowledge and all prospect of amelioration. . . . Reflection and stirrings of mind, with all their restlessness, and all the errors that result from their imperfection . . . are come into the world. . . . Books are in every hovel.

The literate worker reads books and journals "which render it impossible for the man to be treated or governed as a child" (SM, 39–40). In his Omniana, Coleridge compares the attempt to stifle the education of the lower classes with the Philistines' blinding of Samson.[10]

Reform-minded writers like Coleridge and Johann Heinrich Pestalozzi, who favored sending all children to school, faced a strong prejudice against universal education. The upper class in England and Europe feared that if the poor people were educated, they would become dissatisfied and start revolutions like the one in France. Because of this prejudice, most schools for the poor were "designed to inculcate mainly practical religion, social obedience and low-level occupational skills."[11]

The monitorial system was established to educate many poor British children cheaply. It was invented in the late 1790s by Joseph Lancaster, a Quaker, and Andrew Bell, a Church of England clergyman, each working independently of the other. Both Bell and Lancaster advocated extending their "new system" into a national program for educating the poor. Under the monitorial system, one adult teacher supervised a large classroom containing hundreds of students. The more advanced pupils served as monitors for the others. Each monitor— all of ten or eleven years old—supervised ten to twenty children and drilled them in basic reading, writing, and arithmetic. Rewards and punishments were used to keep students working. The main problem with the system was that monitors had no special training and were seldom very far ahead of their students. Also, the supervising "master" teachers were often inadequately trained. Kate Silber points out that in the monitorial system, "learning was purely mechanical, superficial, and by rote." Furthermore, the method did not develop the child's character or potential. Despite its defects, this system was very popular in Great Britain until about 1850.[12]

Coleridge often praises the monitorial system of Andrew Bell. Coleridge knew Bell and read his book, *The Madras School* (1808), which Coleridge drew on for his lecture on education at the Royal Institution in May 1808. In *The Statesman's Manual*, Coleridge praises Bell's system as "an especial gift of Providence to the *human* race." However, he continues, "It would yet appear to me a most dangerous delusion to rely on it as if this of itself formed an efficient national education." He warns his readers that merely teaching all the people to read and write is not sufficient (*SM*, 40–41). Similarly, Coleridge told H. C. Robinson in 1812 that it was an "error" to consider "reading and writing to be in themselves education."[13] Two years later, Coleridge insists in an essay published in *The Courier* that reading and writing are "the *means* of education," not the *end*, which is developing the understanding and the morality of students (*EOT*, 2:395). Coleridge often urges members of the upper classes to develop their own intellects and to take an interest in spreading knowledge among the people. He disagrees with those who argue that it is enough "to make the Ignorant religious." He insists, "All effective Faith presupposes Knowledge and individual Conviction" (*SM*, 42, 47; *Friend*, 1:103–5; 2:70–71).[14]

Much of Coleridge's discussion about teaching and learning is a commentary on and a criticism of John Locke's *Some Thoughts Concerning Education* (1693). Locke's empirical philosophy was dominant at Cambridge, which Coleridge attended, and he mentions in *Biographia Literaria* that he studied the works of Locke (*BL,* 1:93). In *Some Thoughts Concerning Education,* Locke contends that nine-tenths of a man's character and ability are shaped by education. (However, Locke uses the term "education" to include all aspects of bringing up children, not just schooling.) He views education as the development of mental and physical powers, rather than as the mere acquisition of facts. Like Coleridge, Locke emphasizes that the goal of education is to prepare the student for life and for independent study. Locke advises tutors to give a young man an overview of the various studies so that the student can later, if he desires, "penetrate deeper . . . by his own Genius and Industry." Thus, the tutor should "settle in his Pupil good Habits, and the Principles of Vertue and Wisdom; . . . and . . . give him Vigour, Activity, and Industry." The goal of studying is not to learn every detail of Latin grammar or to cover every field intensively, but rather to generate "a love and esteem of Knowledge." Locke advocates stimulating the child's activity and curiosity instead of having a student hear long lectures or memorize rules. He wants children to learn through discovery and direct experience, not by passively accepting the dicta of authorities. He recommends that children's studies be "made easy to them, and as pleasant as possible." The teacher should help them when they are puzzled. However, in subjects that exercise the reason, students should be given problems to "accustom the Mind to imploy its own Strength and Sagacity in Reasoning." Locke suggests discussing the material with pupils and asking them questions, instead of reading lectures or dictating. Discussion allows students to practice the principles that they are learning and fixes the ideas in their minds.[15]

Locke differs from Coleridge in advocating teaching by appealing to the senses. Locke believes that knowledge results from sensations; thus children should learn best when they use concrete objects like dice or blocks with the alphabet or syllables on them. He recommends a game resembling Scrabble to teach spelling. If students must study Latin, Locke suggests that new vocabulary should be linked with their "Knowledge of *Minerals, Plants,* and *Animals.* . . . But more especially *Geography, Astronomy,* and *Anatomy.*" All these fields are "obvious to the Senses." Appealing to sight is especially important.[16] In contrast, Coleridge attacks the practice of teaching mathematics "by making the illustrations obvious to the senses. Nothing can be more absurd or injurious: it ought to be our never-ceasing effort to make people think, not feel" (*SC*, 2:71). Similarly, he condemns "the teacher of geometry who should present his circles, triangles, etc to the scholar in gaudy and variegated colours" (*Logic*, 15). Coleridge contends that such appeals to the senses frustrate the development of abstract thought.

Like Schiller, he believes that education is a prerequisite for citizens, who need to understand both their rights and their duties. Furthermore, Coleridge adapts Fichte's idea that scholars raise the spiritual level of the state. In *On the Constitution of Church and State* (1830), Coleridge stresses the importance of the "clerisy"—clergymen, scholars, and teachers—who can mediate between the landowners and the merchants, the manufacturers and other professionals. The clerisy's task is to protect and accumulate knowledge and thus to educate and civilize the entire country. Coleridge envisions most members of this group dispersed across the nation to provide guidance and instruction for all residents. The clerisy is not limited to one social class but rather includes any person well educated in culture and morality. However, because true wisdom and goodness are so rare, "these acquirements and powers of the understanding . . . fall to the lot of two or three in each several group, club, or neighbourhood" (*CCS*, 43–44, 46–47, 52–54, 69, 87–88).[17]

Coleridge took his own role as a writer/teacher very seriously. According to Shawcross, "Coleridge was essentially a teacher, and conscious of a message to his age" (Preface, *BL*, 1:iv). In his prose, Coleridge often refers to his role as a teacher and his desire to expand the consciousness of his public. A letter to J. Britton of the Russell Institution is a good example. Here, Coleridge argues that he selects material for his lectures which will "keep the audience awake and interested during the delivery, and . . . leave a *sting* behind—*i. e.* a disposition to study the subject anew, under the light of a new principle" (*SC*, 2:325). The epigraph that Coleridge chose for *Biographia Literaria* also emphasizes the need for the experienced adult "to instruct others" in order to spare them "those circuitous paths, on which he himself had lost his way" (Shawcross's translation of Goethe, *BL*, 1:iv).

Another writer who shared Coleridge's sense of having a mission was Johann Heinrich Pestalozzi. The Swiss educator established several schools during his life (1745–1827). His schools at Burgdorf and Yverdon attracted teachers, students, and visitors from Britain, Europe, and America. Pestalozzi also wrote and had published numerous books and essays, including *Leonard and Gertrude* (1781), *How Gertrude Teaches her Children* (1801), *The Method* (1800), and *My Inquiries into the Course of Nature in the Development of Mankind* (1797). Coleridge praises Pestalozzi's analysis of the human intellect (*Letters*, 4:806). Coleridge also corresponded with Gioacchino de' Prati, who had taught at Pestalozzi's school at Yverdon (*Letters of Coleridge*, 5:452–53 and n. 1). Pestalozzi's ideas were advocated in Britain by writers and educators such as Elizabeth Hamilton and Maria Edgeworth. Madame de Staël commended his work in her book, *De l'Allemagne*, which was published in England in 1813.[18]

Like Coleridge, Pestalozzi condemns contemporary schools because they cram facts into children's heads rather than develop originality. Pestalozzi emphasizes that his system results in active minds, in contrast to the passivity of students trained by using traditional methods. He writes, "In the one case the child and all his capacities will be stimulated earlier and activated, in the other the innermost being of the child will be forced into an emptiness, a desert." Pestalozzi agrees with Coleridge that teachers should stimulate dynamic thought in students. At Yverdon and Burgdorf, the education consisted not of "teaching pupils about thought, but of forming their capacity to think." Like Coleridge, Pestalozzi stresses that students need to understand basic principles, instead of memorizing formulas. Only by approaching education in this way can teachers help students to solve problems by themselves.[19]

Locke, Pestalozzi, and Coleridge agree that true learning cannot occur in an atmosphere of frequent beatings. All three anticipate the twentieth-century psychologist, Jean Piaget, when they argue that children do not need severe punishments if teachers present material at the right time and at the right pace for the students. The ideal education is individualized in order to accommodate the differing needs of children in various stages of development. For example, Coleridge argues that the secret of teaching "is to begin low enough. If a boy cannot learn three lines, give him two; if not two, one; if not one, half. The level of the capacity must be found." Furthermore, children should not be confused by material that is too difficult for them. The ideas of a child "should not be palsied by obliging it to utter sentences which the head could not comprehend nor the heart echo" (*SC*, 2:290, 292, 294, 296). Coleridge suggests that a teacher must "remember [his or her] own state of mind when the subject was new" in order to understand the pupil's unfamiliarity with the material.[20] Coleridge views education as "a *progress*" (*SC*, 2:296)—a journey, a process of continuous improvement (see the *Oxford English Dictionary,* definitions 1, 3a, 4b). This developmental concept of learning is widely accepted in the twentieth century but was unorthodox in the early 1800s.

Both Coleridge and Pestalozzi contend that without self-knowledge, people cannot develop their innate benevolence. Education helps students to overcome selfishness and thus to achieve social awareness and morality. While the pursuit of self-knowledge may appear egocentric, it paradoxically leads to sympathy for others. Coleridge writes in his *Notebooks* that moral life begins "at the first exertion of reflective Self-consciousness."[21]

The problem with conventional schooling is that it emphasizes the accumulation of facts and the superficial skills of debate. Such a system tempts students to become arrogant show-offs who despise other people's ideas but are unaware of the "shallowness" of their own knowledge (*EOT,* 2:396). In contrast, a genuinely liberal education promotes "intellectual activity," by which the mind is expanded and the individual develops sympathy and benevolence for other people.[22]

Similarly, Hazlitt argues that a good education enables people to transcend their egos and petty everyday pursuits in order to learn abstraction. Such schooling "accustoms the mind to take an interest in things foreign to itself; to love virtue for its own sake; . . . and to fix our thoughts on the remote and permanent, instead of narrow and fleeting objects." Those who lack a thorough education "have no power of abstraction, no general standard of taste, or scale of opinion. They see their objects always near, and never in the horizon." Such people lack coherent principles that would enable them to prevent inconsistency and prejudice.[23]

Coleridge views literature as an ideal means of aiding students to transcend their egos and to develop their imaginations. He stresses the importance of the imagination more than Locke and Pestalozzi do. Coleridge argues that "works of imagination" develop both the intellect and the morality of a child because such works

> carry the mind out of self, and show the possible [*sic*] of the good and the great in the human character. . . . In the imagination of man exist the seeds of all moral and scientific improvement. . . . The imagination is the distinguishing characteristic of man as a progressive being.[24]

Without the sympathetic imagination, mankind cannot make progress. Coleridge argues that both poetry and religion help people to transcend "their own narrow sphere of action" and help to merge "the individual man in the whole species." Therefore, both poetry and religion aid the development of the sympathetic imagination (*SC*, 2:147). Note that this view of the imagination differs greatly from the stereotype of romantic subjectivity.[25]

Over and over, Coleridge recommends that parents and teachers give children imaginative literature to read, rather than didactic tales about goody-goody youths. When children read a blatantly moralized book, they will imitate the actions of the virtuous young heroes and heroines and expect praise. Coleridge feels that this teaches vanity, not goodness. He is reacting against both utilitarian and evangelical prejudice against imaginative literature.[26] Instead of didactic stories, Coleridge suggests that children read works of imagination like the *History of St. George*, the *Seven Champions of Christendom*, and *Arabian Nights*. These books implicitly teach children to "feel and reverence the nature of man and . . . feel deeply for the afflictions of others" (*SC*, 2:109–10).[27] Such sympathy is the root of true morality, Coleridge believes, not artificial maxims, which do not engage the emotions. Imaginative literature enables children to "forget themselves" because it concerns events "beyond their own sphere of action" (2:11–14, 293). Such books also help children to think in terms of wholes rather than to focus on component parts (*Letters of Coleridge*, 1:354).

Coleridge excludes many contemporary novels from his category of imaginative literature. These books merely make the reader cry without provoking him or her to take action. Because such novels lack a core of imagination, Coleridge compares them to the exposed props and backdrops of a theater when no drama is being performed (I will explore this important first association later in this chapter). Nineteenth-century fiction excites curiosity without producing "an activity of the intellectual faculties" (*MC*, 195–96). Coleridge consistently denigrates "curiosity" and praises "love of knowledge" (*Friend*, 2:276).

Though Coleridge emphasizes that young students should not be overwhelmed by material that is beyond their capacity to absorb, he also criticizes "the practice of . . . making learning easy" for children (*SC*, 2:13). If schooling is too simplistic, the intellect will never be stimulated. He tries in his own lectures and writings to challenge the public. Alice D. Snyder points out that Coleridge's interest in the art of teaching was spurred by his own "difficulties . . . in trying to communicate ideas that demanded a new vocabulary and a new imaginative approach."[28]

The Art of Method

Coleridge was criticized by contemporaries for the alleged obscurity and disorganization of his work. Henry Crabb Robinson complained that his friend was "always digressing" in his lectures and that "it was impossible for him to be methodical." Robinson worried that the 1811 to 1812 series of lectures on Shakespeare's and Milton's poetry would not be popular because Coleridge "supposes so much unusual attention and rare faculties of thinking, even in the hearer" (*SC*, 2:17, 211, 227, 223–24). Even loyal Charles Lamb whispered to Robinson that the comments on *Romeo and Juliet* were so digressive that Coleridge appeared to be "'delivering the lecture in the character of the Nurse'" (2:216).[29] Pater considered Coleridge's "influential" books, *Aids to Reflection, The Friend,* and *Biographia Literaria,* to be among those works that are "furthest from artistic form—bundles of notes." Similarly, the twentieth-century critic René Wellek argues, "Coleridge, even when he writes for a periodical, meditates almost oblivious of his audience."[30]

In various passages, Coleridge answers his critics. For example, he defends Plato from similar charges in the "Essays on the Principles of Method" found in *The Friend.* While Plato's works may seem "tortuous and labyrinthine in their progress," they in fact "exemplify the art of METHOD." According to Coleridge, Plato's intention

> is not so much to establish any particular truth, as to remove the obstacles, the continuance of which is preclusive of all truth. . . . The EDUCATION of the intellect, by awakening the principle and *method* of self-development, was his proposed object, not any specific information that can be *conveyed into it* from without: not to assist in storing the passive mind with the various sorts of knowledge most in request, as if the human soul were a mere repository or banqueting-room, but to place it in such relations of circumstance as should gradually excite the germinal power that craves no knowledge but what it can take up into itself, what it can appropriate, and re-produce in fruits of its own. (*Friend,* 1:472–73)

Coleridge designs his own writings to change his readers/students by activating their minds. He urges the readers of his *Logic* to undertake a periodic "self-examination" to review and master the material that they have studied and also to ask themselves,

> "*Have I reason to believe that my faculties are improved and my means enlarged?*" For that alone is truly knowledge in relation to the individual acquirer which reappears as power, and the improve-

ment of the faculties, the only sure measure and criterion of the attainments. (*Logic*, 42)

Coleridge clarifies what he means by power in *The Statesman's Manual:* "every idea is living, productive, partaketh of infinity, and . . . containeth an endless power of semination" (*SM*, 23–24).[31] If readers can actively engage in developing ideas that they have understood, they become part of this infinite process. Coleridge also intended *The Friend* and *Aids to Reflection* to stir the readers to more active thinking. He chooses words to provoke his audience to self-examination.

> The aim of every sentence is to solicit, nay *tease* the reader to ask himself, whether he *actually* does, or does not understand *distinctly?*—whether he has reflected on the precise meaning of the word, however familiar it may be both to his own ear and mouth? (*Friend*, 1:16, n. 3)

Coleridge hopes that the reader will use *The Friend* as a point of departure for original and creative thinking.

> The Writer wishes . . . not so much to shew my Reader this or that fact, as to kindle his own torch for him, and leave it to himself to chuse the particular objects, which he might wish to examine by its light. (1:16; 2:276–77)

The torch metaphor emphasizes the enlightenment that Coleridge wishes to spread by engaging the intellectual potential of his public.[32]

Coleridge is careful not to underestimate his audience's capacity to meditate independently. He favors metaphors that present his relationship to the reader/student as informal and low-key, rather than as autocratic or dictatorial. Thus, "Coleridge poses as the reader's friend, his host, his guide on a chamois-hunting expedition, his fellow laborer, or his tutor."[33] In 1811, Coleridge told his London lecture auditors,

> I consider myself, not as a man who carries moveables into an empty house, but as a man who entering a generally well furnished dwelling, exhibits a light which enables the owner to see what is still wanting. I endeavour to introduce the means of ascertaining what is, and is not, in a man's own mind. (*SC*, 2:113)

Note that light imagery reoccurs here in a slightly different context. Coleridge portrays himself as a consultant for the interior decorating of one's mind. These informal poses tend to ingratiate him with the reader.

Coleridge views true method as the ability to bring together and to unify distinct ideas and perceptions in new and original ways. "Where the habit of Method is present and effective, things the most remote and diverse in time, place, and outward circumstance, are brought into mental contiguity and succession, the more striking as the less expected" (*Friend*, 1:455; *SC*, 2:340).[34] He often uses Shakespeare as an example of this kind of organization. Coleridge compares the conversation and writing of educated and uneducated people. He argues that well-educated men arrange their words carefully to relate each part to the whole, while those who lack schooling have trouble organizing their ideas and sentences: their diction is characterized by "*disjunction . . .* in the component parts." In contrast, a well-educated person can achieve a "*surview*" of his whole argument "and by this means so to subordinate and arrange the different parts according to their relative importance, as to convey it at once, and as an organized whole" (*BL*, 2:44). Similarly, Coleridge insists in *The Friend*, "However irregular and desultory his talk, there is *method* in the fragments." In contrast, one who is ignorant narrates by first associations and connects all sentences with the meaningless conjunction "and." Mistress Quickly in *Henry IV*, part 1, is used as an example of lack of method, while Hamlet's speeches are cited as specimens of methodical organization. Coleridge admits that Hamlet's "exuberance of mind . . . interferes with the *forms* of Method"; however, "sterility of mind, . . . wanting the spring and impulse to mental action, is wholly destructive of Method itself." An intelligent person may overlook the importance of selecting and arranging thoughts to suit the listeners, but an "unreflecting talker overlooks *all* mental relations" (*Friend*, 1:448–54; *SC*, 2:334–35, 339). Perhaps thinking of his detractors, Coleridge distinguishes between the appearance of method and true method: the former results from "learned and systematic ignorance—arrangement guided by the light of no leading idea, mere orderliness without METHOD!" (*Friend*, 1:513).

Coleridge views his own work as fundamentally organized around certain ideas, despite his minor lapses. In his lecture notes, he contends, "Illustration of principles [is] my main object; therefore [I am] not so digressive as might appear" (*SC*, 1:203). He uses questions in his lectures and essays to focus the audience's attention on an important critical issue, such as the difference between copies and imitations ("On Poesy or Art," *BL*, 2:256), or a dramatic problem, such as the witches in *Macbeth*. He challenges various assertions made by other writers and then spends the rest of his lecture gradually developing his own theory and provoking the auditors to do the same. For example, for a lecture on the subject of Shakespeare's genius and judgment, Coleridge starts by asking, "Are the plays of *Shakespeare* works of rude uncultivated genius, in which the splendor of the parts compensates . . . for the barbarous shapelessness and irregularity of the whole?" Coleridge poses additional questions to gradually move the audience closer to his own position (*SC,* 1:222–23). Those who demand detailed explications of literature from Coleridge are missing the point. He explains to his auditors that he has "taken the great names of Milton and Shakespeare rather for the purpose of illustrating great principles than for any minute examination of their works" (2:110). These principles were designed to stimulate his audience to develop skill in reflective thought, which Coleridge viewed as an art, and he wished to make his students capable of drawing their own conclusions about literature and other topics.

One way to teach people how to think profoundly is to show them how to evolve ideas and link them to one another. Coleridge appears conscious of using this teaching method. In a letter to Thomas Poole, Coleridge argues that digressions in essays are useful and instructive because "they are the *drama* of Reason—& present the thought growing, instead of a mere Hortus siccus" (*Letters,* 3:282). Thus, parentheses show the reader how a writer derives his idea and are superior to a mere summary of conclusions.

In some works, Coleridge intentionally presents the reader with fragments and expects him to fill in the blanks with his own reflections. Good examples are the "Introductory Aphorisms" of *Aids to Reflection.* Coleridge may have had works such as the Proverbs and *Pirke Avot* (*Ethics of the Fathers*) in mind as models for structuring this kind of literature. He explains that his "Appendix Containing Comments and Essays" affixed to *The Statesman's Manual* is "desultory" because it is designed to be "a String of Hints and Materials and Materials for Reflection [*sic*]. The Object too was to rouse and stimulate the mind—to set the reader a-thinking." Coleridge hopes that the public will question various fashionable opinions (*IS,* 201). Another example of this use of fragments is found in *On the Constitution of the Church and State.* Here, Coleridge ridicules the illogical modes of thinking that his contemporaries substitute for true reasoning. The passage reads like prose poetry and forces the reader to make connections between the images in the list. "Idealess facts, misnamed proofs from history, grounds of experience, &c., [are] substituted for principles and the insight derived from them. State-policy, [is] a Cyclops with one eye, and that in the back of the head!" Coleridge views his task as a writer as that of stimulating his readers to "supply the commentary" for his books (*CCS*, 58, 66).[35]

Creative Reading

Many of Coleridge's writings identify weaknesses in the reading habits of his contemporaries. Over and over, he insists that reading must be an active endeavor, and he tries to convey the pleasure that creative mental activity can give. According to Coleridge, most readers do not derive much knowledge from a challenging text because they hate analytic thinking and "all intellectual effort" (*Friend*, 1:22; 2:152). In general, he considers his century a "much-reading, but not very hard-reading age" (*CCS*, 134). He classifies readers into four categories:

> 1. Sponges that suck up everything and, when pressed, give it out in the same state, only perhaps somewhat dirtier. 2. Sand glasses, or rather the upper half of the sand glass, which in a brief hour assuredly lets out what it has received—and whose reading is only a profitless measurement and dozing away of time. 3. Straining bags, who get rid of whatever is good and pure, and retain the dregs. . . . And lastly, the Great Mogul's diamond, sieves. . . . But imperial or culinary, these are the only good, and I fear the least numerous, who assuredly retain the good while the superfluous or impure passes away and leaves no trace. (*SC*, 1:249; see also 2:64)[36]

The majority of readers seems unwilling or unable to confront a text actively and to judge it objectively.

Coleridge was well aware that the increase in the number of book clubs, reading rooms, circulating libraries, and used book stores in the nineteenth century had made books and periodicals available to more people. Cheaper printing methods also resulted in more affordable publications. While some circulating libraries were scholarly and served the educated middle and upper classes, many libraries specialized in novels and other "light literature" for patrons with little schooling. Richard D. Altick describes these novels as "hair-raising, scandalous, or lachrymose." Beginning in the late eighteenth century, many attacks on fiction and on circulating libraries were published. The mass reading public was associated with low-grade fiction in these attacks. Many critics opposed to the novels and the libraries were conservatives who feared that social unrest would result from working-class literacy.[37]

We have already seen that Coleridge did not fear that literacy would lead to revolutions and that he advocated universal education. However, he does question the new readers' choice of books and their casual approach to reading. Most circulating libraries seem useless to him because they offer corny novels and tales of chivalry to a public that needs more intellectually stimulating works. Coleridge argues in *Biographia Literaria* that people who check out frivolous books are wasting their time.

> I dare not compliment their *pass-time*, or rather *kill-time*, with the name of *reading*. Call it rather a sort of beggarly day-dreaming, during which the mind of the dreamer furnishes for itself nothing but laziness and a little mawkish sensibility.

Coleridge classifies such poor novels and chivalric romances not as reading but as a "species" of the genus that includes "gaming, swinging, or swaying on a chair or gate; spitting over a bridge; smoking . . ." (*BL*, 1:34; see also *IS*, 206; *SC*, 2:57; *Friend*, 2:11).[38] He complains that most of his contemporaries cannot read analytically, so they choose books which will spare them "the trouble of thinking" (*BL*, 1:25–27). Such "lazy half-attention amounts to a mental yawn." When reading a new work, nineteenth-century readers are tempted to declare an author "unintelligible," but the truth is that they have not been paying close attention to the text (*Friend*, 1:25–26). As a case in point, Coleridge quotes from an abusive letter that accused him of writing "learned non*sence* and unintelligible Jar*gin*." He questions the "Erudition" of anyone who spells so poorly. Though Coleridge admits that an author's work may be obtuse, he insists that problems with communication may often result if the reader lacks "understanding" (*Friend*, 2:275).

Coleridge finds a close connection between the literary style of an era and the sophistication of the public. He strongly objects to the short, choppy sentences which were becoming prevalent during the early nineteenth century. These easy-to-read sentences produce a style that gives the impression of having been "invented for persons troubled with the asthma to read, and for those to comprehend who labour under the more pitiable asthma of a short-witted intellect." Such prose will lead to intellectual sloth, he believes.

> It cannot but be injurious to the human mind never to be called into effort: the habit of receiving pleasure without any exertion of thought, by the mere excitement of curiosity and sensiblity, may be justly ranked among the worst effects of habitual novel reading. . . . Those who confine their reading to such books dwarf their own faculties, and finally reduce their understandings to a deplorable imbecility.

Coleridge fears that his own style can never be popular because he has been influenced by "the stately march and difficult evolutions, which characterize the eloquence of Hooker, Bacon, Milton, and Jeremy Taylor" (*Friend,* 1:20–21; *IS,* 110–11). These authors, unlike many nineteenth-century writers, increase one's "power of thinking in long and connected trains" (*Friend,* 1:20). Though Coleridge praises *The Spectator,* he worries that the short, simple articles and excerpts from literature that were published by Addison, Steele, and later editors of periodicals have reduced the public's attention span for longer works and more complex styles of writing. Coleridge intends *The Friend* to bridge this gap.

> Consider too the very different Objects of the Friend & of the Spectator: & above all, do not forget, that these are AWEFUL TIMES!—that the love of Reading, as a refined pleasure weaning the mind from grosser enjoyments, which it was one of the Spectator's chief Objects to awaken, has by that work, & those that followed (Connoisseur, World, Mirror &c) but still more, by Newspapers, Magazines, and Novels, been carried into excess: and the Spectator itself has innocently contributed to the general taste for unconnected writing—just as if 'Reading made easy' should act to give men an aversion to words of more than two syllables, instead of drawing them *thro'* those words into the power of reading Books in general.—In the present age, whatever flatters the mind in it's ignorance of it's ignorance, tends to aggravate that ignorance— and I apprehend, does on the whole do more harm than good. (*Letters of Coleridge,* 3:281)

Even educated people who could read reviews misused the periodicals. Because most British schools failed to teach pupils how to think analytically and independently, graduates tended to rely on the opinions of a self-proclaimed authority, rather than forming their own judgments. Coleridge stresses the need to think for oneself. He worries about "the unreasoning multitude" that lacks learning and tends to "live as alms-folks on the opinions of their contemporaries" (*Friend,* 1:211–12; 2:138–39).[39] He traces this problem in British history. According to Coleridge, the eagerness of Renaissance scholars to learn later degenerated into "an abasement of mind under authority. Authority was substituted for reason and the *ipse dixit* of a philosopher for a due appreciation of those grounds which justified the philosopher in the formation of his judgement" (*SC,* 2:101). Coleridge attributes much false criticism to

> the effect, and at first the very painful effect, of really *thinking,* really referring to our own inward experiences, and the ease with which we accept as a substitute for this, which can alone operate a true conviction, the opinions of those about us, which we have heard or been accustomed to take for granted, etc. (*SC,* 1:248)[40]

Repeatedly, Coleridge condemns those who rely on reviews to form opinions of books and writers. The authors of contemporary reviews are incapable of training anyone to judge a work objectively because they do not appeal to universal standards of taste. Furthermore, the readers of journals passively adopt a book reviewer's opinion instead of approaching the text analytically and without biases.

> Reviews are generally pernicious, because the writers determine without reference to fixed principles—because reviews are usually filled with personalities; and, above all, because they teach people rather to judge than to consider, to decide than to reflect: thus they encourage superficiality, and induce the thoughtless and the idle to adopt sentiments conveyed under the authoritative WE, and not, by the working and subsequent clearing of their own minds, to form just original opinions. (*SC,* 2:57–58; see also *Friend,* 2:138)

Coleridge returns to this topic in other passages, using metaphors of masters and servants to convey his disgust with such laziness. "As men often employ servants, to spare them the nuisance of rising from their seats and walking across a room, so men employ reviews in order to save themselves the trouble of exercising their own powers of judging" (*SC,* 2:61). Similarly,

> These reviewers might be compared with the Roman *praegustatores* whose business it was to tell you what was fit to be eaten, and like the *praegustatores* the reviewers gave their opinions, but carefully

concealed all the reasons for such judgements." (*SC*, 2:105; see also 1:246–48; *BL*, 1:44, 49; 2:86–87, 90)[41]

Instead of relying on other people's minds, each individual should learn the importance of introspection and self-knowledge. In *Aids to Reflection*, Coleridge complains that most people manifest an "angry aversion to think" and avoid examining their own biases; thus, their judgments are "irrational." Introspection is a prerequisite for attaining active states of thought. However, Coleridge finds it difficult "to fix the attention of men on the world within them. . . . For, alas! the largest part of mankind are nowhere greater strangers than at home" (*AR*, 117–19).[42]

In the first issue of *The Friend* in 1809, Coleridge lists among its main topics "Education in its widest Sense, private, and national" (2:18). One of his primary goals is to teach his readers to be introspective and to use universal principles instead of prudence to make judgments. Like failures in education, the neglect of principles has both "private and . . . national Consequences" (*Friend*, 2:281–82). Coleridge argues in the *Opus Maximum* that most people lack principles but fool themselves that their "prudential motives" are objective standards.[43] In *A Lay Sermon*, he asks his educated readers to act in accordance with their knowledge of principles, not by relying on "Custom." He urges his middle- and upper-class audiences to use their increased leisure time to expand their knowledge. The comprehension of "universal laws" will improve both private morality and public zeal (*LS*, 124–25).

An underlying cause for mental laziness, according to Coleridge, is his contemporaries' overreliance "on the immediate impressions of the senses." He links this fault to a lack of insight and blames readers for attacking a good writer simply because they have no insight into literature (see *BL*, 1:19–20; *SC*, 1:221; *Letters of Coleridge*, 1:354). The ultimate problem is again their shortage of learning and their inability to achieve abstraction.

Because most of his contemporaries were enslaved by their senses, Coleridge believed that they were obsessed with commerce and the accumulation of wealth. He accuses his era of a "general neglect of all the austerer studies." This neglect has resulted in "the non-existence of a learned and philosophic Public." In contrast, the Renaissance produced truly learned men, fit to govern others (*LS*, 170–72; see also *SM*, Appendix E, 101).

Coleridge views himself as different from his contemporaries because he has tried to distance himself from his senses and has devoted himself to reading and philosophy. He describes himself in a letter to John Thelwall as "a great reader" who has "read almost everything—a library-cormorant— . . . *deep* in all out of the way books. . . . Almost always reading" (*Letters of Coleridge,* 1:260). Furthermore, Coleridge informs Thomas Poole that reading imaginative literature when he was a child enabled him to develop skill in abstraction. He learned to disregard "[his] *senses* . . . as the criteria of [his] belief." Coleridge explains, "I regulated all my creeds by my conceptions not by my *sight*" (1:354). He feels alienated from his contemporaries because they cannot transcend their senses and thus make it very difficult for an author to communicate with them. In a moment of despair, Coleridge writes to Poole, "I am assured, that such is the depravity of the public mind, that no literary man can find bread in England except by misemploying & debasing his Talents—that nothing of real excellence would be either felt or understood" (2:710).

Coleridge yearns for communion between writers and their public, a state which he believes existed during the Renaissance. Authors like Bacon could address " '*learned* readers' " who respected books. However, gradually, "the amateurs of literature" became the incompetent judges of literary merit. By the nineteenth century, "all men being supposed able to read, and all readers able to judge, the multitudinous PUBLIC . . . sits nominal despot on the throne of criticism." Coleridge charges that the general public is an intellectual eunuch, unfit for "the guardianship of the muses" (*BL,* 1:41–42).

Coleridge tries to recreate for himself the "learned" reader of the Renaissance. He attempts to wean the public from the senses by championing the importance of principles and by choosing subjects that force the reader to think more abstractly. Coleridge vows to Humphry Davy that *The Friend,* unlike Cobbett's journal, will not report on specific contemporary events and people because *The Friend* is aimed at a different audience, a public capable of reflection.

> I do not write in this Work for the *Multitude;* but for those, who by Rank, or Fortune, or official Situation, or Talents and Habits of Reflection, are to *influence* the Multitude. I write to found true PRINCIPLES, to oppose false PRINCIPLES, in Criticism, Legislation, Philosophy, Morals, and International Law." (*Letters of Coleridge,* 3:143)

Similarly, Coleridge addresses *The Statesman's Manual* to educated men with " '*sound book learnedness*' " and the ability to handle "philosophic thought." He spurns the "READING PUBLIC," which he considers an "ERUDITULORUM NATIO," a nation with little learning (*SM*, 39, 36). In a letter to William Blackwood, Coleridge admits that his writings are not best sellers because they are "addressed to the higher interests and blameless predilections of men," in contrast to typical contemporary works, which are "constructed on the plan of flattering the envy and vanity of sciolism, and gratifying the cravings of vulgar curiosity." He wants to avoid gossip, slander, and factionalism in his prose (*Letters of Coleridge*, 5:168). When a writer like Coleridge directs his work to a certain type of reader, the work will be "unintelligible" to "an incompetent reader" (*Friend*, 1:54; 2:48). He is willing to sacrifice many incompetent readers to reach a meditative segment of the population. Coleridge claims in *The Friend* that his high-mindedness has "precluded three-fourths of the ordinary readers of periodical publications, whether Reviews, Magazines, or Newspapers" (2:273).

Hazlitt takes a different stance on this problem of public ignorance. He agrees with Coleridge that "most people take their opinions on trust from others" and fail to develop their own "unfettered, independent opinion." However, Hazlitt attributes this habit to the government, which has kept the people ignorant and "in a state of vassalage" and has treated them like "lunatics, incapable of self-government" (*Works of Hazlitt*, 7:272). In his reviews of Coleridge's books, Hazlitt strongly objects to the mockery of the reading public in *The Statesman's Manual* and elsewhere. Hazlitt finds Coleridge's position elitist and prejudiced against the dissenters' Lancasterian system of education (16:106, 112–13; 7:126). Unlike Coleridge, Hazlitt often maintains that the public's ignorance is a result of centuries of oppression. In "What Is the People?" (1817), he argues "that the tide of power constantly setting in against the people, swallows up natural genius and acquired knowledge in the vortex of corruption." He also expresses less confidence than Coleridge in the ability of well-educated politicians, lawyers, ministers, and teachers to benefit the lower classes. At the same time, Hazlitt has a higher opinion of periodicals and the press in general. He asks,

> For what one measure of civil or religious liberty did our own Bench of Bishops ever put themselves forward? What judge ever

proposed a reform in the laws! Have not the House of Commons
. . . voted for every measure of Ministers for the last twenty-five
years, except the Income-tax? It is the press that has done every
thing for the people. (7:269)

He compares the government's abuse of common people to Oliver's
mistreatment of Orlando in *As You Like It*. Hazlitt summarizes Orlando's position: "You teach us nothing, and you will not let us learn."
Hazlitt also attacks the pablum reading material published by the
Church of England and by the government to keep the people in line
(7:273).[44]

Recent critics like Jerome McGann have repeated Hazlitt's charge
that Coleridge's *Statesman's Manual* is elitist because it justifies the status quo. McGann views Coleridge as a "reactionary" romantic writer.
"Because his position is a conceptual-idealist defense of Church,
State, and the class interests which those institutions support and
defend, Coleridge's ideas are, in a Marxist view, clearly deplorable."[45]
However, Hazlitt and McGann ignore Coleridge's radical and consistent support for universal education and self-realization in *The Statesman's Manual* and elsewhere. Also, neither critic quotes Coleridge's
condemnations of the ruling classes and politicians. In one passage,
Coleridge compares British statesmen of the nineteenth century to a
cyclops with one eye in the back of its head: because the statesmen lack
knowledge and philosophic principles, they find themselves "walking
backwards, under the fascination of the Past," instead of preparing
their country for the future (*SM*, 42–43). Would a firm defender of
established institutions publish such a hostile analogy? While some of
Coleridge's statements do seem to belittle the lower classes, his primary concern is not with social classes as defined economically.
Rather, he asserts that one cannot discuss complex ideas with uneducated people of any social stratum. This is why he favors universal
education: communication among people in a modern state requires
literacy and the ability to analyze and evaluate an argument. A well-educated person can compare ideas and make distinctions; furthermore, he or she can use this mental agility to create new ideas. However, an uneducated person is isolated from the flow of philosophic
concepts.

Other proof that Coleridge's so-called elitism is really exasperation with his contemporaries' inability to think analytically can be
found in his comments about the reception of *The Friend*, which he
designed in 1809 for educated and reflective citizens. Coleridge had

hoped for both thought and attention from the readers of the journal (*Friend*, 2:277). However, by 1810 he had become disillusioned because his readers preferred light subjects which did not demand much attention. He complains,

> The way to be admired is to tell the Reader what he knew before, but cloathed in a statelier phraseology, and embodied in apt and lively illustrations. To attempt to make a Man wiser is of necessity to remind him of his ignorance: and in the majority of instances, the pain actually felt is so much greater than the pleasure anticipated, that it is natural that men should attempt to shelter themselves from it by contempt or neglect.

Coleridge complains that when the public cannot understand a writer, it is too "indolent" to do more than condemn the writer as inferior (*Friend*, 2:282). In a notebook entry around the same time, Coleridge expresses the same disappointment: the readers of *The Friend* are capable of neither thought nor attention (*Notebooks*, 3:no. 3670).

The results of this ignorance and mental laziness go far beyond the sales of *The Friend*, according to Coleridge. Because his contemporaries cannot transcend their five senses to contemplate "the principles of truth," human history cannot truly progress. He blames "the deficiency of good" on "the general unfitness and aversion of men to the process of thought" (*Friend*, 1:61–62).

The Value of Literary Studies

Coleridge values the study of language and literature because these disciplines develop one's capacity to contemplate abstract ideas and wean him or her away from relying solely on physical sensations. He hopes that through reading literature, society may perfect itself. "Ideas may become as vivid and distinct, and the feelings accompanying them as vivid, as original impressions. And this may finally make a man independent of his Senses. One use of poetry" (*IS*, 150). Literary study will eventually "emancipate the mind from the despotism of the eye" (*Logic*, 242). By drawing the reader away from the humdrum sensations of ordinary life, writers like Shakespeare and Molière implant the ideas of human nobility and "possible greatness" in the receptive mind (*Friend*, 2:217–18).

Sense impressions and easy-to-read works are seductive because of their clarity. In contrast, the ideas contained in good literature are complex and often obscure. To understand these ideas, a reader must invest a lot of energy and creativity. He must risk the stage of uncertainty and puzzlement in order to achieve the mastery of a text which results in intellectual growth and the awareness of the sublime (*Notebooks*, 2:no. 2509).[46] Coleridge argues that a good education should also challenge a student even in the early stages by presenting "unindicable notions." While the advanced classes can move toward more clarity, Coleridge believes "nothing more unfavorable to intellectual progression, than a too early habit of rendering all our ideas distinct & indicable" (1:no. 902).

In *The Friend*, Coleridge argues that the arts, education, and private life are all governed by the same basic principles (2:276–77). In his essays and lectures, he tries to demonstrate these principles to the public in order to enable his contemporaries to approach all situations analytically and dynamically. The close connection between his ideas about educating citizens and his ideas about reading literature is clear in the imagery that he uses to discuss both subjects. Just as Coleridge uses the metaphor of the agile chamois hunter to clarify the importance of teaching young students how to think creatively (see the "Teaching and Learning" section above in this chapter), he also applies this same metaphor when discussing the effort needed by an ideal reader. He contends that a reader must exert himself to follow the argument of a philosophic writer. Though the guide may show aspiring hunters shortcuts and warn his protégés about

> many a mock road that had formerly led himself to the brink of chasms and precipices, or at best an idle circle, . . . he cannot carry us on his shoulders; we must strain our own sinews, as he has strained his; and make firm footing on the smooth rock for ourselves, by the blood of toil from our own feet.

Coleridge worries because most people can sustain "self-torture" more easily than the "exertion of the Will . . . to *think*" (2:48–49).

In the lectures of 1811 to 1812, Coleridge emphasizes that good literature, like Milton's *Paradise Lost*, stimulates the readers' minds rather than offering them a platitude or an obvious metaphor.

> The grandest efforts of poetry are where the imagination is called forth, not to produce a distinct form, but a strong working of the mind, still offering what is still repelled, and again creating what is again rejected; the result being what the poet wishes to impress, namely the substitution of a sublime feeling of the unimaginable for a mere image. (*SC*, 2: 138; see also 2:77–78, 260–61)

The reward of this exertion of the imagination and the analytic powers of the mind is "a certain joyousness" (*Notebooks*, 3:no. 4422).[47] In his lecture notes, Coleridge mentions the "pleasurable emotion, which the exertion of all our faculties gives in a certain degree." This pleasure requires "the full play of those powers of mind, which are spontaneous rather than voluntary" (*SC*, 1:164). Similarly, Coleridge writes in *Biographia Literaria*,

> The reader should be carried forward, not merely or chiefly by the mechanical impulse of curiosity, or by a restless desire to arrive at the final solution; but by the pleasurable activity of mind excited by the attractions of the journey itself. (*BL*, 2:11)[48]

Note the emphasis on the reader's willing attitude and the need for readers to be active.

Coleridge contends that both writers and readers of literature need to have active minds. In *Biographia Literaria*, he defines the ideal poet as one who "brings the whole soul of man into activity" (*BL*, 2:11–12). In order to challenge the reader, the poet needs to penetrate the surfaces of reality to reach profound truths. Similarly, a good reader must be able to follow the writer on this journey of discovery. Coleridge views the ideal poet as one "who, with a soul unsubdued by habit, unshackled by custom, contemplates all things with the freshness and the wonder of a child." This open-mindedness should be accompanied by the "knowledge, admiration," and "the inquisitive powers" of an adult (*SC*, 2:148). Like the poet, the ideal reader needs to approach literature without biases and with a willingness to cooperate with and appreciate the writer's originality. Coleridge praises Wordsworth's "Ode on the Intimations of Immortality" and emphasizes that this poem "was intended for such readers only as had been accustomed to watch the flux and reflux of their inmost nature, to venture at times into the twilight realms of consciousness, and to feel a deep interest in modes of inmost being" (*BL*, 2:120). Most readers, who are too unimaginative to risk this exploration, will find Wordsworth obscure.[49]

After defining poetry in his lecture notes, Coleridge proceeds to discuss the ideal reader of poetry. In order to understand the "pleasurable emotion" and the "excitement" that the writer is trying to communicate, ideal readers "must combine a more than ordinary sympathy with the objects, emotions, or incidents contemplated by the poet . . . with a more than ordinary activity of mind in respect of the fancy and the imagination" (*SC*, 1:163–64).[50] Coleridge requires an analogous sympathy and mental agility from great authors.

Coleridge feels that Renaissance literature was designed to activate the readers' minds. He contrasts the complex, intriguing texts of the Renaissance with the oversimplified writing styles of the early nineteenth century.

> There was, in truth, an energy in the age, an energy of thinking, which gave writers of the reigns of Elizabeth and James, the same energy. At the present, the chief object of an author was to be intelligible at the first view; then, it was to make the reader think— not to make him understand at once, but to show him rather that he did not understand, or to make him to review, and re-meditate till he had placed himself upon a par with the writer. (*SC*, 2:86)

Coleridge views Shakespeare as the quintessential Renaissance poet. Shakespeare's genius inspires the willing reader to develop imaginative powers. This is possible because Shakespeare is so sensitive to his audience that he designs his plays to involve the readers and spectators emotionally and intellectually. Coleridge told his auditors in 1818 that *The Tempest* reveals how Shakespeare "tempered every thing . . . to the feelings of his audience" (*SC*, 2:322). Shakespeare has enabled anyone with imagination to attain insight into the nature of poetry by reading the dramas and the sonnets. For example, Sonnet 33 is great literature because it shows "the activity of the poet's mind, which, in one image, has merged so many associations. You feel him to be a poet, inasmuch as, for a time, he has made you one—an active creative being" (2:94; see also 2:202).[51]

Coleridge argues that he himself has become more introspective as a result of reading Shakespeare and that the insight gained by this process may affect all readers (*SC*, 2:269). In his notes, Coleridge asserts that, since the age of ten, he has read Shakespeare "almost daily." As his own knowledge and learning have increased, his understanding of the playwright has also deepened (*SC*, 1:210).

Coleridge views Shakespeare as demanding effort from the audience. "If, says he, you will listen to me with your minds and not with your eyes . . . and assist me with your imaginations, I will do so and so" (*SC*, 2:315). Note the consistent emphasis on transcending the senses. Coleridge may have in mind various invocations of the imagination in Shakespeare's plays. For example, "In your imagination hold / This stage the ship, upon whose deck / The sea-tossed Pericles appears to speak" (*Pericles,* 3.Chorus.58–60). Coleridge summarizes the Prologue to *Henry V* in his lectures (*SC,* 2:85) as evidence that Shakespeare called upon his audience to supply with the imagination what his primitive stage lacked.

> . . . Can this cockpit hold
> The vasty fields of France? Or may we cram
> Within this wooden O the very casques
> That did affright the air at Agincourt?
> . . .
> . . . Let us, ciphers to this great accompt,
> On your imaginary forces work.
> . . .
> Piece out our imperfections with your thoughts.[52]

Readers who lack active, creative minds can never appreciate Shakespeare's genius because his plays require mental agility. Coleridge derides those who categorize Shakespeare as "wild" or "irregular." Such commentators do not have "intellect enough to comprehend, or soul to feel" (*SC,* 1:220). Because most people are overly reliant on their senses, they cannot respond to drama that requires reflection. "To those who do not think, and have not been made to think, Shakespeare has been found . . . difficult of comprehension" (2:71). Coleridge wrote to Godwin that the nineteenth-century audience did not appreciate good tragedy. Coleridge speculates that if Shakespeare's plays had premiered in the 1800s, the "Rabble . . . would hiss them into infamy" (*Letters of Coleridge,* 1:653).

Coleridge makes fun of writers who flatter the common reader while they attack literary and philosophical geniuses. Such writers reveal "presumption" when, in their prefaces, they "have prostrated themselves before the superiority of their Readers, as supreme Judges," but spend much of the books criticizing "Plato, Milton, Shakespeare, Spenser, and their Compeers" (*Friend,* 2:278). Many of Coleridge's prose writings are designed to teach his public to appreciate the genius of great authors like Shakespeare and to read literature produced by such a genius carefully and reflectively.

Performance of Shakespeare's Plays

Repeatedly, Coleridge condemns stage performances of Shakespeare's plays and insists that the texts must be *read* to be fully understood. These statements have been taken out of context by twentieth-century critics who insist that Coleridge lacked knowledge of the stage. Allardyce Nicoll asserts in *A History of the English Drama,* "Coleridge had no idea as to what constituted a good play. . . . He . . . wholly neglected the practical side of those very masterpieces which were chosen as his models." Coleridge failed to comment on Shakespeare's "dramatic construction." Furthermore, Nicoll considers Coleridge's criticism too "abstract" to discuss adequately "those concrete elements which are of such importance in drama." Raysor complains, "It is characteristic of Coleridge that he says nothing of plot or structure. His criticism of Shakespeare was poetic rather than dramatic criticism" (*SC,* 1:206, n. 1). Note that Raysor makes this remark after a passage in which Coleridge has listed "a dramatic poet's characteristics," not the prerequisites for a good play. J. A. Appleyard faults "the persistent one-sidedness of romantic criticism in treating Shakespeare's dramas as though they were only character studies." Coleridge's analysis is merely "an examination of character and feeling, with scarcely any mention made of plot, of structure, and particularly of the representative function of the drama as a whole." In general, Appleyard finds Coleridge's position overly subjective. Paul S. Conklin accuses Coleridge of "ignoring matters of dramatic relevance" in his interpretation of *Hamlet.* Coleridge "could not see Hamlet's real relation to the plot in which he moves." In a recent *PMLA* article, Robert DeMaria argues that Coleridge tends "to see the poetic as more valuable than the dramatic." Furthermore, Coleridge approaches all literary works as if they were lyrical poems.

> Through Coleridge's lyrical spectacles drama quite frequently appears to be simply an extension of the lyric mode or a format for its presentation. Coleridge looks for the essential Shakespeare in the early poems, and he places unusually heavy emphasis on the early plays, in which the poetic predominates over the dramatic.[53]

Critics who draw a line of demarcation between "poetic" comments about the characters, imagery, and mood of a play, and "dramatic" comments about plot and structure miss the point: imagery, characters, and mood are inseparable from the structure of a play, and the plot cannot function without them. Furthermore, many passages in Coleridge's notes and lectures refute the assertions that he lacked knowledge of drama, ignored structure, and overemphasized lyrical elements in plays. For example, while he is intrigued by the early plays, he condemns the self-consciously ornate and parenthetical style of *Love's Labor's Lost* because it is not appropriate to the dramatic situation. The language is "suited neither to the passion of the speaker, nor the purpose of the person to whom the information is to be given, but manifestly betraying the author himself" (*SC*, 1:96). Similarly, Coleridge criticizes Shakespeare for passages in tragedies like *Romeo and Juliet* where "the poet is not . . . entirely blended with the dramatist. . . . Capulet and Montague not unfrequently talk a language only belonging to the poet, and not so characteristic of, and peculiar to, the passions of persons in the situations in which they are placed." In such dialogue, Shakespeare fails to individualize the characters (2:136–37). In general, Coleridge faults the tragedy because it lacks unity (2:127). Thus, he insists on the need for the playwright to be vigilant lest he depart from sympathetic identification with his characters and organic unity of action, character, and dialogue.

Coleridge's concern with structure is evident in his repeated demand that literature have a "total effect" (*SC*, 2:79). When defining a good poem, he insists that "the parts . . . mutually support and explain each other" (*BL*, 2:10). Great literature can "communicate from each part the greatest immediate pleasure compatible with the largest sum of pleasure on the whole" (*SC*, 1:164). Coleridge analyzes the characters, the language, the structure, and the underlying themes of Shakespeare's plays in order to prove that "the judgement of Shakespeare is commensurate with his genius" (*SC*, 1:126). In the best of Shakespeare's dramas, the most minute details are part of a master design: "he never introduces a word, or a thought, in vain or out of place" (*SC*, 2:145). Though Shakespeare works with a wide variety of characters and moods and combines comic and serious scenes in his plays, he has the true poet's imaginative gift, "that capability of reducing a multitude into unity of effect" (*SC*, 2:91; see also *BL*, 2:14). Coleridge gives *Lear* as an example: Shakespeare spreads Lear's "deep anguish" and "the feeling of ingratitude and cruelty over the very elements of heaven" (*SC*, 1:213). Coleridge also uses *Lear* to exemplify Shakespeare's subordination of comic elements to the overall tragic mood. The fool's remarks during the storm scene increase the king's distress. "Thus even his comic humour tends to the development of tragic passion" (*SC*, 2:266).[54]

Coleridge's lectures on *Richard II* also reveal his awareness of dramatic structure. He points out that most of the characters in the play tend to "ease . . . anguish with words instead of action." In the dialogue between the Queen, Bushy, and Bagot in act 2, scene 2, we find "the characters all talking high, but performing nothing." Similarly, the Duke of York is "a man giving up all energy under a feeling of despair." When Richard returns from Ireland in the third act, his words convey "his resolution and determination of action." However, when he hears the bad news, he allows "despondency" to overcome him. Richard thus has "great activity of mind, without any strength of moral feeling to rouse to action." The only exception to this dramatic pattern is Bolingbroke, who takes strong measures to dethrone the king. However, Bolingbroke resembles the other characters in that there is a discrepancy between what he says and what he does: "In Bolingbroke is defined the struggle of inward determination with outward shew of humility" (*SC*, 2:280–83). In comments like these, Coleridge fuses analysis of character with analysis of plot and situation. Similarly, he argues that *Romeo and Juliet* is given coherence by the hastiness, rashness, and spring fever that affect the main characters, young and old (2:265; see also 1:8–9).

Coleridge demonstrates the importance of minor characters and seemingly trivial events by linking them to the overall structure of the play and to the need to involve the audience in the dramatic action. For example, Mercutio's death is intimately connected to the catastrophe of *Romeo and Juliet*. "Had not Mercutio been rendered so amiable and so interesting, we could not have felt so strongly the necessity for Romeo's interference, connecting it immediately, and passionately, with the future fortunes of the lover and his mistress" (*SC*, 2:133). Coleridge also emphasizes how Shakespeare interweaves lyrical and dramatic scenes while still advancing the plot. The dialogue between Laertes and Ophelia in act 1, scene 3, of *Hamlet* is one example (1:23). Coleridge also praises Hamlet's discussion with the players in act 3, scene 2, because it reveals "Shakespeare's power of diversifying the scene while he is carrying on the plot" (1:30).

While Coleridge worked for the *Morning Post* in London (1799–1800), he attended Drury Lane Theatre four times a week to become acquainted with the staff and the manager, Sheridan.[55] One can assume that this familiarity with contemporary productions also taught Coleridge some details about dialogue and staging.

There is more evidence for Coleridge's interest in drama per se in the letters. He writes to Sir George Beaumont in 1804,

> Each scene of each play I read, as if it were the whole of Shakespere's Works—the sole thing extant. I ask myself what are the

characteristics—the Diction, the Cadences, and Metre, the character, the passion, the moral or metaphysical Inherencies, & fitness for theatric effect, and in what sort of Theatres—all these I
write down with great care & precision of Thought & Language—
/ and when I have gone thro' the whole, I then shall collect my
papers, & observe, how often such & such Expressions recur / &
thus shall not only know what the Characteristics of Shakespere's
Plays are, but likewise what proportion they bear to each other.
(*Letters of Coleridge,* 2:1054)

Coleridge emphasizes here that he considers each scene in detail sepa-
rately from the rest of the drama *and* in proportion to "the whole." He
is concerned with many matters besides the poetry and the characterization, including word choice, theme, and theatricality. The letters
often stress his awareness of dramatic structure. For example, in a
letter to Godwin, Coleridge praises "the *Sequence* of Scenes" (1:621) in
Schiller's *Wallenstein,* which he was translating. Addressing Robert
Southey, Coleridge declares that he is proud of "the simplicity and
Unity of the Plot" in his tragedy *Remorse.* The play is unified by the
theme of remorse and by the central character, Ordonio (3:433–34). Of
course, *Remorse* had a successful run of twenty nights and went
through three editions in 1813. J. R. de J. Jackson comments, "In terms
of profit and public recognition it was Coleridge's most successful
literary enterprise."[56]

Richard M. Fletcher finds evidence in *Remorse,* which is a revised
version of *Osorio* (written in 1797), that Coleridge had improved his
command of structure. A new first scene clarifies the previous action,
and many speeches throughout the play are condensed or extended to
streamline or to illuminate dialogue. Fletcher cites three successful
revised scenes to demonstrate "the care and skill with which Coleridge synthesized and juxtaposed the previously chaotic elements of
Osorio to form a dramatic unity."[57]

Coleridge also structures the plot of *Remorse* to create more suspense than *Osorio* has. The acts in *Remorse* are short and are based on
confrontations between characters. Coleridge heightens the dramatic
irony of the play by beginning *Remorse* with Alvar's landing in Spain
and assuming a Moorish disguise. The reader or audience knows Alvar's true identity, but the other major characters do not. This allows
the protagonist to test the consciences of Teresa, his beloved, and of
Ordonio, his brother. The reader/spectator also learns before Alvar
that Teresa is innocent of adultery and that Ordonio lied to the assas-

sin, Isidore, about Teresa's behavior. The dramatic irony makes the reader or theatergoer feel closer to Alvar and more concerned about his fate.

Other plot elements are more carefully integrated in *Remorse* than in *Osorio*. By having the Inquisition interrupt Alvar's conjuration rites in act 3 of *Remorse* to arrest the much-wronged freethinker, Coleridge more adequately works into the action his criticism of religious intolerance and abuse of prisoners. Furthermore, in *Osorio*, Alhadra has the last words of the play, but in *Remorse*, the stature of Alvar is again enhanced by Coleridge's assigning the last speech to him. The character of Valdez, the father of Alvar and Ordonio, contributes more to the plot of *Remorse* than does the parallel character in *Osorio* because, in *Remorse*, Valdez becomes quite suspicious of Ordonio (see 3.2) and is reunited with Alvar in the final scene.

Coleridge even changes the personality of the protagonist. In *Osorio*, Albert is portrayed as awkward, passive, and indecisive. He has been "loitering" in Spain for three weeks, but he has taken no action.[58] Hypersensitive Albert is so upset when Osorio, his guilty brother, visits him that Albert can hardly talk. Albert resembles Hamlet in his hesitancy to take action. However, in *Remorse*, Alvar is much more active, subtle, and decisive. As soon as he lands in Spain, he begins to investigate and to make plans. His self-possession enhances his stature for the reader/spectator.

Alan Richardson argues in *A Mental Theater: Poetic Drama and Consciousness in the Romantic Age* (1988) that romantic playwrights like Coleridge, Byron, and Shelley were not substituting poetry for drama but were creating a new dramatic form. They were "fusing the objective portrayal of action with the subjective lyrical voice. Dramatic action would not function to portray or set off character; rather, character becomes plot as the dramatic interest centers on the history of a protagonist's consciousness." Many of these protagonists, like Beatrice Cenci and Ordonio, suffer from isolation from others and what Richardson terms "a divided self-consciousness." The goals of romantic dramatists are "problematizing literary conventions and received ideas" and also "deeply engaging and . . . directly challenging the reader."[59]

Coleridge certainly considered his plays dramatic, and he kept trying to improve his mastery of dramatic structure. He writes to Byron in 1815 that in *Zapolya*,

I have endeavored to avoid the faults and deficiencies of the *Remorse* by a better subordination of the characters, by avoiding the duplicity of Interest, by a greater clearness of the Plot, and by a deeper Pathos. Above all, I have labored to render the Poem at once tragic and dramatic. (*Letters of Coleridge,* 4:598)

Coleridge has some positive things to say about the stage. He views the theater as an antidote to the boredom "and ever-increasing sameness of human life." The stage can renew strong emotion and excitement for the deprived nineteenth-century public and cure the "dead palsy of the public mind." When great works like those of Shakespeare are performed, they reach people who are unlikely to read his masterpieces (*SC,* 1:209–10).

Coleridge's comments on acting for Shakespeare's dramas also reveal a critic who is genuinely interested in how plays can be rendered most convincingly on stage. Coleridge gives instructions for actresses when he discusses how to speak Viola's lines in act 2, scene 4 (ll. 113–15), of *Twelfth Night* (*SC,* 1:107). His comments show an interest in character motivation and elocution. Similarly, his lecture notes give advice on how "a good actress" should handle Hermione's dialogue in *The Winter's Tale,* act 1, scene 2 (*SC,* 1:122), and portray Miranda in *The Tempest* (2:180).

Perhaps Coleridge's most famous hostile statement about the performance of Shakespeare is a digression in his lecture on *Richard II* given at Bristol in 1813. After observing that *Richard II* was seldom acted, Coleridge insists that "he never saw any of Shakespeare's plays performed, but with a degree of pain, disgust, and indignation." Even the best actors, Mrs. Siddons and Kemble, could not perform tragic heroes like the Macbeths effectively (see figure 5 for an artist's rendering of the two actors). The oversized Covent Garden and Drury Lane "drove Shakespeare from the stage, to find his proper place in the heart and in the closet" (*SC,* 2:278–79). Coleridge explains why Shakespeare's greatest dramas may be awkward when produced on stage. For example, *Richard II* is too laden with "long speeches," and the causes of many historical events are not shown to the audience (1:142). Also, Coleridge doubts that any actor is "capable of representing Richard" because of the extreme moodiness of the king and his "rapid transitions" from one mood to another (2:188). These problems make what Coleridge considers Shakespeare's "most admirable" historical drama for the closet inappropriate for nineteenth-century theaters (1:142).

5. *John Philip Kemble and Sarah Siddons in* **Macbeth,** *a painting by Thomas Beach, courtesy of the Garrick Club, London.*

The supernatural phenomena in plays like *Macbeth* are also awk-ward in a theater. Coleridge speculates about whether Banquo's ghost should appear to the audience. Coleridge concludes that the matter "depends on the overbalance of the educated to the uneducated" (*MC,* 450). This implies that a sophisticated audience would not need to see the bloody ghost: the horror would then arise solely from Macbeth's mental imbalance and the spectators' ability to imagine the ghost.

If Shakespeare's plays must be represented, Coleridge prefers the simple stage and acting styles of the Renaissance to nineteenth-century productions. During Elizabethan times, drama was presented "without scenery" in a manner very close to "recitation." Scenery and acting were subordinate to the poetry. "Description and narration supplied the place of visual exhibition: the audience was told to fancy that they saw what they only heard described; the painting was not in colours, but in words" (*SC*, 1:232; 2:85, 169).[60] Thus a play like *The Tempest* appeals "to the imagination," not to "any sensuous impression . . . of time and place" (2:169). In general, the advantage of Renaissance staging was that the members of the audience were stimulated to exert their minds rather than to absorb passively the elaborate and sensual details of nineteenth-century spectacles. "The idea of the poet was always present, not of the actors, not of the thing to be represented. It was at that time more a delight and employment for the intellect, than [an] amusement for the senses." As we have seen earlier in this chapter, such cerebral drama was possible because the Renaissance encouraged "a general energy of thinking, a pleasure in hard thinking" (2:84–85). The simple stage and this commitment to deep thought "compelled the actor, as well as the author, to appeal to the imaginations, and not to the senses of the audience" (2:160; see also 1:232; 2:97). In a similar passage, Coleridge contrasts nineteenth-century plays, which emphasize spectacle, to Shakespeare's dramas, which stress poetry and verbal effects. While Coleridge's contemporaries distract the audience with gimmicks, Shakespeare could spellbind his audience. When one attends

> modern plays, . . . the glare of the scenes, with every wished-for object industriously realized, the mind becomes bewildered in surrounding attractions; whereas Shakespeare, in place of ranting, music, and outward action, addresses us in words that enchain the mind, and carry on the attention from scene to scene. (2:279–80)

Coleridge insists that an undue emphasis on spectacle and gestures distorts dramatic literature. He ridicules poorly written German tragedies "in which the dramatist becomes a novelist *in his directions to the actors,* and degrades tragedy to pantomime" (1:207). Similarly, Coleridge compares Imogine in Maturin's *Bertram* to a "puppet-heroine, for whom the showman contrives dialogue without any skill in ventrilo-quism" (*BL,* 2:197). Note that Coleridge's comments here resemble those of Rowe, Goldsmith, and Fielding on the problems of the stage.

In a play like *The Tempest,* which "addresses itself entirely to the imaginative faculty," elaborate scenery, props, and costumes are "dangerous," according to Coleridge.

> For the principal and only genuine excitement ought to come from within,—from the moved and sympathetic imagination; whereas, where so much is addressed to the mere external senses of seeing and hearing, the spiritual vision is apt to languish, and the attraction from without will withdraw the mind from the proper and only legitimate interest which is intended to spring from within. (*SC,* 1:131–32)

In labelling both vision and hearing as superficial, Coleridge goes beyond Horace and other earlier commentators.[61] A careful analysis of the above passages reveals that Coleridge's animosity is directed not at the theater itself but at the tendency of any production to appeal to the audience's senses rather than to the intellect. The stage distorts the cerebral nature of Shakespearean drama, according to Coleridge, and impoverishes the spectators' imaginations.

Dramatic Illusion

Coleridge's many comments about the nature of dramatic illusion clarify that he knew and appreciated the theater much more than many twentieth-century critics give him credit for. Coleridge rejects both the French neoclassical claim that the audience must be "deceived" into believing dramas to be "reality" and Samuel Johnson's insistence that the audience is completely conscious "of the falsehood of the presentation."[62] Coleridge takes a position between these anti-thetical views:

> There is a state of mind between the two, which may be properly called illusion, in which the comparative powers of the mind are completely suspended; as in a dream, the judgment is neither beguiled, nor conscious of the fraud, but remains passive. (*SC,* 2:321–22; see also 1:127–29, 204; *Letters of Coleridge,* 4:642)

Coleridge contrasts the effects of paintings and dramas on spectators. Paintings are designed for viewers who are fully aware that they are looking at a picture, not a real scene. However, in a play "a forest-scene is not presented to the audience as a *picture,* but as a forest." Drama is designed

> to produce as much illusion as its nature permits. These and all other stage presentations are to produce a sort of temporary half-faith, which the spectator encourages in himself and supports by a voluntary contribution on his own part, because he knows that it is at all times in his power to see the thing as it really is. (*SC,* 1:199–200)

This "half-faith" requires a reader/spectator who actively cooperates with the playwright.[63]

Coleridge also contrasts the state of illusion produced by a drama to that state we experience in dreams. He writes to Daniel Stuart in 1816,

> It is not strictly accurate to say, that we believe our dreams to be actual while we are dreaming. We neither believe it or disbelieve it—with the will the comparing power is suspended, and without the comparing power any act of Judgement, whether affirmation or denial, is impossible.

In contrast, the spectator's will actively participates in dramatic illusion.

> Add to this a voluntary Lending of the Will to this suspension of one of it's own operations (i.e. that of comparison & consequent decision concerning the reality of any sensuous Impression) and you have the true Theory of Stage Illusion. (*Letters of Coleridge,* 4:641–42)[64]

Coleridge uses similar terminology in *Biographia Literaria* when he discusses his handling of the supernatural incidents and characters in *Lyrical Ballads.* He designed poems like "The Rime of the Ancient Mariner" with a specific goal: "to transfer from our inward nature a human interest and a semblance of truth sufficient to procure for these shadows of imagination that willing suspension of disbelief for the moment, which constitutes poetic faith" (*BL,* 2:6; see also 2:107). Not surprisingly, Coleridge was fascinated by scenes in Shakespeare's plays that, similarly, induced the audience to suspend disbelief in "ghosts, wizards, genii" (2:189), and other supernatural phenomena.

According to Richard Haven, Coleridge views the poet's task as "the transformation of ordinary language and ordinary perception into a kind of 'mythic' language and 'mythic' perception." In order to communicate imaginative insights to readers, a good poet must dissolve "that conceptual order in which 'normal' discursive apprehension is imprisoned." The personae of Coleridge's poems move toward "an expanded consciousness." Coleridge also tries to move his readers in this direction. Haven examines the revisions of "This Lime-Tree Bower my Prison" to show Coleridge's attempts to improve the passages that prepare the public for new insights. The revised poem is successful because the poet immediately involves his readers in reflection and communicates with them by means of a shared experience.[65]

Coleridge's poems reveal the same interest that we find in his prose in how readers pass from normal consciousness to imaginative states. His poetry also demonstrates Coleridge's fascination with the interaction of authors with their readers by means of the written text. "The Rime of the Ancient Mariner" (1798) is a good example. In the opening of this literary ballad, the poet stresses the conflict between the Ancient Mariner, a bard, and the Wedding-Guest, his audience. At first, the Wedding-Guest tries to escape, annoyed at the "grey-beard loon" (l. 11) who has detained him. But eventually, the Wedding-Guest stops resisting: he "stood still, / And listens like a three years' child" (ll. 14–15). At this point, "He cannot choose but hear" (ll. 18 and 38). Coleridge's 1817 marginal gloss for stanzas four and five (ll. 13–20) emphasizes the psychological state of the Wedding-Guest, who "is *spellbound* by the eye of the old seafaring man, and *constrained* to hear his tale" (italics are mine). Note the use of "spellbound" with its connotations of magic and enchantment. This imagery is consistently employed by the romantics to indicate a state of full dramatic illusion. Of course, Coleridge hopes that his readers have been drawn into the poem and "spellbound" like the Wedding-Guest. Throughout "The Rime," the Guest serves as a model for the readers' reactions.[66] His choric commentary is vital to the structure of the narrative. For example, part 1 of the poem concludes with the Wedding-Guest's concerned query, " 'Why look'st thou so?' " and the Mariner's shocking admission that he shot the innocent Albatross. Though the Guest is silent during parts 2 and 3, he opens part 4 by expressing his "fear" that the Mariner may have died along with two hundred shipmates. His sympathetic imagination aroused by the narrative, the Guest experiences the terror that the Mariner must have felt. Coleridge allows the Guest a six-verse speech here, the longest outburst by that character in the poem. The phrase "I fear" is repeated three times to emphasize the emotion (ll. 224–29). The Guest's interruption focuses the reader's attention on the Mariner's answer that he survived, "alone" (ll. 231–33). The Guest's growing sympathy for the Mariner mirrors the pattern of the poem's climax: the egotistic Mariner finally acknowledges his relationship to all creatures by blessing the water-snakes in an act of sympathetic imagination (ll. 282–87). The concluding passage of "The Rime" stresses the effect of the tale on the Wedding-Guest/reader. Though the Mariner has gone, the Guest "Turned from the bridegroom's door" (l. 621) of his own accord. The narrative has left the Guest in no mood for a frivolous wedding party. He no longer needs the bard's "glittering eye" to restrain him. Coleridge uses the Guest much as the ancient Greeks used the members of the chorus, "as . . . the ideal representatives of the real audience" (*SC,* 1:174).[67]

While the Wedding-Guest tends to draw the readers into "The Rime," the marginal glosses give the readers more perspective by making them self-conscious and by distancing them from the text. Jerome McGann explains that the many different points of view contained in the poem encourage "a diversity of interpretations" by readers. He believes that Coleridge intended this symbolic method to spur readers to generate their own analyses of the poem's meaning.[68]

A listener responds in a similar way to a narrative in the lesser known poem "Love" (1799). The young bard, in love with Genevieve, sings to her the story of a scornful lady and the knight she maddens and kills with her neglect. Genevieve is so moved by the ballad that it releases her repressed love for the singer. Genevieve's reaction to the narrative is more important to this poem than the story itself, which is broken off by the bard.[69] As in "The Rime," the tale changes the listener by evoking her sympathetic imagination. However, this poem lacks the complexity of point of view and interpretation that we find in "The Rime."

Coleridge is especially interested in how dramatic illusion is created and maintained by Shakespeare for his audience. The creation of illusion is not a problem in dreams because "in sleep we pass at once by a sudden collapse into this suspension of will and the comparative power." However, the playwright must generate illusion in the opening scenes and maintain it for two or three hours as the plot and characters develop. Coleridge insists on the importance of the audience's cooperation in sustaining dramatic illusion.

> In an interesting play, read or represented, we are brought up to this point . . . gradually, by the art of the poet and the actors; and with the consent and positive aidance of our own will. We *choose* to be deceived. (*SC,* 1:129)

Patricia Ball comments, "As Coleridge sees it . . . our state of mind in the theatre is one of a particular 'inward excitement', a heightened and receptive condition where imaginative expectation supersedes our ordinary judgments."[70] Unlike a dream, a drama requires the audience's voluntary exertion of the imagination.

Coleridge compares this "poetic faith" to people's belief in historic events. Paradoxically, our faith in imaginative literature is stronger than our belief in history. He uses *The Tempest* as an example. In the first two scenes of this comedy,

> what is called poetic faith is required and created, and our com-
> mon notions of philosophy give way before it: this feeling may be
> said to be much stronger than historic faith, since for the exercise
> of poetic faith the mind is previously prepared. (*SC*, 2:175)

Coleridge emphasizes how precarious this state of illusion is: the playwright "solicits us only to yield ourselves to a dream; and this too with our eyes open, and with our judgement *perdue* behind the curtain, ready to awaken us at the first motion of our will" (*BL*, 2:189). In his lectures on Shakespeare, Coleridge argues that scene changes in the theater "destroy" dramatic illusion "by arousing [us] from that delightful dream of our inner nature" (*SC*, 2:110).[71] Realistic spectacles are dangerous because they focus attention on material objects rather than on the author's ideas.

Coleridge attacks those critics who watch Shakespearean drama not for pleasure but to find minor details that conflict with realism. Pure stage realism "is yet never attainable." Furthermore, those who demand that drama should copy reality misunderstand the art and reveal "an utter want of all imagination" (*SC*, 1:79).[72] Coleridge returns to his distinction between imitation and copy:

> the drama is an *imitation* of reality, not a *copy*—and that imitation is
> contradistinguished from copy by this: that a certain quantum of
> difference is essential to the former, and an indispensable condi-
> tion and cause of the pleasure we derive from it. (1:127–28)

Like Charles Lamb, Coleridge argues that "domestic tragedy," which was popular in the early nineteenth century, is too realistic to yield true pleasure (2:83).[73] In contrast, Shakespearean drama does give pleasure because it is designed to appeal "to the imagination rather than to the senses" and helps the readers or spectators to understand profoundly human emotions and psychology (1:198). Because of

Shakespeare's imaginative power, the unities of time and space and other trappings of realism are irrelevant to his plays.

> And if only the poet have such power of exciting our internal emotions as to make us present to the scene in imagination chiefly, he acquires the right and privilege of using time and space as they exist in the imagination, obedient only to the laws which the imagination acts by. (1:198)

Coleridge points out that Shakespeare often purposely violates theatrical illusion in his comedies, demonstrating that the Elizabethan playwright is consciously avoiding stark realism. In *The Merchant of Venice*, Portia claims, "I have a poor pennyworth in the English" (1.2.76–77). The humor here arises from our knowledge that the play is written in English, although it is set in Italy. Coleridge comments, "How boldly Shakespeare outsoars the absurd system of cold-blooded probability (i.e., facsimile of real life) in the drama" (*MC*, 452). Coleridge insists that the audience must remain aware that drama is an imitation, not reality: "The true pleasure we derive from theatrical performances arises from the fact that they are unreal and fictitious" (*SC*, 2:72).

Those who can suspend disbelief and exercise the imagination will be "drawn away from ourselves into the music of noblest thoughts in harmonizing sounds" (*SC*, 1:79). Similarly, Hazlitt contends that a tragedy like *Othello* "substitutes imaginary sympathy for mere selfishness. It gives us a high and permanent interest, beyond ourselves, in humanity as such" (*Works of Hazlitt*, 4:200). This transcendance of the ego is an advantage that great literature, especially Shakespeare's plays, offers the imaginative reader.

The First Scenes of Shakespeare's Dramas

Because the opening scenes of a play are so important in enthralling the reader or spectator and in embodying the central idea, Coleridge devotes a large percentage of his lectures and notes to an examination of Shakespeare's first acts. These early scenes carefully introduce the main characters, capture the overall mood of the play, and gradually prepare the audience for subsequent action. Though exposition is difficult to write, it may violate certain rules that later dialogue cannot defy. In his 1818 lecture on *The Tempest*, Coleridge insisted

> that many natural improbabilities were innocent in the groundwork or outset of the play, which would break the illusion after-

wards; and the contrary. The temper of mind in the spectator must be considered; a strong improbability in the story, founded on some known tradition, does not offend in the outset of a play; but the interest and plot must not depend upon that improbability. Again, violent emotions must not be excited at the very commencement; for if the mind is not prepared, the judgment is awakened and the illusion vanishes at once. (*SC*, 2:322)

All elements of a good drama are designed as "means . . . of producing and supporting this willing illusion" (1:130).

Coleridge contrasts Shakespeare's occasional use of improbable circumstances in some opening scenes with Beaumont and Fletcher's dependence on such events. While the first scene of *King Lear* is not realistic, the dialogue is based on "an old story, rooted in the popular faith." Coleridge then demonstrates that the improbable conduct of Lear in scene 1 fits the second criterion quoted above: the tragedy is not completely dependent on this unlikely sequence because "it is merely the canvas to the characters and passions, a mere *occasion*—not (as in Beaumont and Fletcher) perpetually recurring, as the cause and *sine qua non* of the incidents and emotions" (*SC*, 1:59).

Furthermore, different dramatic genres require different degrees of illusion. Although straight drama gradually prepares the reader or spectator for the following action, farce can be sloppier in its exposition. "The definition of a farce is, an improbability or even impossibility granted in the outset; see what odd and laughable events will fairly follow from it!" Coleridge gives *Comedy of Errors* as an example of "a pure farce" (*SC*, 2:355). Historical plays also require special techniques. Because the audience usually knows the basic plot of a drama based on history, "An historic play requires more excitement than a tragic; thus Shakespeare never loses an opportunity of awakening a patriotic feeling" in *Richard II* (2:279).

Coleridge often stresses the organic nature of Shakespeare's plays: "*Growth* as in a plant. No ready cut and dried [structure]; and yet everything *prepared* because the preceding involves or was the link of association" (*SC*, 1:233). Coleridge adapts Schlegel's distinction between mechanical and organic form: the former imposes external rules, while the latter develops from within in a more natural way. Walter Jackson Bate views Coleridge's drama criticism as organic because it explores "the relation . . . of expression to character and of both to over-all structure." Similarly, Joseph W. Donohue contends that Coleridge is preoccupied with the first scenes of Shakespeare's plays because these passages are "striking examples of organic growth." M. M. Badawi is more specific: Coleridge judges a scene to be "valuable in proportion to its contribution towards the total effect of the whole play."[74]

Coleridge is especially impressed by the organic coherence of the first scenes in *Hamlet*. He praises the choice of language, the pace of the action, the portrayal of the guards' anxiety, the creation of suspense, and the introduction of Hamlet and Horatio. The guards' nervousness is revealed in the brief interchange between Francisco and Bernardo (1.1.1–14). Coleridge commends the details from ordinary life that "produce the sense of *reality*." For example, he cites Francisco's report, "Not a mouse stirring" (l. 10). Several lines before Horatio first appears, Bernardo mentions his acquaintance's name (l. 12). This is part of the careful introduction of this minor character:

> Bernardo's enquiry after Horatio, and the repetition of his name, and in his own presence, [indicate] *respect* or eagerness . . . [?] that implies him as one of the persons who are to appear in the foreground. (*SC,* 1:42–43)

Coleridge notes that Horatio has a special function in act 1, where Horatio serves as "the representative of the ignorance of the audience" (1:20).

Coleridge pays close attention to the suspenseful introduction of the supernatural in *Hamlet*. He may be elaborating on Joseph Addison's remark in *The Spectator*:

> The Appearance of the Ghost in *Hamlet* is a Masterpiece in its kind, and wrought up with all the Circumstances that can create either Attention or Horrour. The Mind of the Reader is wonderfully prepared for his Reception by the Discourses that precede it.[75]

Coleridge finds that the Ghost invariably enters when someone is in the middle of a sentence, as when Bernardo begins his leisurely narrative of his previous sighting of the Ghost (1.1). This is a perfect time for the spirit's first entrance in *Hamlet* because the reader's curiosity has been aroused, and the reader is caught up in Bernardo's story. Similarly, Horatio's silence for four lines after the Ghost enters reinforces the frightening reality of the apparition (*SC,* 1:44).[76] In act 1, scene 4, the men watching for the Ghost speak of "trivial objects and familiar circumstances" in order to ease the tension. Coleridge demonstrates that the small talk is "obliquely connected . . . with the expected hour of the visitation." Hamlet's long speech on Danish drinking bouts enables Shakespeare to succeed in "entangling the attention of the audience" in the prince's rhetorical flourishes while the playwright "takes them completely by surprize on the appearance of the Ghost" (2:274–75).

Coleridge compares the introduction of the supernatural in *Hamlet* and *Macbeth*. In both tragedies, the protagonist speaks about neutral topics right before ghosts or witches enter. Coleridge stresses the effect of this dramatic presentation on the reader. "Thus, in both cases, the preternatural appearance has all the effect of abruptness, and the reader is totally divested of the notion, that the figure is a vision of a highly wrought imagination" (*SC*, 2:193). Shakespeare convinces the reader of the dramatic reality of these phenomena in this way.

Coleridge also focuses on Hamlet's first speeches at court in scene 2. This dialogue with Gertrude and Claudius reveals the prince's most important traits and develops his character, especially "the aversion to externals, the betrayed habit of brooding over the world within him, and the prodigality of beautiful words" (*SC*, 1:38).

Coleridge emphasizes that Shakespeare's opening scenes are not stock dialogues and that they differ greatly from play to play. Each exposition is tailored to the dramatic situation and the character of the protagonist. For example, *Hamlet* begins with the "easy language of ordinary life, contrasted with the direful music and wild rhythm of the opening of *Macbeth*" (*SC*, 1:38). Also, Hamlet's first speech in scene 2 is a "play of words, the complete absence of which characterizes *Macbeth*." Coleridge considers *Hamlet* a psychological tragedy that appeals to the mind, while *Macbeth* is more superficial (1:20, 38). The pacing of these two tragedies is also different. The exposition of *Macbeth* is more sudden and appeals less to the intellect than the exposition of *Hamlet*. This contrast in pacing is characteristic of the two plays as dramatic wholes: *Hamlet* "proceeds with the utmost slowness," while the action in *Macbeth* moves "with breathless and crowded rapidity" (1:67; 2:273).[77] Coleridge explains the reason for this difference. *Macbeth* can move rapidly because the protagonist is less introspective: there are "no reasonings of equivocal morality, which would require a more leisurely state and consequent activity of mind; and no sophistry of self-delusion, except only that previous to the dreadful act" (1:80).

Like Thomas Whately and other earlier commentators, Coleridge praises Shakespeare's invention of characters who have the same occupation but are distinct individuals.[78] Coleridge contrasts the reactions of Macbeth and Banquo to the predictions of the witches in the third scene of *Macbeth*. These reactions reveal the different personalities of the two men: Banquo has no illicit ambitions, but Macbeth does. After the witches depart, "Banquo's wonder [is] that of any spectator." Note that Coleridge's use of the word "spectator" to describe Banquo links his innocence to that of the audience. In contrast, Macbeth is obsessed with the witches' promises and broods on them. Coleridge analyzes the scene as foreshadowing Macbeth's future conduct: "So truly is the guilt in its germ anterior to the supposed cause and immediate temptation" (*SC*, 1:69; see also 2:270). Similarly, Coleridge notes how upset Macbeth is when Duncan declares Malcolm the Prince of Cumberland. The critic stresses Macbeth's conflicting thoughts in the aside (1.4.48–53): "the alarm of his conscience appears, even while meditating to remove this bar to his own advancement, as he exclaims, 'Stars! hide your fires!' " Coleridge interprets this psychological confusion as a foreshadowing of Macbeth's "total imbecility and helplessness when the crime had been committed, and when conscience can be no longer dallied with or eluded" (2:270). Also, this scene establishes a "contrast between the honest king and the already scheming Macbeth." Duncan greets the thane warmly and praises him, while Macbeth's reply is rhetorical and insincere (*MC*, 448; see also *SC*, 1:70–71). Likewise, Banquo's openness in scene six is a foil for Lady Macbeth's hypocrisy when talking with Duncan. Coleridge compares her speaking style to her husband's: both are insincere and lack "personal sense" in their compliments to the king (*SC*, 1:73–74). Another important contrast is that between Macbeth's "forced flurry of talkativeness" after he has killed Duncan and the grooms, and Macduff's concise responses (*MC*, 449).

Coleridge frequently explains how Shakespeare makes his villains sympathetic characters for the reader. For example, Macbeth experiences a "struggle of conscience" before he murders Duncan. Similarly, Lady Macbeth is portrayed neither as a "desperate reprobate" nor as a "moral monster": in act 2, scene 2, she compares Duncan to her father, a very human touch. Even the second murderer in *Macbeth*, a minor character, is humanized by his explanation that he has turned to crime because of his hard life (3.1.108–11; *MC*, 448–50).

As in *Macbeth*, the early scenes in *Richard II* contain skillful foreshadowing. Coleridge praises

the judgment with which Shakespeare always in his first scenes prepares, and yet how naturally and with what a concealment of art, for the catastrophe. How he presents the *germ* of all the after events, in Richard's insincerity, partiality, arbitrariness, favoritism, and in the proud, tempestuous temperament of his barons. (*SC*, 1:153; see also 2:279)

Note the typical use of an organic metaphor here. King Richard's character is revealed in his demand that Mowbray and Bolingbroke swear never to plot against him in their exile. "Already the selfish weakness of Richard's character opens. Nothing which such minds so readily embrace, as indirect ways softened down to their quasi-consciences by policy, expedience, etc." The opening scene also introduces the antagonist, Bolingbroke, and contrasts him to Mowbray. Coleridge enjoys the deft strokes with which Shakespeare sketches the two nobles. Bolingbroke reveals

> a decorous and courtly checking of his anger in subservience to a predetermined plan, especially in his calm speech after receiving sentence of banishment compared with Mowbray's unaffected lamentation. In the one, all is ambitious hope of something yet to come; in the other it is desolation and a looking backward of the heart. (1:147-48)

Coleridge frequently praises the way Shakespeare allows his complex characters to reveal themselves to the reader gradually. An inferior dramatist would take away all the challenge by making the characters more obvious in the first scene. Instead of showing only one side of a protagonist, Shakespeare allows the readers to discover what the character's friends and enemies say about him or her. Each perspective is slightly distorted: even "the character himself sees himself thro' the medium of his character, not exactly as it is. But the clown or the fool will suggest a shrewd hint; and take all together, and the impression is right, and all [the spectators] have it." Thus, the personality of the character is "*inferred* by the reader, not *told to him*." The reader must work hard to reconstruct the "whole" personality from the playwright's clues (*SC*, 1:227, 232). For example, Coleridge finds the fourth scene of *Richard II*

> a striking conclusion of the first act—letting the reader into the secret [of Richard's weakness], having before impressed the dignified and kingly manners of Richard, yet by well managed anticipations leading to the full gratification of the auditor's pleasure in his own penetration. (1:148)

Thus, the good reader, like Coleridge's ideal educated man, takes an active part in interpreting the text. Coleridge's tactic as a lecturer is to stimulate this kind of discovery.

Villains, as well as heroes, usually appear in the first acts of Shakespeare's plays. This gives readers an opportunity to understand the motives, the strategies, and the underlying patterns of the antagonists' actions. Coleridge notes that in both *King Lear* and *Othello* Shakespeare introduces the villain in scene 1. In *Othello,* Roderigo serves "as the dupe on whom Iago first exercises his art" (*SC,* 1:44–45, 56–57). Thus, the opening scene foreshadows Iago's later treachery.

Othello is introduced in scenes 2 and 3 of act 1. Coleridge considers these dialogues crucial in building the reader's sympathy for the Moor. Coleridge strongly disagrees with Samuel Johnson's suggestion in the notes for the 1765 edition of Shakespeare's plays that *Othello* should be made to follow the three unities by beginning with the second act in Cyprus. Johnson's scheme would alienate the reader/spectator from Othello. "In how many ways is not Othello made, first, our acquaintance—then friend—then object of anxiety—before the deep interest is to be approached" (*SC,* 1:49–51). Such passages are additional evidence of Coleridge's interest in dramatic structure. Furthermore, he points out, act 1 of *Othello* is full of subtle foreshadowing that the careful reader will notice and use to understand later actions. Coleridge stresses that Shakespeare's plays should be reread and that only a thorough reader will be sensitive to *Othello*'s intricacy. Coleridge cites the parting words of Brabantio and Othello's response (1.3.293–95) and comments,

> In real life how do we look back to little speeches, either as presentimental [of], or most contrasted with, an affecting event. Shakespeare, as secure of being read over and over, of becoming a family friend, how he provides this for *his readers,* and leaves it to them. (1:49)

Coleridge's italics here emphasize the special relationship that readers have with Shakespeare, his characters, and his plays.

The opening scenes of *Romeo and Juliet* introduce the themes and motifs that dominate the tragedy: family feuds and the passion of love. Coleridge compares the first scenes to a musical "prelude." The theme of love is presented in the middle of scene 1 when "Romeo is introduced already love-bewildered." Coleridge contrasts Romeo's fleeing from Rosaline to his later "rushing to Juliet" (*SC,* 1:5–7).

Of all the comedies by Shakespeare, *The Tempest* receives the most attention from Coleridge. The first act of this play seems designed to interest the audience from the start, capture the lively and imaginative mood of the piece, introduce the main characters, and present exposition in a very natural way. Throughout his commentary, Coleridge stresses that Shakespeare's awareness of his audience influences the dialogue and structure of *The Tempest*. The dialogue aboard the storm-tossed boat in scene 1 is a good example. This sequence captures "the bustle of a tempest" in an imaginative and "poetical" fashion, rather than in a realistic mode. The scene gives "the keynote" for a drama that Coleridge describes as supremely imaginative because its "interests . . . are independent of all historical facts and associations" (*SC*, 1:131). Continuing the analogy to music, he compares the opening dialogue to a "tuning" of the audience because the play's conversation captures the mood in a subtle manner, like music. Coleridge frequently uses musical metaphors to express Shakespeare's careful structure and subtlety in building dramatic illusion. In *The Tempest*, "The same judgment is observable in every scene, still preparing, still inviting, and still gratifying, like a finished piece of music" (1:132; 2:178; see also 1:79).

Coleridge emphasizes the contrast between "the noise and confusion" on the ship and "the silence of a deserted island," where Prospero and Miranda converse in scene 2 (*SC*, 1:131). Like the storm, this conversation captures "the main character of the drama." Prospero's long tale, his magic that lulls Miranda to sleep, and the entrance of Ariel all conform to the "fanciful" texture of this comedy. Furthermore, each event prepares the readers for the next one: "In this way the entrance of Ariel, if not absolutely forethought by the reader, was foreshewn by the writer." At the same time, Prospero's magical powers are gradually exhibited to the audience (2:172–75). As in *Othello*, the opening scenes generate sympathy for Miranda. The young heroine's tender concern for her father in scene 2 "puts the reader in a frame of mind to exert his imagination in favour of an object so innocent and interesting" (2:175).

Scene 2 also introduces Caliban, who is contrasted with Ariel. Coleridge again stresses the gradual "preparation" for the monster's entrance: first Prospero describes Caliban, then we hear the creature's voice, then he enters as Ariel exits (*SC*, 2:177). Such commentary indicates Coleridge's awareness of dramatic structure and its relationship to characterization.

Similarly, act 2, scene 1 "prepares the feelings of the reader" for the murderous plot of Sebastian and Antonio. Shakespeare portrays them as "unsocial" men who constantly mock worthy old Gonzalo and other courtiers. The conduct of these two noblemen reveals their villainous "vanity and self-love" many lines before they decide to kill Alonzo (*SC*, 2:178).

Coleridge defends Prospero's speech, "The fringèd curtains of thine eye advance, / And say what thou seest yond" (1.2.408–9), against Pope and Arbuthnot, who found it bombastic. Coleridge believes that such facile condemnations ignore the dramatic situation, Prospero's stature, and his motives for drawing Miranda's attention to Ferdinand. Coleridge seems to use the passage as an excuse to exhort his lecture audience to read texts carefully. He concludes his analysis with an admonition which appears to be directed less at Pope and Arbuthnot than at his listeners:

> It is much easier to find fault with a writer by reference to former notions and experience, than to sit down and read him, recollecting his purpose, connecting one feeling with another, and judging of his words and phrases, in proportion as they convey the sentiments of the persons represented. (*SC*, 2:179–80)

Coleridge hopes that his public will take this advice when reading all great literature.

Conclusion

Coleridge develops earlier critics' objections to staging drama by emphasizing that performances make spectators passive and inhibit the formation of abstract ideas. Like many popular novels and waxworks, the theater merely appeals to the senses when it tries to copy reality. In contrast, by reading good plays, one can use the imagination actively to transcend the senses and the ego, to become spellbound by ennobling concepts, and to sympathize with the sufferings of other people.

Coleridge challenges Locke's empirical view of education by insisting that important principles should not be taught by appealing to the senses. Students will never be capable of abstraction if they think that knowledge must be palpable. A truly liberal education must free students to think creatively and to achieve self-realization.

Coleridge's insistence that a good education requires the mastery of basic principles, not the memorization of isolated facts, should strike a chord in many twentieth-century educators. Writing in 1929, Alfred North Whitehead discusses education and defines culture in terms very much like those of Coleridge. Both stress that true learning is active and creative and that the various disciplines are linked.

> Culture is activity of thought, and receptiveness to beauty and humane feeling. Scraps of information have nothing to do with it. . . . We have to remember that the valuable intellectual development is self-development. . . .
> In training a child to activity of thought, above all things we must beware of what I will call "inert ideas"—that is to say, ideas that are merely received into the mind without being utilised, or tested, or thrown into fresh combinations.
>   . . .
> The result of teaching small parts of a large number of subjects is the passive reception of disconnected ideas, not illumined with any spark of vitality.[79]

More recently, William G. Perry and his team of researchers have examined the intellectual phases that a college student moves through as he or she develops skill in analytic thinking. Learners often begin with what Perry calls a "dualistic" framework: something is either right or wrong, and authorities have all of the facts. Eventually, students can progress to a more advanced stage in which they commit themselves to acknowledge the complexity of issues and to evaluate different perspectives. In order to reach this level, learners need to become self-conscious of their own thought processes, question all assumptions, and begin to think independently.[80] Perry's definition of a liberally educated person is close to Coleridge's definition in the 1826 letter to James Gillman, Jr.

Perry argues that his developmental theory of learning has significant implications for educators. Instead of stressing the memorization of facts, teachers need to challenge students' assumptions and help students to test different solutions for a problem. The classroom should "encourage risking, groping, analytic detachment and synthetic insight."[81] Coleridge would agree with Perry's emphasis on the risky and synthetic process of learning to think, rather than on the accumulation of facts.

Many of Coleridge's comments on reading and on education resemble twentieth-century discussions of "discovery learning," especially analysis of what is called "guided discovery." In a guided discovery framework, the teacher clarifies the relevant principles and shows students how to apply these principles but encourages the students to finish solving the problem by themselves. This differs markedly from "expository teaching," in which the teacher reveals both the principles and the solutions to the students. Proponents of discovery learning like Lee J. Cronbach argue that the method "has special power to make a practicing intellectual out of the student." Jerome S. Bruner lists the advantages of discovery learning: it increases the student's intellectual ability, it motivates the student more than expository teaching, it teaches the student problem-solving techniques that are applicable to many fields, and it helps the student to retain knowledge because the information has been organized by the learner.[82]

Bruner's article reflects many Coleridgean concepts, although "The Act of Discovery" never cites the nineteenth-century writer. For example, Coleridge consistently stresses that a good education prepares students to engage in active thought and independent analysis for the rest of their lives. Similarly, Bruner writes,

> Our aim as teachers is to give our student as firm a grasp of a subject as we can, and to make him as autonomous and self-propelled a thinker as we can—one who will go along on his own after formal schooling has ended.

Bruner also argues that discovery learning will result in students who know how "to discover regularity and relatedness" in information and how to use the knowledge. This approach recalls Coleridge's insistence that facts should not be presented like frog eggs in disorganized clumps but should be conveyed as illustrations of universal principles. Finally, Coleridge's belief that learning must be motivated from *within* the student rather than by outside rewards or punishments is shared by Bruner.[83] Both men insist that the act of discovery is a reward in itself and that creative use of knowledge is an important component of any person's self-realization.

Coleridge's writings and lectures seem designed to clarify central concepts and principles for his contemporaries and to prompt his readers and auditors to think independently. He often appeals to his public by using striking images and metaphors, such as the torch and the chamois hunter. These figures of speech enliven his prose and make his ideas more comprehensible to those unfamiliar with aesthetic theory. He urges the public to develop active and dynamic strategies when reading literature or when solving any other complex problem. Coleridge purposely does not give detailed explications of literary texts because he believes that once his readers and auditors learn a principle, they will be able to apply it successfully to the rest of a play or a poem. He structures many of his lectures so that the students are presented with various literary problems and the principles needed to resolve the controversy. He often applies a principle to the first act of a Shakespearean drama and leaves further application of the concept to his audience.

J. R. de J. Jackson argues that Coleridge condemns the performance of Shakespeare's plays because of "specific shortcomings of the nine-teenth-century stage." Jackson proceeds to discuss various "technical problems" of the theater in the early 1800s.[84] Though this discussion is insightful, Jackson fails to see the connection between Coleridge's comments about the theater and his insistence on active thinking. Even though the late twentieth century has more sophisticated stage machinery than what was available 180 years ago, Coleridge's remarks about the tendency of elaborate spectacle to make the audience passive and intellectually lazy are still applicable today.

4. Hazlitt's Appeal to Readers in His Drama Criticism

Many twentieth-century critics view romantic writers as overly subjective. Irving Babbitt argued in 1919, "There is in fact no object in the romantic universe—only subject." According to Babbitt, the romantics corrupt Aristotle's concept of *katharsis* and apply it primarily to the egocentric writer/artist and not to the reader/spectator: "*Katharsis* has been appropriated . . . to describe the relief one gets by expressing oneself freely." Art is then reduced to self-revelation. M. H. Abrams does not go that far in *The Mirror and the Lamp*, but he characterizes Wordsworth, Coleridge, Hazlitt, and others as writers who refer "to the poet to explain the nature and criteria of poetry," while eighteenth-century authors stressed the readers' concerns. Similarly, René Wellek contends that romantic theories of literature emphasize "the mental processes and equipment of the artist: the work itself hardly enters into the discussion." The ultimate consequence of this subjectivity, according to Frank Kermode, is that romantic writers become alienated from their public.[1] Do these remarks really apply to a critic like William Hazlitt?

This alleged subjectivity is said to lead to the lack of a clear structure in romantic writing. Hazlitt's essays, especially *Characters of Shakespear's Plays*, are a frequent target for such criticism. George Saintsbury calls *Characters* mere "notes" and argues that the essays are "desultory." Wimsatt and Brooks classify Hazlitt as an "impressionistic" critic. Recently, these accusations have been repeated by Charles I. Patterson, Jr., who faults Hazlitt's "fragmentary quality and incompleteness" in *Characters* and his overall "impressionistic" stance. "He would usually begin with an incisive statement or insight, and then a flood of associations followed, finally subsiding without in any sense concluding."[2]

However, there has been a growing awareness among critics that the romantic writers are indeed interested in their audience, and some attempts have been made to find coherence in their essays. According to Walter Jackson Bate, a thorough "self-absorption" is found only "in extreme romanticism." He points out that Hazlitt attacks the egotism of Rousseau and praises the extroversion of Shakespeare. Bate views Hazlitt and "the majority of romantic critics" as "strongly interested in the way in which the human mind and emotions react in creating or responding to art." Recently, Morris Eaves has expanded Abrams's "expressive" theory to accommodate the romantics' interest in their audience. Citing evidence from the writings of Blake, Wordsworth, and Shelley, Eaves demonstrates that even though these authors *begin* with art as self-expression, they move toward a conviction that readers must participate fully in the act of communication. According to John L. Mahoney, Hazlitt and the other romantics believe that the arts expand the mind of the reader or spectator "by involving him . . . at the same level of imagination and passion" that the writer or artist experiences. Furthermore, critics like Peter Hoheisel have explored the "method amid the rhetoric" of Coleridge's prose, and Richard Haven and John R. Nabholtz have discussed the structure and the careful revisions of romantic essays.[3]

In this study, I hope to show that Hazlitt, like Coleridge and Lamb, is as concerned with the reader's responses to literature as he is with the poet's creative powers, and that this concern influences his aesthetic judgments. Hazlitt's insistence on the need for the public to become actively involved in works of imagination leads him to condemn most performances of Shakespeare's plays. Like eighteenth-century critics, Hazlitt was fascinated by Shakespeare's dramatic characters, and he continued earlier efforts to determine how they evoked the sympathy of audiences and readers. Furthermore, I will argue that Hazlitt used similar techniques in his own work: while his literary criticism appears self-indulgent and disorganized, it is in fact a carefully structured rhetoric designed to arouse the reader's sympathetic imagination. I will draw most of my examples from Hazlitt's studies of drama, especially the much maligned *Characters of Shakespear's Plays.*

The notion of sympathy occurs frequently in Hazlitt's prose, including his early philosophical writings. On the first page of *An Essay on the Principles of Human Action* (1805), he argues "that the human mind is . . . naturally interested in the welfare of others" and that the imagination "must carry me out of myself into the feelings of others." According to Hazlitt, one must transcend the self because it "binds" and "deadens" the mind. The same principle is important in Hazlitt's later work. He defines imagination in 1828 as a mental faculty that requires sympathy: "Imagination is another name for an interest in things out of ourselves, which must naturally run counter to our own." In an essay about drama in 1820, he insists, "This is the true imagination—to put ourselves in the place of others, and to feel and speak for them."[4]

Conversely, Hazlitt deplores literature that features the writer's "devouring egotism" (5:53). While Byron's self-centered poetry encourages intolerance, the novels of Sir Walter Scott transcend egotism and thus release his readers "from petty, narrow, and bigotted prejudices" (11:69-77).

The drama, especially tragedy, is a unique medium for generating public sympathy, Hazlitt believes. He considers drama superior to lyric poetry because good playwrights like Shakespeare can transcend their egos in order to sympathize with many different characters' perspectives. This sympathy can be transferred to the public if the protagonist's situation and motives are universal in their appeal (5:47-52). Hazlitt often praises Shakespeare's ability to create characters who evoke the sympathetic imagination of the reader or spectator. For example, Shakespeare involves the audience intimately during the tragedy of *Macbeth*.

> What he represents is brought home to the bosom as a part of our experience, implanted in the memory as if we had known the places, persons, and things of which he treats. . . . The castle of Macbeth . . . has a real subsistence in the mind; the Weïrd Sisters meet us in person on 'the blasted heath'; the 'air-drawn dagger' moves slowly before our eyes; the 'gracious Duncan,' the 'blood-boultered Banquo' stand before us; all that passed through the mind of Macbeth passes, without the loss of a tittle, through ours. (4:186-87)

Elsewhere, Hazlitt commends Shakespeare's ability to design tragedy that "stirs our inmost affections" and "rouses the whole man within us" (5:6).[5]

In contrast, Hazlitt gives short shrift to plays and operas which fail to evoke the passions and the sympathetic imagination. For example, he faults *Measure for Measure* because none of the main characters can engage the readers'

> cordial interest. . . . There is in general a want of passion; the affections are at a stand; our sympathies are repulsed and defeated in all directions. . . . In this respect, there may be said to be a general system of cross-purposes between the feelings of the different characters and the sympathy of the reader or the audience. (4:345-46)

Note the centrality of the reader/spectator in Hazlitt's argument. Similarly, he concludes his comparison of Macbeth and Richard III with a comment on their differing appeals to the sympathetic imagination. Richard is "hardened" and "fiendish" in his villainy, but Macbeth is a victim of "passion" and "destiny," so the Scottish king appeals more to the public. We can identify with Macbeth's situation; however, in the last scene of *Richard III*, "we can only regard him as a wild beast taken in the toils: while we never entirely lose our concern for Macbeth; and he calls back all our sympathy by that fine close of thoughtful melancholy—'My way of life is fallen into the sear' " (4:193). Hazlitt seeks to distance his readers from the character of Richard by using subhuman images, such as the comparison of the king to an entrapped beast. This distancing was necessary because fast paced, action-packed *Richard III* was a popular entertainment in the eighteenth and nineteenth centuries and a favorite vehicle for actors such as David Garrick, Edmund Kean, and George Frederick Cooke. Hazlitt insists that the drama's "noise and bustle" cannot compensate for the king's lack of "common humanity" (4:192, 272).[6] Even serious grand opera fails to please Hazlitt: it is designed to soothe the elite patrons and leave them in "their sleek and sordid apathy," rather than to arouse their sympathy for the poor and the oppressed. He considers opera a form of "*euthanasia . . .* hardening the heart, while it softens the senses" (20:94–96).

He justifies his emphasis on sympathy and his condemnation of egotism in an 1816 review of Schlegel's *Lectures on Dramatic Art and Literature*. Here, Hazlitt often departs from the objective stance of a book reviewer to insert his own aesthetic speculations. He condemns French tragedy because it is too generalized and thus frustrates the reader's identification with the heroes.

> The true [dramatic] poet identifies the reader with the characters he represents; the French poet only identifies him with himself. . . . We never get beyond conjecture and reasoning—beyond the general impression of the situation of the persons. . . . We never get at that something more, which is what we are in search of, namely, what we ourselves should feel in the same situations. The true poet transports you to the scene—you see and hear what is passing—you catch, from the lips of the persons concerned, what lies nearest to their hearts;—the French poet takes you into his closet, and reads you a lecture upon it. The *chefs-d'oeuvres* of their stage, then, are, after all, only ingenious paraphrases of nature.[7]

I have cited this passage at length because it is central for Hazlitt's dramatic theory. He repeats it in *Lectures on the English Comic Writers* in 1819 (*Works of Hazlitt*, 6:27–28) and *Lectures on the Dramatic Literature of the Age of Elizabeth* in 1820 (5:205–6).

Just as a good playwright helps the reader to identify with the characters, the best literary criticism should arouse the reader's imagination. In his essay "On Criticism" in *Table Talk* (1821–1822), Hazlitt attacks critics who show off their learning and opinions rather than grapple with the essence of a text. He calls for essays that illuminate books by "transfusing their living principles" instead of applying stale rules of composition to "dissecting the skeletons of works." Hazlitt concludes,

> A genuine criticism should, as I take it, reflect the colours, the light and shade, the soul and body of a work: here we have nothing but its superficial plan and elevation. . . . We know every thing about the work and nothing of it. The critic takes good care not to baulk the reader's fancy by anticipating the effect which the author has aimed at producing. (*Works of Hazlitt*, 8:217–18)

Good criticism should help the reader by highlighting the writer's primary aesthetic goals.[8]

Characters of Shakespear's Plays, contrary to popular critical opinion, is perhaps Hazlitt's most successful attempt to implement his theory of drama criticism. He highlights Shakespeare's primary effects, enabling the reader to concentrate on the most important themes and characters. Furthermore, Hazlitt tries to transfer his own enthusiasm to the reader. According to Herschel Baker, *Characters*

> exemplifies the gusto, power and passion that [Hazlitt] regards as the unique effect of art. His chief distinction as a critic lies precisely here, in his ability to perceive the imaginative truth of art and to convey the rapture that he feels.[9]

Leigh Hunt, a contemporary, found Hazlitt's approach an advantage for drama criticism. In an 1817 review of *Characters of Shakespear's Plays,* Hunt praises his friend's "general enthusiasm . . . for his author" and emphasizes

> the very striking susceptibility with which he changes his own humour and manner according to the nature of the play he comes

upon; like a spectator in a theatre, who accompanies the turns of the actor's face with his own.

Hunt proceeds to cite the first paragraph of Hazlitt's essay on "Hamlet" as "a striking specimen of the tendency . . . in this author to give himself up to his poet."[10] Because Hazlitt can do this, he can fully appreciate Shakespeare's greatness.

The experience of reading Hazlitt's criticism is unique because he establishes intimate bonds between the reader and dramatic characters, and between his own sensibility and that of the reader. In an 1821 review of *Table Talk*, Charles Lamb discusses the intimacy of Hazlitt's essays and links him to the prose tradition established by Plutarch, Montaigne, Johnson, and Steele. Like his predecessors, Hazlitt was not afraid to fill his works with his own opinions and "personal peculiarities," which unify the essays and have a very strong "appeal to the reader." Twentieth-century critics such as W. P. Albrecht and John Kinnaird echo Lamb's reaction.[11] In the present era of reader-response criticism, Hazlitt's work can be reevaluated in terms of the effect of his subjectivity on his audience.

He admits his designs on his readers in a letter to Macvey Napier in 1816. Hazlitt insists that his emphatic and "paradoxical" statements are intended to catch readers' attention. He adds that his opinions are "abstract principles" which require deductive logic. Instead of working out every step in his essays, he has decided "to leave the public to find out."[12] Like Coleridge, Hazlitt has no desire to fill in all the blanks by doing exhaustive explications: both romantic writers demand active readers.

In *Hazlitt and the Spirit of the Age*, Roy Park defines Hazlitt's aesthetics as "experiential." The experiential response requires both great writers and sensitive readers to have an imaginative openness and a capacity for deep feeling. By exercising these two faculties, an individual can transcend his or her ego to sympathize with other people's experiences. As a result, one gains an appreciation of the complexity and variety of human life. Ideally, the writer helps the reader to achieve openness and insight.[13]

Hazlitt worries that the stage can impede this potential insight by oversimplifying and distorting dramatic literature, especially the plays of Shakespeare. In many chapters of *Characters*, he insists that a particular role is not or cannot be portrayed adequately in the theater. For example, Hazlitt complains about actors who present "caricatures" of Shylock, instead of well thought out interpretations. The critic concludes,

The stage is not in general the best place to study our author's characters in. It is too often filled with traditional common-place conceptions of the part, handed down from sire to son, and suited to the taste of *the great vulgar and the small*. (*Works of Hazlitt*, 4:324)

This argument is an extension of the remarks of earlier commentators like Schlegel, James Beattie, and Leigh Hunt.[14]

The only works of Shakespeare that Hazlitt likes to see performed are *The Winter's Tale* and *Richard III*. Hazlitt had witnessed successful performances of these two plays. He recalls an 1802 production of *The Winter's Tale* starring Mrs. Siddons as Hermione, John Philip Kemble as Leontes, and John Bannister as Autolycus. The critic laments, "We shall never see these parts so acted again." While the spectator is dependent on the cast, which may age and change, the reader's reaction to the play is independent of time and place. "True poetry, like nature, is always young; and we still read the courtship of Florizel and Perdita, as we welcome the return of spring, with the same feelings as ever" (*Works of Hazlitt*, 4:326). Similarly, Hazlitt has mixed feelings about *Richard III*. He considers it "properly a stage play" and praises Edmund Kean's "perfectly *articulated*" acting as King Richard. However, certain aspects of the character elude Kean: "It is possible to form a higher conception of the character of Richard than that given by Mr. Kean" (4:298). Also, in the final paragraph of his essay, Hazlitt cites two moving lyrical speeches by minor characters in the tragedy and comments, "We do not insist on the repetition of these last passages as proper for the stage: we should indeed be loth to trust them in the mouth of almost any actor" (4:303).

In *Lectures on the Dramatic Literature of the Age of Elizabeth*, Hazlitt explains why he prefers to *read* good plays. Books

are the nearest to our thoughts: they wind into the heart; the poet's verse slides into the current of our blood. We read them when young, we remember them when old. We read there of what has happened to others; we feel that it has happened to ourselves. (*Works of Hazlitt*, 6:247)

In other words, the act of reading stirs the mind and the sympathy of the participant, and a book involves the reader more than the passive experience of witnessing a performance. In a review of *Richard II* in 1815, Hazlitt criticizes all productions of Shakespeare's dramas, "even by the best actors," because theaters neglect poetic imagery and "minuter strokes of character" to emphasize physical distress and other obvious claptraps. Like earlier critics, Hazlitt distinguishes between true drama and mere pantomime. He agrees with Coleridge that the best elements of a play arouse the mind to meditation, while the most intensely physical aspects of plays distract the spectators from the essence of the works.

> It is only the *pantomime* part of tragedy . . . which is sure to tell, and tell completely on the stage. All the rest, all that appeals to our profounder feelings, to reflection and imagination, all that affects us most deeply in our closets . . . is little else than an interruption and a drag on the business of the stage. . . . Those parts of the play on which the reader dwells the longest, and with the highest relish in the perusal, are hurried through in the performance, while the most trifling and exceptionable are obtruded on his notice, and occupy as much time as the most important. . . . Hence it is, that the reader of the plays of Shakespear is almost always disappointed in seeing them acted; and, for our own parts, we should never go to see them acted, if we could help it. (5:222)

Similarly, Hazlitt finds that Covent Garden's production of Milton's *Comus* in 1815 overemphasizes the physical aspects of the drama, rather than its poetry and its allegorical meaning. Such a performance discourages abstraction: "Every thing on the stage takes a literal, palpable shape, and is embodied to the sight. So much is done by the senses, that the imagination is not prepared to eke out any deficiency that may occur." By appealing so exclusively to the senses, the theater reduces a serious drama to "a speaking pantomime" (*Works of Hazlitt*, 5:230–31).

Despite Hazlitt's stream of criticism of the London stage, its managers, and its most prominent stars, he clearly loved the theater. After praising Kean's Romeo, Hazlitt remarks parenthetically, "Actors are the best commentators on the poets" (*Works of Hazlitt*, 4:256). When Covent Garden was in danger of closing in 1829, Hazlitt wrote two articles to advocate keeping the theater open (see 20:283–88). While Coleridge consistently denigrates the performance of drama, Hazlitt and Lamb celebrate many aspects of the theater. In "The Free Admission" (1830), Hazlitt lists the pleasures of attending live productions, which liberate the audience from everyday cares and renew "the social principle" that links us to our neighbors. Paradoxically, the theater can also promote "solitary musing" by evoking memories of older actors and bygone performances. However, the stage also creates problems: "it kills time and saves the trouble of thinking"; the spectator may become "callous and inert with perpetual excitement" (17:366–70). Hazlitt never recommends the abolition of dramatic performances; instead, he emphasizes that the public needs to understand the limitations of the stage, especially when Shakespeare's plays are mounted.

Not even Hazlitt's favorite actor, Edmund Kean (see figure 6), satisfies the critic in many Shakespearean roles. While he finds Kean's portrayal of Richard III powerful, Hazlitt doubts that anyone can play Macbeth. "We can conceive a common actor to play Richard tolerably well; we can conceive no one to play Macbeth properly, or to look like a man that had encountered the Weïrd Sisters" (*Works of Hazlitt*, 4:194). Note that Hazlitt agrees with Thomas Whately and other eighteenth-century critics in viewing Macbeth as a far more complex character than Richard.[15] Similarly, Hazlitt believes that Hamlet's role is not actable (4:237). Although he extolls Shakespeare's skill in creating unique and believable heroines, Hazlitt discovers that most performances fail to capture these traits. "His women are certainly very unlike stage-heroines; the reverse of tragedy-queens" (4:180).

Shakespeare's most fanciful characters—witches, sprites, strange beasts—are perhaps the hardest to represent. Hazlitt contends that this factor makes *The Tempest, Macbeth,* and *A Midsummer Night's Dream* impossible to act. Caliban is a case in point: "It is not indeed pleasant to see this character on the stage any more than it is to see the god Pan personated there" (4:239). Likewise, Hazlitt finds the witches in *Macbeth* "ridiculous on the modern stage" (4:194). Hazlitt's most extensive discussion of this problem occurs in his essay on *A Midsummer Night's Dream.* In the second paragraph, he praises Shakespeare's "subtlety," "delicacy," and powers of description (4:245–46). These virtues are likely to be obscured by a performance. Because Shakespeare's dramas are so subtle, they are more difficult to stage than those of any other writer. Hazlitt uses images of delicate phenomena to emphasize the subtlety of *Midsummer Night's Dream.* Note that only the reader can fully appreciate the delicate texture of the comedy. "The reading of this play is like wandering in a grove by moonlight: the descriptions breathe a sweetness like odours thrown from beds of flowers" (4:246). Hazlitt considers any staging of this drama a mistake, and he makes it clear that his ban does not apply only to a few awkward nineteenth-century productions. Despite Liston's fine acting as Bottom in one London extravaganza, the performance "failed . . . from the nature of things." The following passage, which concludes the essay, develops Hazlitt's thesis that most of Shakespeare's plays,

6. *Edmund Kean as Sir Giles Overreach in* **A New Way to Pay
Old Debts,** *a painting by George Clint, courtesy of the
Victoria and Albert Museum, London.*

especially his fanciful creations, must be read to be experienced adequately because the stage does not allow enough abstraction from the senses.

> The MIDSUMMER NIGHT'S DREAM, when acted, is converted from a delightful fiction into a dull pantomime. All that is finest in the play is lost in the representation. The spectacle was grand: but the spirit was evaporated, the genius was fled.— Poetry and the stage do not agree well together. . . . That which was merely an airy shape, a dream, a passing thought, immediately becomes an unmanageable reality. Where all is left to the imagination (as is the case in reading) every circumstance, near or remote, has an equal chance of being kept in mind, and tells according to the mixed impression of all that has been suggested. But the imagination cannot sufficiently qualify the actual impressions of the senses. Any offence given to the eye is not to be got rid of by explanation. Thus Bottom's head in the play is a fantastic illusion, produced by magic spells: on the stage it is an ass's head, and nothing more; certainly a very strange costume for a gentleman to appear in. Fancy cannot be embodied any more than a simile can be painted; and it is as idle to attempt it as to personate *Wall* or *Moonshine.* Fairies are not incredible, but fairies six feet high are so. . . . The boards of a theatre and the regions of fancy are not the same thing. (4:247–48)[16]

To the typical spectator, Bottom's head is merely "strange," but for the careful reader, the same head is "a fantastic illusion." Hazlitt implies that the people responsible for staging *Midsummer Night's Dream* are as uncouth as the rustics who think that one can portray moonlight. Note that Hazlitt consistently uses the word "pantomime" in a pejorative sense to attack performances of Shakespeare's plays.

Tragedy presents different problems when produced in a theater. Plays like *Othello* have no supernatural component; they interest the audience by arousing the sympathetic imagination, according to Hazlitt. Shakespeare stirs the imagination by enabling readers to identify strongly with his tragic heroes. Hazlitt speaks about this phenomenon from the reader's point of view, not from the spectator's. For example, Hamlet's speeches become "as real as our own thoughts. Their reality is in the reader's mind" (*Works of Hazlitt,* 4:232).

The clearest statement of Hazlitt's theory of tragedy occurs in the opening paragraph of his essay "Othello." Elisabeth Schneider has pointed out that he begins by reworking Aristotle's thesis that tragedy effects katharsis by evoking terror and pity.[17] Hazlitt argues that be-

cause tragedy stimulates the sympathetic imagination, it enables man
to transcend his usual selfish concerns.

> It has been said that tragedy purifies the affections by terror
> and pity. That is, it substitutes imaginary sympathy for mere self-
> ishness. It gives us a high and permanent interest, beyond our-
> selves, in humanity as such. It raises the great, the remote, and the
> possible to an equality with the real, the little and the near. It
> makes man a partaker with his kind. . . . It opens the chambers of
> the human heart. (*Works of Hazlitt*, 4:200)

These remarks contradict Babbitt's view that the romantics interpret
katharsis as mere self-expression.

Hazlitt's essay on Othello seems designed to help the reader to
identify with the hero. When describing how Shakespeare develops
Othello's character, Hazlitt intentionally implicates his reader in the
Moor's reactions by shifting from third-person singular pronouns re-
ferring to Othello to first-person plural pronouns.

> It is in working his noble nature up to this extremity through rapid
> but gradual transitions, in raising passion to its height from the
> smallest beginnings and in spite of all obstacles, . . . in unfolding
> the strength and the weakness of our nature, . . . in putting in
> motion the various impulses that agitate this our mortal being,
> and at last blending them in that noble tide of deep and sustained
> passion . . . that Shakespear has shown the mastery of his genius
> and of his power over the human heart. (*Works of Hazlitt*, 4:201–2)

The parallel construction of this long sentence also tends to merge
"his noble nature" with "our mortal being." The *our* pronouns emphasize the universality of this tragedy: Othello is Everyman.

Perhaps the most striking example of Hazlitt's awareness of his
readers is the essay "Hamlet" in *Characters of Shakespear's Plays*. "Hamlet" begins and ends with a discussion of the play's appeal for readers,
and the argument is carefully structured to captivate and to manipu-
late Hazlitt's own reading public. In this essay, he reworks material
from his theater review "Mr. Kean's Hamlet," which first appeared in
The Morning Chronicle in March 1814. When one examines Hazlitt's
revisions and compares them to the 1814 review, it is clear that the
chapter for *Characters of Shakespear's Plays* (1817) focuses more on readers and emphasizes the process of sympathetic identification with a
character by means of the imagination. The first two paragraphs of the
1817 version, which develop Hamlet's "reality . . . in the reader's

mind," are 90 percent new, and the third paragraph begins with new remarks stressing the close relationship that Hazlitt feels to the protagonist. (This closeness is also apparent in Hazlitt's letters, where he frequently quotes from *Hamlet*.) The end of the third paragraph contains new observations on the psychological truth of the tragedy for readers, who are "more than spectators" (*Works of Hazlitt*, 4:232–33).

In the original review, Hazlitt had observed that Hamlet is "the most difficult" role for an actor and compared playing this role to "the attempt to embody a shadow" (*Works of Hazlitt*, 5:186). The critic had gone on to analyze Kean's recent performance as Hamlet. However, Hazlitt intensifies his criticism of the stage in his revised essay for *Characters*, arguing in the last paragraph that he is uncomfortable with *any* stage productions of Shakespeare's plays and that *Hamlet* "suffers" the most when acted (*Works of Hazlitt*, 4:237).

Hazlitt catches the reader's attention at the outset of the 1817 version of the essay with a series of clauses which imitate the rhythm and phraseology of Exodus 6:26–27. The King James Bible translates these verses in this way:

> These are that Aaron and Moses, to whom the LORD said, Bring out the children of Israel from the land of Egypt, according to their armies. These are they which spake to Pharoah king of Egypt, to bring out the children of Israel from Egypt: These are that Moses and Aaron.

Hazlitt's slightly blasphemous adaptation catalogs Hamlet's attributes and actions as a herald does before the entrance of a royal personage. This is appropriate, of course, because Hamlet is a prince. Despite the fact that Hamlet lived around 1300, Shakespeare's great dramatic skill enables nineteenth-century readers to identify with the Dane and to "remember" him as if he were an acquaintance.

> This is that Hamlet the Dane, whom we read of in our youth, and whom we may be said almost to remember in our after-years; he who made that famous soliloquy on life, who gave the advice to the players . . . ; he that was mad and sent to England; the slow avenger of his father's death; who lived at the court of Horwendillus five hundred years before we were born, but all whose thoughts we seem to know as well as we do our own, because we have read them in Shakespear. (*Works of Hazlitt*, 4:232)

As in other essays which I have already discussed, Hazlitt insists on first-person plural pronouns here. This forces the reader to recall his or her own responses to the character of Hamlet. Note that the "we" represents *readers* of Shakespeare, not spectators. In the middle of the paragraph, Hazlitt cites various phrases which would stick in the mind of someone who knew the text of *Hamlet* well, not a casual playgoer.

The second paragraph begins by contradicting the spirit and tone of the opening passage: "Hamlet is a name; his speeches and sayings but the idle coinage of the poet's brain." Hazlitt wants the reader to find this sceptical statement flat and colorless after the stately, evocative cadences of the previous sentence. The reader should protest the unfairness of such an unimaginative response. Hazlitt proceeds to challenge this empty assertion and to reassure the reader that Shakespeare's prince cannot be dismissed in this fashion. "What then, are they not real? They are as real as our own thoughts. Their reality is in the reader's mind. It is *we* who are Hamlet" (*Works of Hazlitt*, 4:232). Here Hazlitt moves rapidly from a defense of the validity of dramatic literature to the bold assertion that the readers' responses to Hamlet generate his reality.[18] People with sympathetic imaginations *become* Hamlet when perusing the tragedy, while prosaic individuals distance themselves from what they consider "the idle coinage of the poet's brain."

Hazlitt examines the psychology of the readers' intense involvement with Hamlet: we identify with the prince because we have had analogous experiences. Our emotional response gives the play its validity.

> This play has a prophetic truth, which is above that of history. Whoever has become thoughtful and melancholy through his own mishaps or those of others; whoever has borne about with him the clouded brow of reflection . . . ; he . . . whose powers of action have been eaten up by thought, he to whom the universe seems infinite, and himself nothing; . . . and who goes to a play as his best resource to shove off, to a second remove, the evils of life by a mock representation of them—this is the true Hamlet. (*Works of Hazlitt*, 4:232–33)

Hazlitt's assertion that the "play has a prophetic truth" is clearly related to the parody of biblical language in paragraph one. Both of these heterodox passages are meant to elevate the imaginative truth of the tragedy by likening it to religious verity. Other parallels with the first paragraph are (1) the long sentence cataloging human suffering, which is structurally similar to the bulk of the opening clauses, and (2) the concluding statement, which echoes the first words of the essay. Thus, the first and second paragraphs form a large chiasmus. Both passages are designed to evoke as many as possible of the readers' first associations.

At this point, Hazlitt takes a step back to confess, "We have been so used to this tragedy that we hardly know how to criticise it any more than we should know how to describe our own faces. . . . Whatever happens to him we apply to ourselves" (*Works of Hazlitt*, 4:233). The use of "we" here suggests that Hazlitt sees this problem as a general one: because many readers identify so strongly with the hero, it is impossible to approach Hamlet in the conventional fashion, which requires a critic to maintain distance from a work of literature in order to achieve objectivity.

One may well ask, Why must critics rely only on "objective" approaches? If a tragedy's strength is its capacity to arouse the reader's sympathetic imagination, perhaps a new approach is justified. Hazlitt does not make this argument in "Hamlet"; however, the remarks which I have quoted previously from "On Criticism" indicate that he was consciously trying to evoke "the soul and body of a work" (*Works of Hazlitt*, 7:217) by a new, sympathetic form of criticism.[19]

Hazlitt marvels at Shakespeare's seemingly effortless ability to involve the reader in many characters' lives. "There is no attempt to force an interest: every thing is left for time and circumstances to unfold. The attention is excited without effort" (*Works of Hazlitt*, 4:233). Unlike other writers, who stress external action, Shakespeare reveals the inner workings of his characters. If a reader is attuned to this, he can envision much more than the usual stage spectacle.

> But here we are more than spectators. We have not only 'the outward pageants and the signs of grief'; but 'we have that within which passes shew.' We read the thoughts of the heart, we catch the passions living as they rise. Other dramatic writers give us very fine versions and paraphrases of nature; but Shakespear, together with his own comments, gives us the original text, that we may judge for ourselves. This is a very great advantage. (4:233)

Unlike the French writers whom Hazlitt attacks in several essays, Shakespeare presents the reader with nature herself. However, the playwright's refusal to "paraphrase" nature complicates the reader's job: each person must arrive at his or her own interpretation. The privilege of "judg[ing] for ourselves" demands a great imaginative effort.

Hazlitt tries to help the reader by stressing the unique aspects of

Hamlet's character. Although "Hamlet is as little of the hero as a man can well be," his sensitivity, enthusiasm, and vulnerability should appeal to the reader. Like most of the romantic commentators, especially Coleridge, Hazlitt finds Hamlet's inaction intriguing and tries to answer questions raised by eighteenth-century critics about the delay of the prince's vengeance.[20] The terminology used in the following passage reflects the eighteenth-century commentator's interest in a character's dominant trait. "His ruling passion is to think, not to act: and any vague pretext that flatters this propensity instantly diverts him from his previous purposes" (*Works of Hazlitt,* 4:233–35).

In the sixth paragraph, Hazlitt turns to critics who had questioned Hamlet's morality. He defends the Danish prince, using arguments which anticipate those of Charles Lamb in *The Essays of Elia* (1823). Lamb protests against the behavior of British citizens who seem incapable of imagining a world where the restrictive laws of common life cannot apply. Such people have no tolerance for certain kinds of drama, because plays often violate ordinary codes of conduct. Lamb uses courtroom imagery to satirize this frame of mind.[21] Similarly, Hazlitt points out that Hamlet's behavior does not follow typical social customs because the prince's

> very excess of intellectual refinement . . . makes the common rules of life . . . sit loose upon him. He may be said to be amenable only to the tribunal of his own thoughts, and is too much taken up with the airy world of contemplation to lay as much stress as he ought on the practical consequences of things. (*Works of Hazlitt,* 4:235–36)

If one considers the prince's intellectual bias when evaluating his actions, one sees that Hamlet is, in fact, "amiable" (4:235). Hazlitt appears to direct this paragraph only to literary critics who believe that drama should be rigidly moral. However, his arguments are also designed to challenge the thinking of any readers who may agree with this wrongheaded school of criticism.

Hazlitt gives another reason for admiring Shakespeare's characters, despite the fact that they depart from orthodox morality: "Shakespear was thoroughly a master of the mixed motives of human character" (*Works of Hazlitt,* 4:236). In other words, the playwright presents complex personalities, not pasteboard figures. Hazlitt mentions Queen Gertrude as an example of a complicated individual. Obviously, the more intricate the characters are, the more work a reader must do to understand them. Hazlitt argues that most critics have not analyzed Polonius properly. While many commentators view the courtier as inconsistent, Hazlitt denies this allegation and contends that one must examine Polonius's motives and the different circumstances in each scene. Shakespeare's psychological insight leads him to present men whose conduct belies their intelligence.

Paragraph eight includes a paean to Shakespeare's "tenderness and pathos" in portraying Ophelia. In contrast, Laertes does not win the readers' sympathy at all. Hazlitt dismisses him in one sentence. "Her brother, Laertes, is a character we do not like so well: he is too hot and choleric, and somewhat rhodomontade" (*Works of Hazlitt*, 4:236–37). One wishes that the critic had expanded this useful observation. Perhaps Shakespeare had reasons for obstructing the reader's sympathetic identification with Laertes.

In the final paragraph of the essay, Hazlitt strongly condemns *any* performance of *Hamlet*. "We do not like to see our author's plays acted, and least of all, HAMLET. There is no play that suffers so much in being transferred to the stage. Hamlet himself seems hardly capable of being acted" (*Works of Hazlitt*, 4:237). Even the best English actors could not succeed in this role. Hazlitt found Kemble too inflexible in his portrayal of the young prince, and he found Kean "too splenetic and rash." The part requires extreme subtlety and an awareness of the character's complexity. In order to emphasize the difficulty in acting Hamlet, Hazlitt concludes the essay with this paradox: "He is the most amiable of misanthropes" (4:237).[22]

Experiments in manipulation of his readers are not confined to *Characters of Shakespear's Plays*. Hazlitt's essays on the theater for various periodicals also reveal a self-conscious critic at work. This is especially true of those longer articles which were not written as reviews of single performances. Many of these essays exploit the possibilities of digressions. Although the digression on Ophelia and Laertes in "Hamlet" was left hanging, Hazlitt's later excursions are coherent and well developed. He indicates in parenthetical remarks directed to his readers that he is *purposely* departing from the central topic. However, he often veils his underlying rhetorical strategy.

A good example is the third of Hazlitt's articles for *The London Magazine* (March 1820). He begins by informing the readers that his subject will be the minor theaters and that he intends to "give a furlough to fancy." In the next paragraph, Hazlitt explains that he views the minor houses as "the connecting link" between the most primitive theater and the most elaborate stage pomp. At this point, he digresses to evoke the excitement of an individual's first experience of the theater, usually "a company of strolling players" performing in a barn, booth, town hall, or assembly room temporarily converted into a stage. Hazlitt deemphasizes the importance of the theater building and the spectacle to focus on the pleasure of unadorned drama. He labels the stage world "an anomaly in existence" and compares it to "fairy revels" and a "gay waking dream." Under the influence of a play, the initiate's "childish fancy" paradoxically becomes "the only reality" (*Works of Hazlitt*, 18:291–93).

Throughout this digression, Hazlitt uses first-person plural pronouns to implicate the readers and to involve them more intimately with his argument. When we first see a play, "how glad, how surprised are we! We have no thought of any deception in the scene, no wish but to realise it ourselves with inconsiderate haste and fond impatience. . . . A new sense comes upon us, the scales fall off our eyes" (*Works of Hazlitt*, 18:293). By repeating pronouns such as "we," "us," and "ourselves" in this passage, Hazlitt moves his readers from agreement with the uncontroversial statement, "how surprised are we," to the radical evaluation, "the scales fall off our eyes."

The essay proceeds to gently caricature theater managers as frustrated actors who travel from door to door distributing playbills and verbal propaganda. Hazlitt finds the manager's illusions fascinating:

> he is little less happy than a king, though not much better off than a beggar. He . . . is accompanied, in his incessant daily round of trifling occupations, with a never-failing sense of authority and self-importance. . . . He is not quite mad, nor quite happy. (*Works of Hazlitt*, 18:294–95)

Like people at their first play, the manager is absorbed in a world of fancy.

Actors are also transformed by their profession. Again, Hazlitt stresses the imaginative involvement of each player.

> The poet fancies others to be this or that; the player fancies himself to be all that the poet but describes. . . . He has discovered the true Elixir of Life, which is freedom from care. . . . Offer him twice the salary to go into a counting-house, to stand behind a counter, and he will return to poverty, steeped in contempt, but eked out with fancy, at the end of a week. (*Works of Hazlitt*, 18:295–96)

Because they live in a world of imaginary splendor, actors can transmit the magic of drama to those around them.

Hazlitt recalls one joyous actor, singing and "heart-whole," and speculates about what has happened to the man. Hazlitt lists various possibilities—care, death, sickness, "[o]r is he himself lost and buried amidst the rubbish of one of our larger, or else of one of our Minor Theatres?" (*Works of Hazlitt*, 18:296). Clearly, this last eventuality is the worst. The word "rubbish" jolts the reader intentionally. This sentence concludes the four-page digression, a substantial slice of an eleven-page essay. Hazlitt's descriptions of actors, managers, and playgoers should have made the reader recall exciting moments in the magical world of drama. The reader's sympathetic imagination has been aroused, and he or she has fallen under the spell of the prose incantation. Now Hazlitt pulls the rug out from under his reading public by implying that both major and minor houses violate the joyous world of the actor and are callous to his fate.[23]

After this "intended digression," Hazlitt criticizes the minor theaters, where he witnessed "the heartless indifference and hearty contempt shown by the performers for their parts, and by the audience for the players and the play" (*Works of Hazlitt*, 18:297). Though he came "determined to be pleased," Hazlitt found no satisfaction; none of his expectations was met. By digressing to emphasize the imaginative potential of theater and then disillusioning his readers with the London reality, he forces us to undergo his own disappointment. Hazlitt purposely raises our expectations so that he can frustrate them.

Conclusion

Although Babbitt, Abrams, Wellek, and others assert that the romantics' criticism is dominated by their interest in the writer, Hazlitt's essays on drama reveal an overwhelming concern with the *reader's* responses to literature. This concern links Hazlitt to eighteenth-century critics such as Hume, Johnson, Richardson, and Morgann, who explored audience reaction. Hazlitt differs from Hume and Johnson in stressing the need for one to identify with tragic heroes, instead of maintaining aesthetic distance.[24] His favorite tragedies are those which most involve the reader in the main characters' sufferings and evoke the sympathetic imagination.

Hazlitt is fascinated by the complexity and variety of Shakespearean heroes, and he comes to believe that they cannot be presented adequately on stage. Only a sensitive reader can appreciate the bard's insights into the human psyche. Because Shakespeare's tragedy involves an internalization of the action, Hazlitt feels that the nineteenth-century public needs help in understanding this kind of drama. Awareness of his readers shapes the rhetoric and the overall structure of his essays.

5. Lamb and Reader-Response Criticism

Scholars have recently devoted many books, articles, and conferences to the responses of readers to texts and investigated different authors' concepts of "the implied reader."[1] Writers like Stanley Fish, Walter Slatoff, and Wolfgang Iser have explored the demands that poets and novelists make on the reading public. However, few twentieth-century critics have taken any interest in the reader's reaction to a published play, perhaps because they define drama as solely a performing art.

Since reader-response scholars have neglected plays, one must turn to film criticism to find comparisons of the responses of readers to dramas, novels, and short stories and the responses of audiences to motion pictures based on works of fiction. Adaptations of Shakespeare's plays have generated debates among film critics. While commentators such as Jack J. Jorgens view movies as "truest to the effect of Shakespeare's dramatic verse," other scholars complain that films are overly concerned with setting and other external details and thus neglect poetic language and important themes. According to Siegfried Kracauer, "Film and tragedy are incompatible with each other" because tragedy is "an exclusively mental experience." In contrast, "films cling to the surface of things. They seem to be the more cinematic, the less they focus directly on inward life, ideology, and spiritual concerns." When a drama is made into a motion picture, there is "a shift of emphasis from the dimension of intellectual messages to that of photographable objects." Kracauer believes that the photographic images of Max Reinhardt's *A Midsummer Night's Dream* and Laurence Olivier's *Hamlet* are so obtrusive that they distract the spectator from Shakespeare's use of language. Seymour Chatman and Wolfgang Iser have also observed that films of literary works affect viewers very differently from the way the original novel or short story affects readers. Chatman argues in "What Novels Can Do That Films Can't (and Vice Versa)" that films have an overabundance of images.

> Film narrative possesses a plenitude of visual details, an excessive particularity compared to the verbal version. . . . But . . . unlike painting or sculpture, narrative films do not usually allow us time to dwell on plenteous details. Pressure from the narrative component is too great. Events move too fast.

In *Story and Discourse,* Chatman points out that the reader reacts to "only what is named," while movies present both central and peripheral characters and objects. Because films are so visual, directors have trouble with "nonscenic" narratives, which emphasize "a realm of ideas" rather than a specific location. In contrast, literature can easily convey this "nowhere" realm. Wolfgang Iser goes even further in his discussion of Fielding's novel and the movie version of *Tom Jones.* Iser contends that the numerous details of the motion picture limit viewers' imaginative responses.

> While reading *Tom Jones,* they may never have had a clear conception of what the hero actually looks like, but on seeing the film, some may say, "That's not how I imagined him." The point here is that the reader of *Tom Jones* is able to visualize the hero virtually for himself, and so his imagination senses the vast number of possibilities; the moment these possibilities are narrowed down to one complete and immutable picture, the imagination is put out of action and we feel we have somehow been cheated.

The complex, "round" characters of many novels are flattened when they are portrayed on screen by an actor or actress. According to Chatman, "The all too visible player . . . seems unduly to circumscribe the character despite the brilliance of the performance."[2]

Although Charles Lamb made many of these same arguments—in regard to staged dramas—150 years ago, none of the above critics mentions Lamb's essay "On the Tragedies of Shakspeare, Considered with Reference to their Fitness for Stage Representation" (1811). Here, Lamb insists that all of Shakespeare's tragedies suffer when performed, and he examines *Hamlet, Lear, Macbeth, Richard III,* and *Othello* to determine why they have a greater impact when read. This essay has been considered eccentric by most twentieth-century commentators. For example, Wimsatt and Brooks speak condescendingly of "Lamb's baroque whimsicalities concerning Shakespeare's tragedies."[3] In this chapter, I hope to show that "On the Tragedies of Shakspeare" is not an aberration. The arguments in Lamb's essay are consistent with his overall approach to reading literature. Furthermore, many of his conclusions anticipate those of Chatman, Kracauer, and Iser and are remarkably close in spirit to the film criticism of these men.

It seems strange that Lamb, who often celebrates the theater in his poems, letters, and essays, could write "On the Tragedies of Shakspeare." He frequently attended Drury Lane and Covent Garden (see figure 7), wrote reviews of various plays for London periodicals, com-

7. *New Covent Garden Theatre* (1810), *courtesy of the Henry E. Huntington Library and Art Gallery, San Marino, California.*

posed prologues and epilogues for his friends' dramas, had his comedy *Mr H* produced, and even fell in love with the actress Fanny Kelly. In a note to Robert Lloyd, Lamb insists, "A crowd of happy faces justling into the playhouse at the hour of six is a more beautiful spectacle to man than the shepherd driving his 'silly' sheep to fold—— ——" (*Letters*, 1:271). Also, in "My First Play," Elia calls the theater "the most delightful of recreations" (*Works*, 2:100). However, Lamb carefully distinguishes between dramatic genres that he feels succeed on stage and those that do not. In general, he finds comedy well suited to performance, especially "artificial comedy" (comedy of manners). But Lamb consistently expresses reservations about the staging of tragedy. His main criterion is the effect of the genre on an audience: comedy allows the spectators to escape the "shackles" of their ordinary lives to experience the freedom of a fictional dream world (see "On the Artificial Comedy of the Last Century," in *Works*, 2:141–43), but tragedy is more metaphysical and requires deeper audience involvement and imaginative effort, which reading alone can provide.[4]

John I. Ades has observed, "In all of Lamb's Shakespearean criticism, he commends only one tragic performance as completely successful: a production of *Othello* in which Robert Bensley played Iago."[5] Lamb believed that the best tragedies should be read, not performed. This conviction grew out of his belief, shared by other romantic writers, that reading good literature provides abstraction and actively involves a person, while the stage renders one passive by appealing to the senses. Lamb spent most of his free time with his books, according to his own testimony in *The Last Essays of Elia* (1833): "When I am not walking, I am reading" (*Works*, 2:172). He compares reading to having a private "chapel" or "oratory" (2:458). Furthermore, Lamb castigates those who do not take reading seriously enough. This is his complaint in "Readers Against the Grain" (1825): more Englishmen are literate, and publications are more affordable, but the average reader's experience has degenerated into a fashionable hobby.

> We read to say that we have read. . . . These are your readers against the grain, who yet *must* read or be thought nothing of— who, crawling through a book with tortoise-pace, go creeping to the next Review to learn what they shall say of it. (*Works*, 1:272–73)[6]

This passive, unimaginative response to books disgusts the essayist. If people cannot become actively involved in what they read, they should avoid great literature.

Like Coleridge, Lamb views the ideal relationship between a writer and a reader as that of two intelligent and creative friends. Over and over, Lamb insists that both authors and readers must cooperate with and challenge one another. The writer must avoid patronizing the reader or beating him over the head with an argument. In turn, the reader must allow the writer imaginative freedom, even if the author's statements conflict with the reader's viewpoint. No one who is close-minded can appreciate good literature. For example, Lamb warns the readers of Hazlitt's prose that they must be receptive to new ideas. "Table-Talk is not calculated for cold or squeamish readers. The average thinker will find his common notions a little too roughly disturbed. He must brace up his ears to the reception of some novelties."[7] Readers should also be introspective. Lamb classifies the kind of reader who will appreciate the poems of Charles Lloyd as "one that has descended into his own bosom; that has probed his own nature even to shivering" (*Works*, 1:195). Introspection is valued by Lamb and the other romantics because they believe that great literature must be psychologically profound. A person who never examines his or her emotions and behavior will be blind to many dimensions of literary works.

Lamb was also concerned about the public's tendency to interpret writing too literally. In a proposed "Dedication" to the readers of *Elia,* he urges his audience to avoid interpreting the essays "perversely in [the] absolute and literal sense" (*Works,* 2:299). Lamb elaborates on this overly literal frame of mind when discussing Scotchmen in "Imperfect Sympathies" (2:59–61). Like Coleridge, Lamb wants readers to be open-minded and flexible, instead of biased and rigid.

Lamb often speaks of the writer/reader relationship as if there were a contract between the two parties, and he criticizes any violations of the necessary mutual respect. He complains to Wordsworth that "The Cumberland Beggar" contains passages which

> are too direct and like a lecture: they dont slide into the mind of the reader, while he is imagining no such matter.—An intelligent reader finds a sort of insult in being told, I will teach you how to think upon this subject. This fault, if I am right, is in a ten thousandth worse degree to be found in *Sterne* and many many novelists & modern poets, who continually put a sign post up to shew *where you are to feel.* They set out with assuming their readers to be stupid. Very different from Robinson Crusoe, the Vicar of Wakefie[l]d, Roderick Random, and other beautiful bare narratives.—There is implied an unwritten compact between Author and reader; I will tell you a story, and I suppose you will understand it. (*Letters,* 1:265–66)[8]

Twentieth-century critics like Fish, Slatoff, and Iser share this perspective. They view reading as an active and creative process and attempt to make literary criticism more sensitive to the role of the reading public. Stanley Fish writes in *Surprised by Sin* (1967), "Meaning is an *event,* something that happens, not on the page, where we are accustomed to look for it, but in the interaction between the flow of print (or sound) and the actively mediating consciousness of a reader-hearer." Furthermore, writers such as Milton may try to change the reader's conventional values and opinions. In *With Respect to Readers,* Slatoff frequently cites with approval Coleridge's dictum that literature "brings the whole soul of man into activity." Slatoff argues, "Because literature counts on it, the reader must bring his own consciousness and experiences to bear." This emphasis on the reader's introspection resembles Lamb's contract. In *The Implied Reader,* Iser argues that good authors design texts which "entangle" readers in the process of interpretation to give readers more insight into themselves and their world. He explores how authors like Fielding use various strategies "to open [the reader] up to the workings of the text."[9] This process of preparing the reader to appreciate literature intrigued the romantics as well, as is clear from Coleridge's comments on the opening scenes of Shakespeare's plays, Hazlitt's emphasis on sympathy, and Lamb's analysis of author-reader interaction.

When readers break the unwritten contract described by Lamb, the results are disastrous: literary geniuses suffer from neglect. Reviewing *The Excursion* in 1814, Lamb denounces the public's response to Wordsworth's poetry.

> The causes which have prevented the poetry of Mr. Wordsworth from attaining its full share of popularity are to be found in the boldness and originality of his genius. The times are past when a poet could securely follow the direction of his own mind into whatever tracts it might lead. A writer, who would be popular, must timidly coast the shore of prescribed sentiment and sympathy. He must have just as much more of the imaginative faculty than his readers, as will serve to keep their apprehensions from stagnating, but not so much as to alarm their jealousy. He must not think or feel too deeply. (*Works*, 1:170)[10]

Repeatedly in his criticism, Lamb urges the public to overcome its fear of taking imaginative risks, and he champions the work of difficult, risk-taking writers and artists. Like Coleridge and Hazlitt, he tries to educate reluctant readers to help them benefit more from books and pictures.

The contract between writers/artists and readers/viewers is the subject of much of Lamb's essay "On the Genius and Character of Hogarth" (1811). Toward the beginning of the article, Lamb emphasizes, "In the perusal of a book, or of a picture, much of the impression which we receive depends upon the habit of mind which we bring with us to such perusal." While "superficial" viewers will merely laugh (or sneer) at Hogarth's low-life subjects, more thoughtful people will sympathize with his harlots, drunks, and rakes. Lamb frequently describes the works of Hogarth as "objects of meditation." The ideal viewer considers more than color and style when in an art gallery: he or she can penetrate these external elements to reach an understanding of "the poetical and almost prophetical conception in the artist." Lamb celebrates works of art and literature "where the spectator must meet the artist in his conceptions half way; and it is peculiar to the confidence of high genius alone to trust so much to spectators or readers. Lesser artists shew everything distinct and full" (*Works*, 1:72, 74, 78).

The best writers and artists use understatement and carefully chosen symbols to convey ideas, not obvious phrases or icons. Lamb praises Shakespeare's ability to sustain dramatic understatement. Using the subtle concluding dialogue of *King Lear* as an example, Lamb demonstrates that Shakespeare purposely avoids forcing Lear's recognition of Kent into a tear-jerking reconciliation that ostentatiously displays the dramatist's powers. Instead, Shakespeare "trusts to the judicious few for understanding the reason of his abstinence" (*Works*, 1:345–46). Note that in this passage, as in the essay about Hogarth, Lamb emphasizes the mutual "trust" involved in the writer's or artist's contract with the public.

In "Barrenness of the Imaginative Faculty in the Productions of Modern Art" (1833), Lamb distinguishes between "poetic" and "pictorial" subjects: "In the latter, the exterior accidents are nearly everything, the unseen qualities as nothing." The unimaginative pictorial artist violates the artist/spectator contract because he stresses obvious external details, while the poetic painter probes what is hidden by physical appearance. To illustrate "poetic" handling of characters, Lamb cites Shakespeare's development of Othello and Falstaff. Instead of emphasizing each man's body, the playwright concentrates on "the respective moral or intellectual attributes of the character." Their thoughts and emotions outweigh their forms when the plays are read. However, in most pictures of the two characters, Othello's blackness and Sir John's corpulence predominate, blotting out their "moral or intellectual attributes" (*Works*, 2:233). Similarly, Lamb is outraged by pictures of Shakespeare's heroines. In a letter to Samuel Rogers in 1833, the essayist complains that he feels "tied down" by the portraits of Juliet and Imogen at Boydell's Shakespeare Gallery. Such illustrations of imaginative literature will always fail because they attempt to "confine the illimitable."[11]

In many of his essays, Lamb tries to teach his readers how to go beyond external details and first impressions to reach a more profound understanding of art and literature.[12] The essay "On the Tragedies of Shakspeare" is a good example of Lamb's attempts to broaden his public's imaginative horizons. It was published in 1811, shortly after his article on Hogarth. Just as Lamb emphasized the "meditative" quality of Hogarth's prints, here he stresses Shakespeare's interest in the minds of his dramatis personae. Staged versions of Shakespeare's tragedies distort the protagonists and violate the literary contract because the theater accentuates the bodies and gestures of characters like Hamlet, Lear, and Richard III, while the dramatist is more interested in their intellects and their psychology.

Lamb begins "On the Tragedies of Shakspeare" with a protest against what he considers undue attention to actors at the expense of dramatic geniuses. Specifically, he objects to a plaque in Westminster Abbey equating the talents of Shakespeare and David Garrick, the famous eighteenth-century actor. Lamb argues that there is no ground of comparison between the poet, who understands "the internal workings and movements of a great mind," and an actor, who merely imitates the external "signs" of passion (*Works*, 1:98).[13]

Like Seymour Chatman, Lamb contrasts the "slow apprehension" allowed in reading drama to "the instantaneous nature of the impressions which we take in at the eye and ear at a playhouse." Because of this rapid parade of visual images and the prominence of the players, performances tend to elevate the actor over the playwright and may even cause the audience "to identify in our minds in a perverse manner, the actor with the character which he represents." Note Lamb's insistence here on first-person plural pronouns, which implicate both himself and his reading public in this misapprehension. The temptation to identify an actor with a tragic protagonist is strongest when good actors like John Philip Kemble and Sarah Siddons are on the stage. Lamb praises these "two great performers," but he laments the excessive "distinctness" of the theater:

> When the novelty is past, we find to our cost that instead of realizing an idea, we have only materialized and brought down a fine vision to the standard of flesh and blood. We have let go a dream, in quest of an unattainable substance. (1:98)[14]

Like Iser, Lamb finds that the overly specific images of a performance limit the imaginative freedom of the audience: "How cruelly this operates on the mind, to have its free conceptions thus crampt and pressed down to the measure of a strait-lacing actuality." Moreover, fancy props and elaborate gestures distance the spectators from the play. Lamb complains that an abundance of "non-essentials" forces the audience to watch like "a reviewer" or a "judge," instead of viewing the action sympathetically through the eyes of the protagonists (1:99, 111).[15]

Lamb further denigrates acted drama by linking it to the common practice of excerpting significant passages from Shakespeare's plays for schoolboys and elocutionists to spout. This short digression is very effective rhetorically. Even twentieth-century readers groan when

Lamb reminds us how often one hears "To be or not to be" declaimed out of context and "pawed about" until it has lost all meaning (1:99).[16]

Lamb observes that the subtleties of good drama are usually obscured by the actors' practice of overemphasizing scenes of conflict and anger. These episodes of "coarse" passion appeal to "the eyes and ears of the spectators," just as bad art is merely "pictorial." Lamb acknowledges the popularity of such scenes, but he argues that "the best dramas," especially those of Shakespeare, use dialogue and soliloquy to convey to readers and spectators "knowledge of the inner structure and workings of mind in a character." Here again, the theater distorts drama and violates the contract by emphasizing externals and thus "reduces every thing to a controversy of elocution." The actors' emphasis on declamation wreaks havoc on the more delicate passages of Shakespeare's plays. Lamb uses assonance and consonance to stress the contrast between characters who should declaim loudly and those whose oratory is not appropriate: "Every character, from the *boisterous blasphemings of Bajazet* to the *shrinking timidity* of womanhood, must play the orator" (1:99–100).

"On the Tragedies of Shakspeare" is pervaded with antitheses that emphasize the distinction between reading drama and seeing a performance. Oppositions of the imaginative and the material, the free and the restricted, abound in the essay. I have listed these antitheses below.

POSITIVE ATTRIBUTES Associated with Reading Shakespeare's Plays	NEGATIVE ATTRIBUTES Associated with Performances of Shakespeare's Plays
the imagination	the senses
the mind	the body
the intellectual	the physical, the corporal
the internal	the external
depths of the sea	the surface
meditation	action
visions and dreams	the material, flesh and blood, substance
motives, impulses	gestures, tricks, voice
ideas, conceptions, understanding	ordinary perception, eyes and ears
abstraction	distinct shape, distinctness
thought	appearance, costume
illusion	reality
freedom, free conceptions	restriction, confinement, strait-lacing, laws, courts, cramping, pressing down

Of all Shakespeare's plays, *Hamlet, Richard III,* and *Lear* suffer the most on stage. According to Lamb, Hamlet is a meditative, retiring man. Because of the prince's temperament, it is awkward for him to appear before hundreds of spectators to utter his innermost thoughts in soliloquies. Lamb stresses Hamlet's reticence and contemplative nature by using many synonyms for the concepts. The prince indulges in "solitary musings," "silent meditations," "light-and-noise-abhorring ruminations." Lamb refers to the character as "shy, negligent, retiring Hamlet" (1:100–101).[17]

Lamb admits condescendingly that some members of the audience need the theater because they cannot read Shakespeare and therefore cannot be touched by his thought and passion. Perhaps the critic is thinking of "readers against the grain," as well as illiterate people. Lamb insists, "I am not arguing that Hamlet should not be acted, but how much Hamlet is made another thing by being acted" (1:101).[18]

Actors tend to take certain scenes out of context when *Hamlet* is performed. Lamb notes that players always exaggerate the prince's harshness to Polonius and Ophelia, thus vulgarizing the passion and drawing undue attention to the offensive side of the hero's character. These tragedians neglect Hamlet's "soreness of mind," which is his motive for such conduct. The prince's madness should not be overdone but should fit into the overall pattern, "the whole of his character." Lamb doubts that even Garrick could have performed the role of Hamlet adequately. No matter how commanding Garrick's voice and eyes were, these amounted to mere "physical properties" which could never capture the prince's "intellect" (1:101, 103).[19]

Just as Hamlet's mind is neglected in performance, so the "rich intellect" of Richard III is buried under the "butcher-like representation of him that passes for him on the stage." The audience loses sight of "the profound, the witty, accomplished Richard." Lamb compares G. F. Cooke's King Richard to "the giants and ogres in children's books." The essayist implies that only a childlike audience can applaud such stereotyped acting. In contrast, readers can "qualify" their "horror" at Richard's crimes with an appreciation of his intellect (1:105–6).[20] Lamb uses rhetorical questions and first-person pronouns to implicate his readers in the argument, again reaffirming the author/reader contract.

Macbeth presents similar difficulties for the stage. Reading the tragedy offers a "vantage-ground of abstraction" which prevents "the painful anxiety" of a theater audience. While a reader can concentrate on "the sublime images, the poetry alone," the stage version of *Macbeth* is too close to the reality of murder (1:106).

Likewise, watching old Lear "tottering about the stage with a walking stick, turned out of doors by his daughters in a rainy night, has nothing in it but what is painful and disgusting." The theater emphasizes the king's body too much. Lamb concludes, "The Lear of Shakspeare cannot be acted. . . . The greatness of Lear is not in corporal dimension, but in intellectual." Lear is even harder to act than Richard III or Macbeth because the audience needs to identify intensely with the former in order for the tragedy to have its full impact. "On the stage we see nothing but corporal infirmities and weakness, the impotence of rage; while we read it, we see not Lear, but we are Lear. . . . The play is beyond all art" (1:107).[21] While the spectator at a comedy of manners must distance himself or herself from the characters, the reader of *King Lear* must feel close to the suffering protagonist. Lamb's emphasis on this sympathetic identification clearly influenced Hazlitt's analyses in *Characters of Shakespear's Plays*, where Hazlitt cites the above passage (*Works*, 4:270–71).

In the opening paragraphs of the essay, Lamb had criticized facile comparisons between Shakespeare and Garrick. In the middle of the essay, Lamb attacks another false comparison, the common remark that *Othello's* "natural" quality resembles that of *George Barnwell*. He views Lillo's play as a "nauseous sermon" which cannot be likened to Shakespeare's tragedy because *George Barnwell* lacks the psychological insight of *Othello*. The presentation of *Othello* in a theater tends to flatten the characters until the play seems similar to inferior dramas. Thus, the "common auditor" cannot perceive "the texture of Othello's mind, the inward construction marvellously laid open." Although *Othello* seems more feasible for the stage than *Lear*, it fails almost as miserably. The theater overwhelms our imagination's view of the Moor, and we "sink Othello's mind in his colour" (1:102, 108, n. 1). Clearly, Lamb's argument here resembles his complaints about pictures of Othello in "Barrenness of the Imaginative Faculty in the Productions of Modern Art."

Lamb finds the caresses of black Othello and white Desdemona "extremely revolting" on stage (1:108). Some literary critics have accused Lamb of "a benighted racism" in his remarks. However, the issue seems more complicated. Joan Coldwell points out that "only recently some who saw the 'coal-black' Olivier in the film version confessed to a similar sense of outrage."[22] In the context of "On the Tragedies of Shakspeare," Lamb's objections should not be read as an indictment of intermarriage but rather as a protest against the theater's disfigurement of a powerful tragedy when spectacle impedes the audience's emotional involvement. He clarifies his position in a footnote which compares the portrayal of Adam and Eve in Milton's *Paradise Lost* to the uncomfortably naked figures in most paintings. Milton can bestow "Paradisaical senses" on the reader that prevent anyone from viewing the poem as pornography. *Othello* also causes the reader to perceive the characters in special ways. Lamb concludes, "So in the reading of the play, we see with Desdemona's eyes; in the seeing of it, we are forced to look with our own" (1:108 and n. 1).

Lamb argues that Shakespeare's supernatural characters must fail on stage because they also violate the contract and make "gross attempts upon the senses." While a reader is "spell-bound" by the witches in *Macbeth,* an audience finds them laughable: "the sight actually destroys the faith." Just as ghost stories cannot be effective in a well-lit room full of friends, dramatic ghosts cannot be believed under glaring lights in a crowded theater. Similarly, Lamb questions whether *The Tempest* can be performed on stage effectively. He argues, "Spirits and fairies cannot be represented, they cannot even be painted,—they can only be believed" (1:109–10).[23] Like Hazlitt, Lamb finds that the theater does not allow enough abstraction to enable the audience to respond imaginatively to the supernatural.

Although scenery is useful in comedy of manners and domestic genres, it ruins the more abstract imitation that is necessary to sustain the illusion of Shakespearean drama, which appeals "to the higher faculties." Similarly, Lamb finds the frequent costume changes of contemporary productions disconcerting. They give far too much importance to dress, which is superfluous in Shakespeare's plays. Like acting and scenery, costumes overemphasize the most external aspects of dramatic literature. In contrast, when we read a scene, the "better part of our imagination is employed upon the thoughts and internal machinery of the character" (1:110–11).

In the final paragraph of "On the Tragedies of Shakspeare," Lamb insists that he could extend his argument to prove that the playwright's comic characters "are equally incompatible with stage representation" (1:111). He never wrote such an essay, and he does praise various actors for their portrayal of roles in *Twelfth Night* (see "On Some of the Old Actors," *Works,* 2:132–38). However, his attack on paintings of

Falstaff in "Barrenness of the Imaginative Faculty" and his criticism of productions of *The Tempest* in "On the Tragedies of Shakspeare" indicate how he might have proceeded.

Conclusion

Like Iser, Fish, Slatoff, and other twentieth-century writers, Lamb considered the act of reading a creative process. He envisioned a contract of mutual respect between authors and their public. Over and over, he insisted upon the need for both writers and readers to have imaginative freedom. Lamb felt shackled by theatrical productions of Shakespeare's plays because they limited his imagination and distracted him with costumes, scenery, and elocution instead of exploring the protagonists' psyches.

Twentieth-century film critics such as Kracauer and Chatman agree with Lamb that a realization of a work of literature in the theater or on film appeals more to the senses than reading the same work, a process which is primarily intellectual and psychological. An over-abundance of visual images in a representation of a drama may obscure the poetic language and underlying ideas of the piece.

Lamb argues that Shakespeare is unique because he arouses the imaginative "powers" of his readers so forcefully (1:103), a belief that Lamb shares with Coleridge and Hazlitt. In "On the Tragedies of Shakspeare" and other essays, Lamb tries to make his reading public more receptive to the literary power of great drama by teaching his contemporaries to penetrate external details to reach the text's profound themes. Like Coleridge and Hazlitt, he urges readers to open their minds and to participate actively in the experience of literature.

6. The Metamorphoses of Nineteenth-Century Views of Spectacle

Many nineteenth-century writers besides Coleridge, Lamb, and Hazlitt manifest the ambivalence toward spectacle that runs through British drama criticism. Victorian writers both praise and attack advances in stage technology and lighting that make increasingly realistic sets possible. These critics also discuss the public's new demand for historically correct scenery and costumes. Toward the end of the century, writers like Yeats and Wilde explicitly challenge the assumptions behind the movements toward realism and naturalism in the arts, insisting that the stage should not try to represent eras and locations graphically but rather should suggest and evoke reality more subtly. This outlook has had a profound effect on twentieth-century productions of serious drama.

At the same time that nineteenth-century representations were becoming more realistic, stylized pictorial elements also abounded. In contrast to earlier drama, which stressed rhetoric, passion, and carefully articulated scenes, Victorian drama often emphasizes static tableaux and apocalyptic spectacles.[1] Debating the merits of rhetorical and pictorial drama, nineteenth-century critics revive Horace's ear/eye dichotomy and develop the romantics' distinction between literature that appeals to the imagination and literature that appeals to the senses.

However, the concept of abstraction becomes less important in drama criticism. While Coleridge, Lamb, and Hazlitt consider literature different from painting and sculpture because the written word encourages abstraction and the engagement of the sympathetic imagination, authors like Shelley, Lewes, Wilde, and Yeats believe that all of the arts can be effectively combined in dramatic spectacles and that when spectacle is properly integrated into dramas, it can aid the imagination. This change occurs because the latter critics have a different view of the mind and the relationship between art and the senses. Coleridge, Lamb, and Hazlitt insist on separating art that appeals directly to the senses from art that appeals to the intellect and the imagination. However, writers such as Lewes and Wilde resist what they consider a compartmentalized view of the mind. They believe that appropriate stimulation of the senses can help dramatic productions to appeal to higher faculties. They use the word "beauty" to denote art and literature that stimulate both the mind and the five senses.

In this chapter, I will trace the evolution of these concepts in British drama criticism. Because Wordsworth, Hunt, Byron, and Scott take positions on spectacle and reading literature close to those of Coleridge, I will not discuss their drama criticism here in detail.[2] Basically, these four writers agree with Coleridge, Hazlitt, and Lamb that spectacle can be dangerous because it can make an audience passive. All of these romantic commentators want readers who involve themselves actively with literature by exercising the imagination and the sympathy necessary to make reading almost as creative as the act of composing poetry or prose. Instead of repeating these observations, I will concentrate on British writers who have different perspectives on dramatic spectacle.

To show that the British commentators were not idiosyncratic, I will examine the essays of eighteenth- and nineteenth-century French and German writers who also denigrate performances, especially the staging of Shakespeare's plays. Goethe, Madame de Staël, Maeterlinck, and Mallarmé emphasize Shakespeare's appeal to the imagination, the intellect, and the spirit, not to the senses.

G. H. Lewes, Henry James, and Max Beerbohm depart from the romantics when they argue that staging enhances a drama as long as the spectacle is limited and "beautiful." In the article "Shakespeare's Critics: English and Foreign," Lewes attempts to refute Lamb's conclusions in "On the Tragedies of Shakspeare" by redefining the purpose of drama. Lewes concludes that both Shakespeare's comedies and his tragedies benefit from theatrical representation.

Because Matthew Arnold, John Ruskin, and G. B. Shaw want to reform materialistic Great Britain, they examine ways in which the theaters can be used to educate, civilize, and liberate the public. Defying the prevailing idolatry, Ruskin and Shaw refuse to worship Shakespeare; they question the moral adequacy of the bard's self-centered heroes. Shaw rewrites Coleridge's explanation of the effect of good literature on the reader to include stimulation of the senses and of morality.

In my last section, I will discuss the emphasis on unity of the arts in the drama criticism of Percy B. Shelley, Oscar Wilde, and W. B. Yeats. These writers do not oppose the senses to the intellect; instead, they value performed drama because it can appeal simultaneously to all the faculties. However, they insist that decorative and symbolic staging should replace realistic and spectacular productions.

The Continuity of the Bias against Spectacle in the Works of European Writers

British writers' antipathy to staging Shakespeare's plays is shared by contemporary French and German critics, including Goethe, A. W. Schlegel, Madame de Staël, Maeterlinck, and Mallarmé. Because the British romantics were well acquainted with Schlegel's lectures on drama, I have included his comments earlier in this book, along with those of Coleridge, Hazlitt, and Lamb. A brief survey of other continental writers who object to spectacle will reinforce the point that the British romantics were neither idiosyncratic nor isolated.

Although Goethe had shortened and revised Shakespeare's plays when he directed them in Germany, he argues against staging these dramas in "Shakespeare ad Infinitum" (1813–1816). Shakespeare's plays are designed to stir the imagination, not the senses.

> Shakespeare's works are not for the physical vision. . . .
> . . . Shakespeare speaks always to our inner sense. Through this, the picture-world of imagination becomes animated. . . . But if we study the works of Shakespeare enough, we find that they contain much more of spiritual truth than of spectacular action. He makes happen . . . what can be better imagined than seen. Hamlet's ghost, Macbeth's witches, many fearful incidents, get their value only through the power of the imagination. . . . In reading, all these things pass easily through our minds, and seem quite appropriate, whereas in representation on the stage they would strike us unfavorably and appear not only unpleasant but even disgusting.

Later in the essay, Goethe repeats this distinction and argues that Shakespeare designs his works for the reader, not for the stage. "By his treatment, his revelation of the inner life, he wins the reader; the theatrical demands appear to him unimportant." Although Shakespeare has some theatrical scenes, most of his scenes do not appeal to the eye; in fact, "Shakespeare's whole method finds in the stage itself something unwieldy and hostile." Goethe concludes that the bard is "more of a poet than playwright."[3]

Madame de Staël, who was the patroness of Schlegel, contends in *De l'Allemagne* (1813) that Shakespeare's plays are too full of profound philosophical ideas to succeed on the stage. Like Lamb and Coleridge, she finds that the succession of visual images in the theater distracts the audience from the meaning of the scenes.

> Shakspeare . . . has, perhaps, too philosophical a spirit, too subtle
> a penetration, for the instantaneous perception of the theatre; . . .
> his compositions have so much depth, that the rapidity of the-
> atrical action makes us lose a great part of the ideas which they
> contain: in this respect, his pieces deserve more to be read than to
> be seen.[4]

This bias against spectacle persisted in Europe until the twentieth century. Even playwrights such as Maeterlinck voice their discomfort with the stage. In an 1895 interview with *The Daily Chronicle,* he declares that, though he respects the acting companies that produce his plays, he cannot derive "real pleasure" from any performance of drama. He continues, "I think that almost all plays that are not mere stage-carpentry can be better appreciated in reading than on the stage." Similarly, Maeterlinck informs the reporter for the *Sketch* that reading plays is more enjoyable than seeing them acted because "on the stage the delicate symbolic essence of what every thoughtful writer wishes to convey cannot but escape."[5]

The French symbolist movement, which influenced Yeats, reevaluated the impact of the theater on literature and came to some conclusions that resemble those of the romantics and other conclusions that prefigure the drama of Yeats. In an 1885 essay about Wagner, symbolist poet Stéphane Mallarmé argues that actors and spectacles diminish the spiritual and imaginative power of art. He believes that the heroic dreams which are the basis of true drama cannot be confined or represented on the stage; instead, Mallarmé insists, true myth "must live in our imaginations." In later essays, he develops this concept, which Byron had called a "mental theatre" designed for readers. Like the romantics, Mallarmé is uneasy with performances of *Hamlet* because it "is so well patterned on the theater of the mind alone." In general, Mallarmé concludes that humans cannot construct a stage that would do justice to "the miraculous Theater and Stage which the mind envisions, to which the mind alone can give true existence." Actors and music are superfluous because the mind exists "beyond all materiality." When Mallarmé does imagine an ideal theater, it is a literary one dominated by the poetic aspect of works.[6]

The Pictorial Bias in Victorian Entertainments

Mallarmé and other critics of spectacle were reacting to the increasingly pictorial staging and structure of nineteenth-century dramas. Playwrights, actors, and managers gradually abandoned the rhetorical emphasis of previous eras to highlight forms and techniques that stressed the situation and stage picture. Theater spectacles revealed both stylized scenes with painted backdrops and attempts at realistic costumes and built-up sets. In this section, I will examine the reasons for this change in taste. I will draw on the research of M. R. Booth, Martin Meisel, Richard Southern, and Richard D. Altick, who have investigated cultural trends of the Victorian period in Great Britain.

One underlying cause for the pictorial emphasis was urbanization, which produced an unprecedented demand for entertainment, especially genres that provided both information and amusement. Art exhibitions, galleries, and pictorial prints increased in number and popularity. Illustrated books, magazines, and newspapers with reproductions of current events and exotic landscapes were especially successful. The architecture of urban public buildings of the era manifested "mass, grandeur, and elaborate ornamentation," which influenced theater sets.[7]

At the same time, the nineteenth-century public's interest in history spurred archaeological research and excavations in Greece and the Middle East. The findings were published with lithographs, and these illustrated history books served as models for theater scenery, backdrops, costumes, and ensembles, especially designs for historical plays like Byron's *Sardanapalus*. Spectacular processions, palace scenes, and crowded markets became popular in contemporary dramas. Though historical realism can be traced back to William Capon's designs for Kemble at Drury Lane in 1794, the influence of archaeology on staging peaked in the 1870s and 1880s.[8]

The development of the camera, which was available for professional use by the 1840s, encouraged the era's preference for realistic, concrete images. In the theater, carpenters reproduced courtrooms, steamboats, hotels, and other environments from everyday life. Sometimes genuine antique furniture was used.[9]

Improvements in lighting allowed managers to darken the auditorium, to use different colors of stage lights, and to control the brightness and the location of the beams. The electric carbon-arc light was first used on stage in 1848 and the incandescent carbon-filament light in 1881. Realistic sunrises, sunsets, moonlight scenes, and fires were now possible, and the new technology encouraged more spectacles.

However, the elaborate scenery and the intense glare of the stage distracted the audience from the central characters.[10]

The strong demand for dramas induced managers to construct large theaters. Now the actor and the spectators in the back rows were very far apart, so gestures and poses had to become more obvious and stylized in order to communicate emotions.

As in the eighteenth century, transformation scenes were popular, and scene changes themselves were often part of the show. Because of the audience's fascination with the new technology, the Victorians did not lower the curtain between scenes. Theaters adapted other forms of entertainment, such as the popular panoramas and dioramas. Panoramas were most effective when a drama included a journey. According to Altick, the influence of panoramas on the theater was strongest in the early 1850s, especially in Charles Kean's and Samuel Phelp's mountings of Shakespeare's plays. Managers also featured tableaux vivants based on art, mythology, or history. All of these spectacles were considered educational.[11]

Booth argues that all social classes during the Victorian era demonstrated a preference for spectacular effects. Even when productions lacked harmony of set, costumes, and properties, the displays drew crowds to London theaters. By 1880, the notion that dramatic performance should resemble painting was so predominant that Squire Bancroft installed a two-foot-wide picture frame around the Haymarket Theatre's proscenium, and other theaters imitated this innovation.[12]

The new massive sets were replete with historical and geographical details. For example, Kean's realistic set for *The Merchant of Venice* in 1853 included a canal, sturdy bridges, and moving boats (see figure 8). Such complex designs required long intervals to allow the stage crew to shift from one scene to another. For this reason, managers rearranged and cut scenes in plays like *The Rivals, The School for Scandal,* and *The Merchant of Venice* in order to leave more time for spectacle and to prevent overly frequent scene changes. Another solution was to insert "flat scenes" before and after the three-dimensional "set scenes." The flat scene, commonly known as the "carpenter's scene," took place in the front area of the stage and concealed the crew behind a painted background. Some playwrights complained about the mangling of their dramas. W. T. Moncrieff protests that all of the transpositions, deletions, and additions to make his play *Zoroaster* more pictorial "nearly wholly deprived it of any pretensions to Dramatic construc-

8. *Charles Kean's 1853 production of* The Merchant of Venice, *designed by William Telbin, courtesy of the Victoria and Albert Museum, London.*

tion it might originally have possessed." Despite such complaints, actor/managers like William Charles Macready and Charles Kean applied the spectacle style to Shakespeare. They replaced the bard's long, descriptive passages with scenery in order to speed up the action. Macready wrote in his diary on 2 September 1835 that he omitted "poetical passages" from scripts because he believed that "imagery and sentiment will not supply the place of action."[13]

To counteract this trend, playwrights published the entire uncut versions of their dramas, which could slow down the action to develop the characters and to embellish the language. Edward Robert Bulwer-Lytton explains in his 1839 preface that he had to shorten *Richelieu* for performance. However, he argues that the play should be *read* in its entirety in order to appreciate "the subtler strokes of character, or the more poetical embellishments of description."[14]

By the 1880s and 1890s, most productions of Shakespeare's dramas in England, from London to the provinces, used antiquarian research in implementing the spectacle. A long run was required to pay for the research and construction of these three-dimensional sets.[15]

The nineteenth-century critics' ambivalence toward spectacle may reflect the paradoxical nature of the era's theatrical enterprise. Booth observes that theaters simultaneously affirmed both realism and art: the decor reminded the audience that the stage presented an artistic picture, yet many aspects of the scenes were realistic. Similarly, Meisel stresses the tension between the audience's demand for both realism and deep meaning. Furthermore, the static tableaux of many dramas conflicted with stage movement.[16]

The Victorian drama critics were well aware of these paradoxes, especially the conflict between realism and profundity. Like the romantics, many Victorian writers insist that elaborate spectacles deaden the audience's imagination. Though late nineteenth-century critics do not object to the performance of tragedy or comedy, they do worry that the creation of beautiful stage pictures has relegated the text and the actors to an unfairly subordinate position.

The collection entitled *Essays on the Drama* (1858), by William Bodham Donne, provides a good example of Victorian attacks on spectacle. Donne complains that his contemporaries are obsessed with pictorial splendor:

> To touch our emotions, we need not the imaginatively true, but the physically real. The visions which our ancestors saw with the mind's eye, must be embodied for us in palpable forms . . . all must be made palpable to sight, no less than to feeling.

He points out that the success of sensational novels, which can be read at home, puts pressure on the theaters to provide "something yet more stimulating abroad."[17]

Donne also complains about the Victorian fad of historical accuracy. While former ages were careless in costume and scenery, the late nineteenth-century theaters have gone too far in the opposite direction. The managers

> represent the drama of Elizabeth and Charles with all the anxious precision of an archaeological society. . . . The passion, the poetry, the plot of 'King John' and 'Macbeth' will not now fill pit or boxes, unless the manager lavishes a fortune on pictures of high Dunsinane, or on coats of mail and kilts such as were actually worn by the Earls and Thanes of the English and Scottish Courts.

Such excesses reveal that "the substance of the drama has . . . become less important than its accessories."[18]

Donne recommends that the playwright's text should be the most important element in the best tragedies and comedies and that the actor should be "wholly subservient" to the author. A good actor should not need fancy historical costumes. Donne feels that his era has confused scenery and archaeology with the real purpose of drama: spectacle should be "the framework of the picture, not the picture itself." While some properties and costumes are appropriate, Donne doubts that "exact copies" of ancient weapons and clothing add anything to the dramatic effect; he also deprecates the undue attention given to "real localities." Staging should avoid obvious anachronisms, but the goal of spectacle is to represent "not so much the historical as the poetical element of the drama." He concludes, "Above all things, an artistic sense of the beautiful should preside and predominate over scenical representations. . . . So much of the costume or the scenery as calls off attention from the actor, is excess."[19] Donne's emphasis on "the beautiful" and the actor differs from the perspective of the romantics. He does not argue that tragedy should not be acted but rather he argues that spectacle should be limited in order to concentrate the audience's attention on the language of the play and the acting. This concern with limiting the excesses of staging unifies much of the drama criticism of Donne's contemporaries.

Lewes, James, Beerbohm, and the Concept of Limited Spectacle

George Henry Lewes departs radically from the romantics' bias against spectacle. He confronts their position most directly in "Shakspeare's Critics: English and Foreign" (1849), which is an attempt to refute Lamb's important article entitled "On the Tragedies of Shakspeare, Considered with Reference to their Fitness for Stage Representation" (1811). Lewes finds the British prejudice against performing Shakespeare to be widespread in print and in conversations. Lewes considers this an "extraordinary fallacy."[20]

Anticipating much twentieth-century criticism of the romantics' analysis of Shakespeare, Lewes complains that no previous critics, including Hazlitt, Goethe, and A. W. Schlegel, have discussed Shakespeare's plays as dramas. The bard has been praised "as a poet, as a thinker, and as a delineator of character," but Lewes contends that drama is a unique art that cannot be judged merely as poetry: "the drama is only amenable to the laws of stage representation."[21]

Lewes reaches different conclusions from his predecessors because he defines the purpose of drama differently. According to Lewes, the primary purpose of a play is *"To interest and amuse an audience"* (the italics are his). However, he insists that art must transcend amusement and arouse "finer faculties." Specifically, the playwright appeals to the audience's curiosity, senses, and sympathy in order "to fill our fancy with images of exquisite beauty, and leave in us the abiding influence of great thoughts and noble aspirations."[22] This definition of the purpose of drama departs from that of Coleridge, Lamb, and Hazlitt because Lewes employs a new vocabulary, does not view the senses as a threat to the intellect, and portrays the theater audience, not just the reader, as a qualified judge of artistic merit. Note that the word "imagination" does not appear in Lewes's formulation. The word "beauty" has acquired a meaning that it does not have in the works of the romantics, with the exception of Shelley: beauty now refers to art forms that arouse both the mind and the senses. Lewes's emphasis on "beauty" makes him more tolerant of stage spectacle.

Lewes sees nothing wrong with the audience's craving for "splendid scenery," as long as the drama's poetry is good and portrays the passions well. The best playwrights combine good poetry and knowledge of acting and the theater. Although he admits that Lamb is right about the distractions of the material elements in performed drama, Lewes finds that the acting in staged productions enhances a play by creating "more intense" and more "vivid" impressions than one can obtain when reading a play. For example, despite the fact that Edmund Kean was not a perfect actor, "Kean's Shylock and Othello produced an infinitely grander effect than could have been reached by any closet reading."[23] This argument inverts Lamb's thesis in "On the Tragedies of Shakspeare."

Unlike Lamb, Lewes does not see the experiences of reading a play and witnessing a performance as mutually exclusive or as contradictory. Lewes insists, "The same persons who are most delighted in reading the plays at home, will be those who are most delighted at seeing them well acted." Furthermore, he points out, Shakespeare wrote his dramas "for the theatre and not for the study." In contrast to the romantics, Lewes emphasizes Shakespeare's theatrical expertise, the fusion of "poetic truth" and "theatrical effect." Very few playwrights can handle this combination.[24]

Despite the defense of spectacle in "Shakspeare's Critics," Lewes's essays and theater reviews often condemn the overuse of scenic effects. In the introduction for *Selections from the Modern British Drama-*

tists (1867), he laments that, on the stage, "Music and Spectacle are daily growing more and more important: wit and poetry daily becoming rarer." Like Donne and many other Victorian commentators, Lewes has little use for stage spectacle when it is not accompanied by good acting. Lewes believes that Charles Kean, the manager of the Princess's Theatre, has pandered to the public demand for pictorialism. As a manager, Kean

> has added nothing to the elucidation of the characters, he has given no fresh light to players or public; but he has greatly improved the scenic representation, and has lavished time and money on the archaeological illustration of the plays.

After seeing Kean's elaborate production of *Sardanapalus*, Lewes queries in his review,

> Is the Drama nothing more than a Magic Lantern on a large scale? Was Byron only a pretext for a panorama? It is a strange state of Art when the mere *accessories* become the aim and purpose of representation—when truth of archaeology supplants truth of human passion.

Lewes accuses Kean of "subordinating drama to spectacle" because the Princess's Theatre troupe is "so incompetent." In a pronouncement that recalls the romantics' analysis of theater, Lewes declares that dramatic productions should stress "poetical conception and execution" and appeal "to our higher faculties, and not to the lower appetites." Similarly, he finds that Kean's version of *Macbeth* is rearranged as spectacle but lacks "poetical" insight and violates Shakespeare's intentions.[25]

Lewes links overdone spectacles to the genre of melodrama, which appeals to the senses, not the intellect. Coleridge would have agreed with the following analysis of excessive appeals to the senses: "it is the fatality of melodrama to know no limit. The tendency of the senses is *downwards*. To gratify them stimulants must be added and added, chili upon cayene, butchery upon murder." Spices like chili and cayenne dull the taste buds so that one requires more and more of the spices to achieve the same effect. Similarly, spectacle dulls the literary taste of the audience. Despite fancy scenery, costumes, sword fights, trap doors, and special effects, melodrama is intellectually in a state of "bankruptcy."[26]

However, Lewes does not condemn spectacle outright because it may enhance the beauty of literature. "There is no need of abjuring the picturesque adjuncts of dress, scene, and distant time. Poetry moves more freely in a world of beauty and magnificence." He contends that Shakespeare's weakest dramas, especially histories such as *King John*, may benefit from stage spectacle since

> we must have some accessory attraction to replace that literary and historical interest which originally made Shakespeare's historical plays acceptable. . . . Scenery, dresses, groupings, archaeological research, and pictorial splendour, can replace for moderns the poetic and historic interest which our forefathers felt in these plays.

Although Hazlitt considered all of Shakespeare's dramas except *Richard III* and *The Winter's Tale* inappropriate for the stage, Lewes contends that the bard's best plays are eminently actable. As evidence, Lewes points out that *Hamlet, Othello, Macbeth,* and *The Merchant of Venice* are popular all over Great Britain, from "the most cultivated audiences" to "barns, strolling companies, and the lowest theatres."[27]

Lewes felt that he was writing his dramatic criticism "during a period of dramatic degradation. The poetic drama had vanished with Macready and Helen Faucit." Ironically, romantic writers like Hazlitt made this same complaint about the degeneration of drama when Macready was still on the stage. Lewes argues that the theater has declined because "Amusement" has replaced "Art" as the goal of playwrights and audiences. Authors like Molière and Shakespeare subordinated amusement to "great ideas." However, gradually "Amusement has usurped the throne of Art—all the attractions of decoration, scenic pomp, and stirring events, are sought, because they are 'amusing,' and the *material* stifles the *spiritual*." As a result, the English public lacks the attention span required to appreciate Shakespeare's poetry. Because managers design dramas to amuse the public, most aspects of the art have been neglected, including "poetry, character, passion, consistency." These have been replaced with bustle, intrigue, special effects, and costume changes. Consequently, the audience learns no more than it would if it had "but just gaped at a tight-rope dancer!" Spectators leave with no feeling of exultation or enlightenment but with "a sense of fatigue."[28] Many spectacles are no better than a circus.

To revive the drama, Lewes advocates the establishment of a specialized theater devoted to works of true art. "It must avoid spectacle, scenic 'effects,' and encroachments on the domains of melodrama and burlesque." He concedes that such a theater would appeal "only to the intellectual classes" because most people prefer familiar and domestic concerns in drama to profundity and exploration of the ideal. "Art is for the *élite*. Some portion of the genius which creates is indispensable to the mind that appreciates."[29] Like Coleridge, Lewes envisions an educated elite that can preserve culture.

Lewes compares the dramatic tradition in Great Britain to that of various European countries. In general, he finds that the theaters in France and Germany tend to be more literary and less reliant on spectacle than those in Great Britain. According to Lewes, French drama emphasizes "stately diction and harmonious versification." In contrast, English plays stress "action, passion, and imagery." While French playwrights tend to error in composing prolix dialogue and description, English dramatists tend to rely on "melodramatic exaggeration." In both France and Germany, the drama grew out of court festivities and addressed "highly cultivated audiences." However, English plays were designed to appeal to the masses.[30] This accounts for the emphasis on literary excellence in European dramas and the preference for spectacle in Great Britain. The French and German traditions are closer to Lewes's ideal theater. Note that Lewes resembles earlier critics who associate a low social class and a low level of education with the desire for overdone theater spectacles.

Lewes's comparison was extended by other cosmopolitan writers like Henry James and Max Beerbohm, who were familiar with both British and French drama. In "The London Theatres" (1877), James argues that London theater audiences lack high standards and good taste, while the French public is more sophisticated and analytical. Though the English public is easily amused, it "is intellectually much less appreciative." In contrast, the Parisian audience, which is "cynical, sceptical, indifferent" when watching plays, "has the critical and the artistic sense," which enables it to evaluate drama more skillfully and, paradoxically, more sympathetically.[31]

Because the British spectators are not very analytic, they mistake elaborate scenery for dramatic excellence. James accuses the British public of "apathy of taste" and argues that such an audience will "accept a pretty collection of eighteenth-century chairs, and buffets, and pottery . . . as a substitute for dramatic composition and finished acting." He also complains that English spectators lack the patience to listen to long dramatic speeches. In fact, he argues that the audiences manifest "an insurmountable mistrust of human speech."[32] Lewes had also noticed this change in taste, but he viewed it as something that drama should accommodate. However, James consistently deplores the contemporary neglect of language in the theater.

This neglect of language has decreased the literacy of the theater audience. According to James, few nineteenth-century adults read plays. "It is one of the odd things of our actual aesthetics that the more theatres multiply the less any one reads a play—the less any one cares, in a word, for the text of the adventure."[33]

Like Lewes, James does not argue that tragedies and other dramatic genres should not be staged. Rather, James laments that contemporary British drama neglects literary elements and declamation while emphasizing scenery. He uses his reviews to plead for the priorities to be changed so that dramas will appeal more to the spectators' ears and less to their eyes. Plays are performed

> with a great reinforcement of chairs and tables and articles of clothing, of traps and panoramas and other massive carpentry.
> . . . The ear of the public, that field of the auditive intelligence which is two-thirds of the comedian's battle-field, has simply ceased to respond for want of use.

In another passage that develops the classical ear/eye dichotomy, James observes sarcastically, "What will it matter what he [the spectator] listens to if he have real buhl cabinets, Persian carpets, and Venetian mirrors to look at?" Similarly, James attacks Henry Irving because the actor relies too much on looking "picturesque . . . ; that is, he depends for his effects upon the art with which he presents a certain figure to the eye, rather than upon the manner in which he speaks his part." Clearly, Irving's neglect of "the art of utterance" is a misunderstanding of the nature of acting. This flaw is especially noticeable when Irving portrays a Shakespearean hero, because the text is so superlative.[34]

James shares Lewes's preference for a limited spectacle. In the dialogue "After the Play" (1889), four characters discuss the use and abuse of spectacle. Dorriforth, who appears to be James's spokesman, contends that a limited spectacle gives more responsibility to the actors and gives more imaginative pleasure to the audience. "The face and the voice are more to the purpose than acres of painted canvas, and a touching intonation, a vivid gesture or two, than an army of supernumeraries."[35]

James worries that his era's emphasis on pictorialism is subverting the structure and poetic value of dramas. For example, he dislikes Irving's production of *Romeo and Juliet* in 1882 because the actor/manager emphasizes spectacle and static tableaux instead of acting, movement, and language.

> The play moves slowly through a succession of glowing and deceptive pictures. . . . The play is not acted, it is costumed; the immortal lovers of Verona became subordinate and ineffectual figures. . . . Its passionate rapidity is chopped up into little tableaus.

If the trend toward pictorial drama continues, language, characterization, and acting will be sacrificed. James imagines a future stage in which the actors will be reduced to "dressed manikins" with no speeches.[36] Such passages resemble Oliver Goldsmith's "On the present State of our Theatres," which condemns spectacles that make actors superfluous (see Chapter 1).

James's position on the staging of Shakespeare's plays is closer to that of the romantics than to that of Lewes. According to James, Henrik Ibsen's prose dramas succeed in the theater because they are designed for "vivification," but Shakespeare's poetic works suffer on stage. "Any acting of Shakespeare is a simplification. To be played at all, he must be played, as it were, superficially." Although James believes that *Othello* and *Macbeth* are appropriate for the stage, he agrees with the romantics that *Lear* cannot be acted because the stage appeals to the senses too much. He terms *Lear* one of "the most sublime . . . of all dramatic poems" and argues that it is too complex for representation. Furthermore, performance "leaves the vastness of the work almost untouched." *Cymbeline* and *Richard III* also resist any attempt to make them stage spectacles because they are, respectively, "a florid fairytale" and "a loose, violent, straddling romance." Victorian theaters present both dramas in too realistic a fashion, which makes them "coarse." Realism

> gives no further lift to the poetry and adds a mortal heaviness to the prose. . . . The more it is painted and dressed, the more it is lighted and furnished and solidified, the less it corresponds or coincides, the less it squares with our imaginative habits. . . . The more Shakespeare is 'built in' the more we are built out.

James declares that he prefers to read Shakespeare's plays. James finds his era's emphasis on scenic realism so absurd that he satirizes this trend by pointing out its ultimate implications: "we shall soon be having Romeo drink real poison and Medea murder a fresh pair of babes every night."[37]

Spectacle and "pantomimic effects" trivialize the poetry and complexity of other great dramas like *Faust* and interfere with the audience's subjective relationship to the plays' language and characters. James objects to "traps and panoramas, processions and coloured lights" because such devices risk "obtrusiveness upon the personal interpretation." Unlimited spectacle warps the universality of a drama by stressing external details. "The theatric is so apt to be the outward, and the universal to be the inward, that . . . they often manage to peck at each other with fatal results."[38] While the romantics would have agreed with James's denigration of unlimited spectacle, they would have objected to his conclusion that managers should try to give equal attention to spectacle and acting.

Max Beerbohm also protests the subordination of the dramatic text to spectacle. Like James and Lewes, Beerbohm contrasts Parisian and London audiences to emphasize the poor taste of the English public. Beerbohm links the Parisian tradition to that of ancient Greece and Elizabethan England because these three audiences enjoy "listening to the declamation of verse" and do not "need any bribe of 'sumptuous production.' " However, the London public

> cares not at all for the sound of words, and will not tolerate poetry on the stage unless it gets also gorgeous and innumerable supers. . . . The poetry must be short and split; must be subordinated to the action of the piece, and to the expensive scenery and the expensive costumes.[39]

Adapting Lewes's analysis, Beerbohm connects good taste to an appreciation of beauty. In contrast to the Parisian public, Londoners lack "a sense of beauty," and this defect characterizes all nineteenth-century British art, especially drama. Like James, Beerbohm views the emphasis on realism in England as a threat to the "obvious beauty of poetry and romance."[40]

However, Beerbohm considers limited and appropriate stage spectacle a useful adjunct to drama. For example, he argues that an effective production of *A Midsummer Night's Dream* must create "the illusion of fairies, illusion of a true dream." When Beerbohm writes that the theater often destroys such illusions because it is too "definite and concrete," one recalls Hazlitt's similar statements in *Characters of Shake-*

spear's Plays (Works of Hazlitt, 4:247–48). According to Beerbohm, a good poet's images do create illusion, but when these images are "materialised," the illusion is dispelled. An exception is Tree's production of *A Midsummer Night's Dream:* Beerbohm finds the fairies, played by children, well trained and convincing.[41] Thus, the critic moves away from Hazlitt's position that the stage is inhospitable to fanciful dramas because it emphasizes the senses and frustrates the imagination.

Beerbohm defends scenery from the attacks of Sidney Lee by pointing out that when spectacle is balanced with the other elements of plays, it can enhance the texts. Scenery must be "kept in the same relation to the figures of the players as real surroundings bear to persons in real life." In fact, Beerbohm finds "skimpy scenery" distracting. Like Lewes, Beerbohm believes that the bare Elizabethan stage should not affect later productions of Shakespeare's plays. Beerbohm thinks that abolishing modern scenery because Renaissance performances lacked it would be like forbidding hansoms and bicycles because they had not been invented in 1600. Departing from the romantics' bias, he asserts that good scenery can be "a means of quickening dramatic illusion" and that appropriate spectacle is compatible with an imaginative audience.[42]

Drama and Social Reform

A concern with social reform dominates the drama criticism of Matthew Arnold, John Ruskin, and G. B. Shaw. Because these writers view performance as a means of educating the public and broadening its horizon, they do not object to stage spectacle per se. In fact, Arnold contends that good theater is "an irresistible need for civilised communities," and therefore the state should support a national theater.[43]

Writing in 1879, Arnold deplores the lack of interest of the puritanical English middle class in theater. Like Lamb, he hopes that the theater can liberate the middle class from "the horrible unnaturalness and *ennui* of its life." Good drama can satisfy the basic human needs "for expansion, for intellect and knowledge, for beauty, for social life and manners." Note that Arnold uses "beauty" where the romantics would use "imagination." His inclusion of "manners" in the list recalls the essays of Steele in *The Spectator* and *The Tatler;* however, Arnold's emphasis is on the overly "prosaic" and "literal" mindset of the classes that he elsewhere calls "the Philistines."[44]

By 1882, the middle class manifested a greater interest in the theater, according to Arnold. He uses his "Old Playgoer" column in *The Pall Mall Gazette* to contrast the theater public and acting of the 1840s and the 1880s. In the 1840s, only the elite and the lower classes attended the theater, and a good actor like Macready lacked an adequate supporting cast. However, in the 1880s, all social classes attend the theater, and the entire acting ensemble is competent. The "Old Playgoer" is delighted with this change.[45]

Although Arnold strongly advocates serious drama, he does not approve of certain genres, especially those that appeal primarily to the senses. Like Coleridge, he rejects much contemporary drama because it appeals to "the average sensual man" and celebrates "the life of the senses." Following Coleridge and Lewes, Arnold associates melodrama with the external and the sensational: "The essential difference between melodrama and poetic drama is that one relies for its main effect upon an inner drama of thought and passion, the other upon an outer drama of . . . sensational incidents."[46]

Despite the success of *La Dame aux Camélias* and *Impulse,* which Arnold considers "idle tales," Shakespeare's masterpieces also continue to fill the theaters. Why is this so? Arnold ascribes the survival of great plays to a primordial desire:

> there is . . . something in human nature which works for Shakspeare's comedy, and against such comedy as the 'Dame aux Camélias' or 'Impulse'; something prompting us to live by our soul and imagination rather than by our senses.[47]

To enjoy Shakespeare's comedies, the audience must be willing to enter "a world of fantasy. Art refreshes us, art liberates us, precisely by carrying us into such a world, and enabling us to find pleasure there. He who will not be carried there loses a great deal."[48] Arnold's analysis here recalls that of Lamb in "On the Artificial Comedy of the Last Century."

Like the romantics, Arnold places Shakespeare in a different category from other playwrights. Most writers produce works that are merely "theatrical," while Shakespeare generates truly "dramatic" texts. In the preface to his own drama *Merope,* Arnold explains that the term "dramatic" refers to "the element of intellect and labour." Because Shakespeare appeals more to the intellect than Molière does, Arnold considers the former a better dramatic writer.[49]

Though he also admires Shakespeare, Ruskin challenges the prevailing bardolatry. Ruskin finds the bard's male characters especially problematic. "Shakespeare has no heroes;—he has only heroines. There is not one entirely heroic figure in all his plays." The only exceptions are Henry the Fifth and Valentine. Other protagonists are too simple-minded (Othello) or too vain (Coriolanus, Caesar, Mark Antony). Ruskin continues, "Hamlet is indolent, and drowsily speculative; Romeo an impatient boy; the Merchant of Venice languidly submissive to adverse fortune." Aside from these flaws, "The catastrophe of every play is caused always by the folly or fault of a man"; Ruskin gives *King Lear, The Winter's Tale,* and *Cymbeline* as examples. This scepticism influenced Shaw's view of Shakespeare's heroes.[50]

Ruskin's concern with the inadequacy of these characters grows out of his insistence that theater can be a potent educational tool. According to Ruskin, good novels and plays promote virtue because they stimulate the readers' or spectators' compassion. He adapts Hazlitt's statements about the moral force of the sympathetic imagination. Ruskin explains,

> The imaginative understanding of the natures of others, and the power of putting ourselves in their place, is the faculty on which the virtue depends. So that an unimaginative person can neither be reverent nor kind. The main use of works of fiction, and of the drama, is to supply, as far as possible, the defect of this imagination in common minds.[51]

Like the romantics, Ruskin insists that readers must be active in order to benefit from literature. Ruskin uses an analogy in the lecture "Of Kings' Treasuries" to clarify what he means by active reading: he compares such reading to the strenuous work of gold miners.

> When you come to a good book, you must ask yourself, "Am I inclined to work as an Australian miner would? Are my pickaxes and shovels in good order, and am I in good trim myself . . . ?" Your pickaxes are your own care, wit, and learning; your smelting furnace is your own thoughtful soul. Do not hope to get at any good author's meaning without those tools and that fire; often you will need sharpest, finest chiselling, and patientest fusing, before you can gather one grain of the metal.[52]

Both Ruskin and Coleridge view themselves as teachers and guides for an intellectually passive public, and both use analogies to explain why mere literacy is not enough. However, Coleridge addresses the well educated while Ruskin directs many of his lectures to working-class audiences with less formal schooling.

Ruskin worries that Victorian materialism has made the British public "incapable of thought" and unable to appreciate literature that contains great ideas. Theater managers exacerbate this problem by mounting superficial plays that do not stimulate the mind. In a letter to the *Journal of Dramatic Reform* in 1880, Ruskin contends that a theater cannot simultaneously educate the people and make money. He urges theater managers to choose the first goal and to eliminate the star system, which gave popular actors too much power. The theaters' obsession with advertisements and profits has decreased the British public's "sense of beauty."[53] Ruskin's concern with cultivating beauty resembles the attitude of Lewes, James, and Beerbohm.

Like the romantics and other Victorian writers, Ruskin deplores the elevation of external details over substance in drama. He insists that the primary concern of drama is emotion: "it despises external circumstance." For this reason, Ruskin laments that London theaters such as Covent Garden spend large sums of money

> in leading our audiences to look for mere stage effect, instead of good acting, good singing, or good sense. . . . Simple and consistent dresses, and quiet landscape exquisitely painted, would have far more effect on the feelings of any sensible audience than the tinsel and extravagance of our common scenery.

Ruskin also scolds English actors and actresses for depending on jewelry and silk instead of on gestures and tones of voice. A less extravagant theater would cost less to operate, and the audience would come "to hear and to feel," not to look at the decorations.[54] He presents the classical ear/eye dichotomy here.

This preoccupation with the external is linked to the nineteenth century's obsession with gratifying the senses. Like Coleridge and Arnold, Ruskin attacks his contemporaries' "ruthless pursuit of sensational pleasure" in art and literature. The craving for sensation leads to a continual demand for "new things." Ruskin shares Lewes's and James's disgust with the poor art and literature ground out to satisfy the public's insistence on novelty. Art has degenerated into a series of fads, each fad lasting no longer than "the coiffure or the bonnet of the day," and art exhibitions have become mere "bazaars of ruinously expensive toys" for the childlike intellects of the spectators. Agreeing with Lamb, Ruskin views portraits of Shakespeare's protagonists as the epitome of the public's ignorance of the bard's profound ideas. Despite the fact that Daniel Maclise's *The Play Scene from "Hamlet"*

(1842) was a very popular and admired painting, Ruskin considers it superficial.[55] (Maclise's painting is reproduced as the frontispiece of this book.)

Going beyond the romantics' condemnation of the senses, Ruskin argues that terrible crimes like murder are connected to "the modern love of excitement in the sensational novel and drama" because the "furious pursuit of pleasure" leads to a craving for horror and death.[56] Thus, he links the degeneration of literature to what he views as his era's moral degeneration.

Although G. B. Shaw would not agree that there is a cause and effect relationship between literature and crimes, he does insist that great art should advocate social change and challenge conventions. In contrast to the romantics, who emphasized highly imaginative literature, Shaw praises writers who criticize corrupt laws, customs, attitudes, and ideals. The romantics considered imaginative Shakespeare the ultimate literary genius, but Shaw prefers the works of John Bunyan and the plays of Henrik Ibsen because they are more oriented toward the reform of society. Like Ruskin, Shaw tries to counteract his contemporaries' mindless idolatry of Shakespeare.

Influenced by Ruskin's opinion that Shakespeare's dramas lack true heroes, Shaw condemns Shakespeare's protagonists as too "self-centred," "selfish," and "vulgarly ambitious." Such characters seem to ignore their "public responsibilities": their self-absorption makes them "princes without any sense of public duty." *Hamlet*, which Shaw considers Shakespeare's best play, is thus inferior to Ibsen's dramas because the Scandinavian author makes "an original contribution to religion and morality." Similarly, Shaw contends, "A Doll's House will be as flat as ditchwater when A Midsummer Night's Dream will still be as fresh as paint; but it will have done more work in the world; and that is enough for the highest genius, which is always intensely utilitarian." In the preface to *Man and Superman* (1903), Shaw argues that Shakespeare and Dickens are not "artist-philosophers" because "they have no constructive ideas" and their characters are motivated by "melodramatic" and "artificial" outside forces. Both Dickens and Shakespeare excel in comedy but have trouble creating tragic heroes. Shaw prefers Bunyan's characters because they strive for purposes larger than personal grievances.[57]

In *The Quintessence of Ibsenism* (1891), Shaw argues that the "accidents" of conventional plots are not effective in dramas because they cannot profoundly move the audience's feelings. For this reason,

"Crimes, fights, big legacies, fires, shipwrecks, battles, and thunderbolts are mistakes in a play, even when they can be effectively simulated." Ibsen succeeds as a playwright because he avoids the conventional plot "accidents," he creates characters who resemble the members of the audience, and he puts the characters in situations that reflect the audience's own lives. This verisimilitude enables Ibsen to arouse powerful emotions and hopes in the spectators. The Norwegian playwright uses these strong feelings to try to change the spectators' outlook and behavior. Shaw portrays Ibsen as a rifleman "sharpshooting at the audience . . . , aiming always at the sorest spot in their consciences."[58]

Similarly, Shaw attempted to stimulate individual and national change in his own plays, which emphasize intellectual discussion of social issues, not action. According to Meisel, Shaw's early work moves from an emphasis on reforming social institutions to an emphasis on reforming "the private imagination." Shaw writes in his 1902 preface to *Mrs. Warren's Profession* that he intends his dramas to invigorate the minds of both the critics and the public by developing "the intellectual muscle and moral nerve."[59]

Like Lewes, Shaw views drama as a form of literature intended primarily for performance. Shaw also admits his debt to Lewes's prose style, which he praises as "clear and vivid." Shaw admires his predecessor's combination of serious, well thought out criticism with a disarming "levity" that strongly appeals to a reader. Shaw considers stage representation to be "the test" of effective drama, and he believes that "the stage certainly does more for Shakespear than for any other dramatic poet."[60]

Unlike the romantics, Shaw does not separate appeals to the mind and imagination from appeals to the senses. In an 1895 review of Max Nordau's *Degeneration*, he argues that great art can "cultivate and refine our senses and faculties until seeing, hearing, feeling, smelling, and tasting become highly conscious and critical acts with us." Shaw also wants such art to "refine our sense of character and conduct, of justice and sympathy, greatly heightening our self-knowledge." Coleridge and Hazlitt would agree with this emphasis on self-knowledge. Shaw insists that the best writers, artists, and craftsmen address both "the physical and moral senses" and "call the heightened senses and ennobled faculties into pleasurable activity."[61] Note that he is rewriting Coleridge's definition of what good literature stimulates in the reader: "The poet, described in *ideal* perfection, brings the whole soul of man into activity, with the subordination of its faculties to each other, according to their relative worth and dignity" (*BL*, 2:11–12). Shaw's redefinition of art places more emphasis than Coleridge did on the morality of art and on the power of art to stir the senses.

In another departure from the romantics' position, Shaw portrays contemporary actors and playwrights as collaborators, not as adversaries. He reveals in "The Heroic Actors" (1907) that he himself designed some plays, including *Caesar and Cleopatra*, for actors like Forbes Robertson. "Without him *Caesar and Cleopatra* would not have been written; for no man writes a play without any reference to the possibility of a performance." In the preface to *Great Catherine* (1913), Shaw goes even further and argues that the actor's art may stimulate and develop the art of a playwright when the actor is "displaying powers not previously discovered by the author." Shaw speculates that Shakespeare's heroes became more sophisticated as Richard Burbage's acting skills developed.[62] These passages should be contrasted to Lamb's complaints that Garrick's prowess was overvalued (see "On the Tragedies of Shakspeare . . .") and Coleridge's insistence that the Kembles mistranslated tragedies like *Macbeth* (*SC*, 2:278).

Despite these differences with the romantics, Shaw is influenced by their writing style and their view of spectacle. As a reviewer, Shaw tends to be subjective and partial. He resembles Hazlitt in his outspoken advocacy of certain actors, managers, writers, and approaches to drama. Shaw praises Hazlitt's descriptions of Edmund Kean's acting.[63]

Shaw agrees with the romantics and with Lewes and James that managers should not emphasize scenic splendor over the language of plays. Shaw often contrasts the attention given to the scenery and costumes of a drama with the playwright's meager literary skill. He observes that by the 1890s, the British stage had replaced painted scenery and awkward costumes with "real walls, ceilings, and doors . . . made by real carpenters; real tailors and dressmakers clothe the performers." However, the plays themselves are often weak. Shaw wishes for "a real poet to write the verse." Even when well-written plays such as those of Shakespeare are performed, Shaw worries that contemporary theaters neglect the "word-music" and emotions of the script. A vicious circle results: the actors and audiences become "deaf as adders" and cannot appreciate the language of Shakespeare's plays; then, to please the public, the theater managers add even more spectacle and neglect the "word-music" even more. In addition, Shaw deplores the trend toward making a production of great dramas such as *Hamlet* "the actor-manager's 'show,'" rather than an authentic performance. He comes closest to the romantics' position on spectacle when he attacks managers like Augustin Daly, who distract the audience with scenery, costumes, and other pictorial effects.

> Every accessory he employs is brought in at the deadliest risk of destroying the magic spell woven by the poet. . . . Most of these absurdities are part of a systematic policy of sacrificing the credibility of the play to the chance of exhibiting an effective "living picture."

Note Shaw's awareness of his era's self-conscious pictorialism. He also echoes the romantics' references to Shakespeare's "magic" poetry that so strongly affects the imagination. Shaw considers it a mistake to try to convey the "enchantment" of Shakespearean plays "by reckless expenditure on incidental music, colored lights, dances, dresses, and elaborate rearrangements and dislocations of the play." He believes that the poetry conveys the illusion to the audience. For example, "The poetry of The Tempest is so magical that it would make the scenery of a modern theatre ridiculous." If this comedy were produced with lavish spectacle, the performance would "spoil the illusion." Although Shaw concludes that *Othello* benefits from scenery, he insists that for *The Tempest* and *A Midsummer Night's Dream*, "the best scenery you can get will only destroy the illusion created by the poetry."[64] Hazlitt had argued along similar lines in *Characters of Shakespear's Plays* (*Works*, 4:239, 247–48).

Just as Shaw protests against altering Shakespeare's plays to accommodate more spectacle, he also opposes making such changes in his own plays. In his 1924 preface to *St. Joan*, Shaw expresses his annoyance at people who advised him to shorten the play. He argues that a shorter version would lack important material about the Church and the feudal system. Furthermore, a truncated *St. Joan* would provide the temptation to add spectacle to fill the vacuum.

> The experienced knights of the blue pencil, having saved an hour and a half by disembowelling the play, would at once proceed to waste two hours in building elaborate scenery, having real water in the river Loire and a real bridge across it, and staging an obviously sham fight for possession of it, with the victorious French led by Joan on a real horse.

Of course, Shaw adds, the coronation of the French dauphin would be an impressive display, and the critics would conclude by having Joan "burnt on the stage."[65]

Like Addison, Shaw objects to the mingling of different levels of reality in the theater. For example, Shaw strongly condemns Tree's bringing real dogs and horses on stage to enliven *Richard II*. Show-stealing animals distract the audience from Shakespeare's emphasis on Richard's "saint-like patience."[66]

Shaw liked the simple staging of William Poel's Elizabethan Stage Society, which avoided elaborate scenery and scene shifts. Shaw insists, "The modern pictorial stage is not so favorable to Shakespearean acting and stage illusion as the platform stage." The platform provides greater intimacy between the actor and the audience and enables the actor to convey both "delicate" and "vehement" gestures.[67]

Shaw worries that his era's obsession with spectacle and the concomitant neglect of texts are making gibberish of printed dramas. He contrasts the plays of his contemporaries with those of Shakespeare:

> Descriptive or narrative recitation did what is now done by scenery, furniture, and stage business. Anyone reading the mere dialogue of an Elizabethan play understands all but half a dozen unimportant lines of it without difficulty; whilst many modern plays, highly successful on the stage, are not merely unreadable but positively unintelligible without visible stage business.[68]

Thus, while Shaw views performance as one test of a drama's viability, he insists that the script should make lively reading material as well. He cannot take seriously dramas that fail this second test.

Beauty and Unity of the Arts

Although Percy Bysshe Shelley was a contemporary of Byron, the emphasis on beauty and the unity of the arts in "A Defence of Poetry" (written 1821, published 1840) and other essays indicates that Shelley's view of spectacle is actually closer to that of Wilde and Yeats. All three writers defend spectacle because it can combine visual arts like painting and architecture with beautiful language, dance, and music to heighten the effect of drama.

Unlike Coleridge and Hazlitt, who contrast the different arts and oppose genres such as opera that mix music, drama, dancing, and pictorial arts (see Hazlitt's *Works*, 20:92–96), Shelley views the imagination as a force that can synthesize many forms of art and also synthesize art with fields not often considered artistic by developing hidden interrelations. In "A Defense of Poetry," Shelley expands the category of poetry to include any human activity that expresses a vision of "order." He lists music, dance, architecture, statuary, and painting as poetic arts and elevates lawgivers, statesmen, teachers, and "inventors of the arts of life" to the rank of poets. Shelley concludes, "Language, colour, form, and religious and civil habits of action are all the instruments and materials of poetry."[69] It is not surprising that one who views poetry as encompassing so many activities believes that drama should be performed and that it should incorporate the other arts.

Shelley considers ancient Greek drama a model for this unification of the arts. "For the Athenians employed language, action, music, painting, and dance, and religious institutions, to produce a common effect in the representation of the loftiest idealisms of passion and of power." According to Marvin Carlson, Shelley anticipates Richard Wagner in praising the Greeks for including all the arts in dramatic performances.[70]

Because performed drama can combine so many different "modes of expression of poetry," more than any other form of art, Shelley argues that drama can be a powerful influence for "social good."[71] This comment prefigures the approach of later critics such as Arnold, Ruskin, and Shaw.

Shelley wanted to see his own plays performed and designed them to teach "the human heart, through its sympathies and antipathies, the knowledge of itself." In his 1819 preface for *The Cenci*, he builds on Hazlitt's discussion of the sympathetic imagination: Shelley considers "antipathies" as useful as sympathy in helping the public to achieve self-knowledge. The characters in *The Cenci* can arouse both strong sympathies and strong hatreds, which create psychological interest and illuminate "some of the most dark and secret caverns of the human heart."[72]

Shelley insists that the true story of the Cenci family, when dramatized, must "increase the ideal, and diminish the actual horror of the events."[73] In fact, the word "incest" is not used at all in the tragedy, and Cenci's rape of his daughter Beatrice takes place offstage. This emphasis on the intellectual meaning of the events rather than on the spectacular presentation of them reveals the influence of Coleridge, Lamb, and Hazlitt on Shelley's view of drama. Shelley avoids sensational scenes in order to provoke thought in the audience.

The Cenci resembles Coleridge's *Remorse* because in both dramas the main characters are shocked that the villain cannot experience remorse unaided, despite his crimes. "Remorse" is a key word in both plays. Also, both villains have unlawful lusts (incest and adultery), sin against family members, and murder other people. However, *The Cenci* differs from *Remorse* in that Cenci is a more hardened villain than Ordonio and has more power over his family than Ordonio does.

Shelley forces the reader of *The Cenci* to undergo a process of self-examination. The reader feels sympathy for Beatrice because she is a rape victim, because she has the courage to confront her father, and because she has a fine mind. However, the reader feels antipathy toward Beatrice because she plots to kill her father and because she lies about the murder when questioned by Church authorities. The reader, like Beatrice, must squarely face the moral and psychological issues that Shelley raises in the tragedy.

Shelley wished to have *The Cenci* performed at Covent Garden with Eliza O'Neil and Edmund Kean heading the cast. Shelley wrote Charles Ollier that *The Cenci* was "singularly fitted for the stage." According to the twentieth-century critic Stuart Curran, *The Cenci* is well adapted to the early nineteenth-century theaters because the tragedy requires "full-bodied, even wildly emotional acting," which was popular in London.[74] However, the play was not performed until 1886, long after Shelley's death, because of its radical subject matter, the theme of incest, and its criticism of the abuse of power by church and state.

Even Shelley manifests some ambivalence toward the stage. He insists that his drama *Prometheus Unbound* (1820) is intended for a very small audience of imaginative readers. In the preface to this work, he declares, "Didactic poetry is my abhorrence. . . . My purpose has hitherto been simply to familiarize the highly refined imagination of the more select classes of poetical readers with beautiful idealisms of moral excellence." In a letter to John Gisborne in 1822, Shelley limits his reading public even more when he asserts that *Prometheus Unbound* "was never intended for more than five or six persons." A similar ambivalence is evident in Shelley's sporadic attendance of the London theaters. On one occasion, Shelley walked out of Drury Lane after seeing Kean in two acts of *Hamlet*. Mary Shelley wrote in her journal that her husband left because of "the inefficacy of acting to encourage or maintain the delusion. The loathsome sight of men personating characters which do not and cannot belong to them."[75] These comments are obviously much closer to the position of Coleridge, Lamb, and Hazlitt in their drama criticism.

In keeping with the romantics' bias against spectacle and frenetic plots, *Prometheus Unbound* has very little action. Even more than *The Cenci* and *Remorse, Prometheus Unbound* focuses on the mental state of the protagonist: as Shelley explains in his 1820 preface, he will emphasize "the operations of the human mind." Instead of action, Shelley structures this drama around debates about key issues. For example, Mercury tempts Prometheus to submit himself to Jupiter's authority by offering the hero freedom and "voluptuous joy,"[76] but Prometheus refuses this bribe. Shelley further slows down the meager action by using minor characters like Ione and Panthea as Greek choruses to reflect lyrically and emotionally on the key ideas and events (see 1.222–39, 1.780–800, for example).

The key moral issue in both *The Cenci* and in *Prometheus Unbound* is, what is the appropriate response of intelligent and sensitive people to tyranny? When Beatrice's pleas for help to friends and family members fail to save her from her father's lust for power, she resorts to murdering him. However, Prometheus's torment ends when he learns to transcend his own consciousness in order to sympathize with Jupiter. In act 1, Prometheus renounces his hatred and feels "pity" (lines 53 and 57) for Jupiter. Prometheus also revokes his curse on Jupiter (lines 303–5). This ability to forgive even his enemy and oppressor makes Prometheus like Jesus. Shelley uses crucifixion imagery frequently to link his hero's suffering to that of Jesus (see 1.20, 473–74, 563, 585). Prometheus's transcendence of his selfish concerns allows his reunion with Asia and his release by Hercules in act 3, scene 3. Unlike *The Cenci*, which emphasizes the tragic isolation of Beatrice, *Prometheus Unbound* celebrates the reunification of Prometheus and Asia with all their friends and relatives. Prometheus's act of sympathy completely changes his world.

After act 3, scene 3, *Prometheus Unbound* has virtually no action. The rest of the play celebrates humans' potential to refine themselves by resisting tyranny, by suffering, by forgiving, by loving, and by hoping for revolutionary change (see 4.570–78). The lyrical emphasis of act 4 demonstrates Shelley's disdain for traditional claptrap endings for dramas.

Recent analyses of *Prometheus Unbound* have emphasized its unconventionality and Shelley's appeals to the readers of this poetic drama. Angela Leighton insists in *Shelley and the Sublime* (1984), "This is not so much a drama of character and action, as of voices and the mind's imaginings."[77] Shelley subtitled the play "A Lyrical Drama in

Four Acts" to stress its combination of lyric poetry and songs with dialogue. Such a work seems to be written in defiance of and in opposition to popular stage spectacles of the nineteenth century. Shelley diminishes stimulation of the senses to focus on poetic language and ideas.

Shelley expects the reader to experience the drama actively. Marlon B. Ross argues that Shelley's "obscure" imagery challenges the reader's mind and imagination. The reader must contemplate paradoxes, negations of visual perception, and the blurring of the boundaries between drama and reality. In order to cope with the difficult text of *Prometheus Unbound*, the reader needs "the capacity to perceive metaphorically." Shelley's complex poem frustrates any simple-minded process of interpretation or any one explanation. According to Ross, the drama emphasizes the world's complexity in order to prepare the reader "to make moral decisions" and to understand how to reform the world.[78] Shelley intends this poetic drama to perplex the reader because thinking about the issues raised by the play will expand the reader's mind. By engendering doubts, the poet can lead his readers to rethink their old ideology and eventually to improve their society.

Although Oscar Wilde and W. B. Yeats do not define poetry as broadly as Shelley, the two writers agree with Shelley that drama is best when it unifies many visual and performing arts. Wilde refers to the stage as "the meeting-place of all the arts," and Yeats insists, "The arts are but one Art." Yeats envisions a community of artists working together to spread culture to the masses:

> I would have all the arts draw together; recover their ancient association, the painter painting what the poet has written, the musician setting the poet's words to simple airs, that the horse-man and the engine-driver may sing them at their work.

Unlike Lewes and James, Wilde does not find that antiquarian staging interferes with dramas. Wilde concludes, "On the stage, literature returns to life and archaeology becomes art. A fine theatre is a temple where all the muses may meet."[79]

Coleridge had viewed drama primarily as literature to be read, and he separated imagination and reason from sense perception. He and the other romantics believed that spectacle, which appeals to the senses, can block the involvement of the imagination. However, René Wellek points out that Wilde "cannot isolate thought from sensation." Wilde's aesthetic leads him to a different view of spectacle. In "Shakespeare on Scenery" (1885), he contends that spectacle can stimulate the taste of an audience in positive ways. Modern scenery manifests "loveliness of form and color," which may "create an artistic tempera- ment in the audience, and . . . produce . . . joy in beauty for beauty's sake." This experience will make the public more receptive to great art. Like Shelley and Lewes, Wilde emphasizes the appeal of dramatic beauty to all the faculties, not just to the intellect. Scenery and acting enable drama to engage the whole spectator. In the following passage, Wilde confronts the romantic bias against spectacle directly.

> To talk of the passion of a play being hidden by the paint, and
> of sentiment being killed by scenery, is mere emptiness and folly
> of words. A noble play, nobly mounted, gives us double artistic
> pleasure. The eye as well as the ear is gratified, and the whole
> nature is made exquisitely receptive of the influence of imagina-
> tive work.

Note that Wilde submerges the classical ear/eye dichotomy by redefin- ing the kind of pleasure that drama should produce. Similarly, in a review of *Henry IV* as presented at Oxford, he insists that Shake- speare's plays do benefit from performance.

> I know that there are many who consider that Shakespeare is
> more for the study than for the stage. With this view I do not for a
> moment agree. Shakespeare wrote the plays to be acted, and we
> have no right to alter the form which he himself selected for the
> full expression of his work. Indeed, many of the beauties of that
> work can be adequately conveyed to us only through the actor's
> art.[80]

According to Wilde, Shakespeare would have approved some aes- thetically pleasing late nineteenth-century mountings of his plays. Wilde cites evidence from *Henry V* and *A Midsummer Night's Dream* to demonstrate that Shakespeare "is constantly protesting against the two special limitations of the Elizabethan stage—the lack of suitable scenery, and the fashion of men playing women's parts."[81]

Wilde justifies modern staging in "The Truth of Masks," pub- lished two months after "Shakespeare on Scenery." He links the mod- ern use of scenery and the modern willingness to allow women actors on stage because both phenomena attest to the public's desire for more realistic details. Furthermore, abolishing advances in stage technology since 1600 would be as ridiculous as returning to the custom of having

"Juliet played by a young man." Plays need to be mounted differently for new generations.

> A great work of dramatic art should not merely be made expressive of modern passion by means of the actor, but should be presented to us in the form most suitable to the modern spirit. . . . Perfect accuracy of detail, for the sake of perfect illusion, is necessary for us.[82]

However, Wilde does not give managers carte blanche to create spectacles unrelated to the dramatic text. He continues, "What we have to see is that the details are not allowed to usurp the principal place. They must be subordinate always to the general motive of the play." Wilde had pointed out in "Shakespeare on Scenery" that bad plays staged with elaborate spectacle have "lured" the audience "by the loveliness of scenic effect into listening to rhetoric posing as poetry, and to vulgarity doing duty for realism." Like Lewes and James, Wilde despises productions with scenery so dominant that it dwarfs the actors.

> As a rule, the hero is smothered in *bric-à-brac* and palm-trees, lost in the gilded abyss of Louis Quatorze furniture, or reduced to a mere midge in the midst of a marqueterie; whereas the background should always be kept as a background.

In fact, Wilde prefers the older tradition of beautifully painted backdrops to the late nineteenth-century built-up sets, which are "overcrowded with enormous properties."[83]

In "The Truth of Masks," Wilde goes beyond Lewes and Shaw to argue that Shakespeare's plays "require" spectacle to fulfill the author's intentions. Specifically, Wilde insists that a Shakespearean drama

> requires the services of a good property-man, a clever wig-maker, a costumier . . . , a master of the methods of making-up, a fencing-master, a dancing-master, and an artist to direct personally the whole production.

As evidence, he cites the frequency of masques, dances, and processions in Shakespeare's plays. Wilde points out how detailed the stage directions are for the processions in *Henry VIII*. According to Wilde, Shakespeare relies heavily on costume to create dramatic illusion, more so than any other English, French, or Greek playwright. The bard's plays abound in disguised heroes or heroines and in characters who change their garments, such as Prospero, to reveal their true station. Finally, costumes are useful because they express "the character of a person on his entrance." Wilde gives examples of Shakespeare's many references to costume in the dialogue of his dramas.[84]

Wilde justifies lovely and historically accurate costumes because the English people are now more appreciative of aesthetic beauty. Incongruous costumes can wreck a late nineteenth-century play. Mixtures of garments from different eras and inauthentic styles cause

> the entire ruin of all dramatic and picturesque effect. . . . To confuse the costumes is to confuse the play. . . . The highest beauty is not merely comparable with absolute accuracy of detail, but really dependent on it.

These statements should be contrasted with the reactions of Lewes and Shaw, who found the emphasis on antiquarian costumes absurd. In an 1884 essay, Bulwer-Lytton had developed his predecessors' objections to the use of archaeological research for dramatic productions. He found such details pedantic and inappropriate, especially when theaters apply archaeological knowledge to Shakespeare's "fairy tale" dramas. To defend historically accurate mounting from Bulwer-Lytton's attack, Wilde points out that Shakespeare based many plays on chronicles and that the bard would have been familiar with various artifacts preserved in England. Wilde believes that Shakespeare would have approved nineteenth-century productions of his dramas that used antiquarian research because "a dramatist who laid such stress on historical accuracy of fact would have welcomed historical accuracy of costume as a most important adjunct to his illusionist method."[85]

Because Wilde is convinced that staging can enhance Shakespeare's plays, he challenges the romantics' assertion that some tragic heroes are impossible to portray. Hazlitt had written in *A View of the English Stage* (1818) that the character of Hamlet "is probably of all others the most difficult to personate on the stage. It is like the attempt to embody a shadow" (*Works*, 5:186). Wilde quotes the last three words of this passage and summarizes the rest in "*Hamlet* at the Lyceum" (1885), attributing the idea to a "great critic" without mentioning Hazlitt by name. Wilde contradicts the romantic writer: "Hamlet seems to me essentially a good acting part" because the prince has many lines to speak, in contrast to a character like Ophelia, who has relatively little dialogue, and because the role of Hamlet combines "poetic grace with absolute reality" when well acted.[86]

Wilde also differs from Hazlitt, Coleridge, and Lamb when he argues that the sympathetic imagination is not crucial in the reader's or spectator's interaction with a work of literature. The romantics had insisted that the best tragic literature enables the public to identify with the characters portrayed. This exercise of the imagination results in transcendence of selfish concerns and sympathy for the sufferings of others. However, in "The Decay of Lying" (1889), Wilde, speaking as Vivian, presents art as so separate from reality that the sympathetic imagination should not become involved.

> The only beautiful things . . . are the things that do not concern us. As long as a thing is useful or necessary to us, or affects us in any way, either for pain or for pleasure, or appeals strongly to our sympathies, or is a vital part of the environment in which we live, it is outside the proper sphere of art. To art's subject-matter we should be more or less indifferent.[87]

Percy Fitzgerald moves from aesthetic to social criticism in *Principles of Comedy and Dramatic Effect* (1870), where he blames the overly elaborate stage spectacles on Victorian commercialism and materialism. His work prefigures Yeats's essays. Fitzgerald complains that contemporary theaters are run with "a purely mercantile and material view of the stage." Paradoxically, the attempt to imitate reality in the theaters calls attention to the impossibility of achieving this feat and ruins the illusion. Fitzgerald concludes that elaborate, realistic sets will fail artistically: "The more realism is aimed at, the more surely will the eye discover where it falls short." Fifteen years later, he published an edition of Lamb's dramatic essays.[88] Fitzgerald's sympathy for the romantics' bias against spectacle is clear in the above passages.

Like Fitzgerald, Mallarmé criticizes the overly realistic spectacles of the nineteenth-century theater, which the French symbolist terms "decadent" and "crude." Instead of realism, Mallarmé recommends the use of myth in drama because myth establishes "amazement and intimacy" with the audience. He contends that successful drama should combine all the arts in order to cast "a spell" on the spectator. He considers music especially effective in creating the "enchantment" which enables a dramatic symbol to overcome the resistance of the reason. Mallarmé praises Wagner's clever synthesis of different art forms to produce "a richer atmosphere of Revery" and "a wave of Passion."[89]

Yeats draws on the ideas of Shelley, Wagner, Mallarmé, and other writers in formulating his new approach to set design. Yeats views drama as a social and literary event that an audience must share. Unlike Coleridge, Hazlitt, and Lamb, Yeats contends that the "delights" of poetic drama "cannot be perfect when we read it alone in our rooms and long for one to share its delights, but that they might be perfect in the theatre, when we share them friend with friend, lover with beloved."[90]

However, he places primary emphasis on the dramatic text, not the spectacle or the action. In "Plans and Methods" (1899), he informs the public that the Irish Literary Theatre will try to publish its plays "before they are acted, and no play will be produced which could not hope to succeed as a book." Yeats cites ancient Greek drama and Shakespeare's plays as precedents for this emphasis on language.

> The ancient drama was all words about action. Nothing at all happened in many of the greatest of Greek plays, and it was Hamlet's soliloquies and not his duel that were of the chief importance in the play. Even in life itself the dramatic moments were those that were inseparable from splendid and appropriate words.[91]

In his emphasis on language, Yeats comes close to the position of the romantic critics.

He strongly objects to his era's preoccupation with pictorial staging. Yeats advocates more subtle effects that leave spectators free to use their imaginations. In the following passage, he contrasts painting and the theater to show why the techniques of pictorial staging are inappropriate.

> Now the art of the stage has three things which the easel painting has not. It has real light and shade, it has real perspective, and it has the action of the player. It is absurd when you have these things to use a painting of light and shade with painted perspective, and a landscape so elaborate that your players are reduced to a picturesque group in the foreground of an old-fashioned picture. It is absurd to paint and set before an audience a meretricious easel painting, a bad academy picture which is so full of fussy detail that the players do not stand out in a clear outline against it, and that takes to itself also some of the attention which should be given to their actions and to their words.

Yeats proposes a simple set that leaves the actors free to move and allows "the free playing of light." He goes beyond Wilde's preference for painted backdrops: Yeats's ideal set would have no painted light and shadow whatsoever. He rejects the pictorial stage because it is too rigid and crowded and too concerned with realistic details.[92]

Like Fitzgerald, Yeats blames English "commercialism and materialism" for the inappropriate pictorial sets and the weak dramas written to feature frenetic action and spectacle. He complains that the theater audience in London prefers "plays of commerce," which substitute a "succession of nervous tremors . . . for the purification that comes with pity and terror to the imagination and intellect." Thus, cheap thrills have replaced the genuine catharsis of "poetical" drama.[93]

Yeats shares Coleridge's conviction that a great writer must overcome the public's poor taste by educating and preparing his audience. Aesthetic appreciation is a "difficult art" because most people prefer to purchase conventional paintings and books and avoid works with new ideas or new forms. In "A Defence of the Abbey Theatre," he insists, "It takes even longer to train an audience than a company of actors."[94]

Yeats argues that urban life has adversely affected public taste by emphasizing what is superficial. Crowded cities "destroy the [intellectual] emotions" required for an audience of drama. In contrast, Irish peasants still appreciate oral poetry, are sensitive to mythopoeia, and can experience intense emotions. Yeats also blames science for the degeneration of literature because science concentrates on "externalities of all kinds." He hopes that the symbolist movement will return the emphasis to "evocation" or "suggestion."[95]

Yeats believes that his era is witnessing a revolt against the external and the material. There is a new appreciation for the visionary essence of life. He predicts that literature will become more "intense," spiritual, and symbolic as a result.

> The literary movement of our time has been a movement against the external and heterogeneous. . . . A movement which never mentions an external thing except to express a state of the soul, has taken the place of a movement which delighted in picturesque and bizarre things for their own sakes.

Yeats views himself as part of this movement away from materialism and superficiality in art. In "An Introduction for my Plays" (1937), he declares that his goal was to combine words and movement in drama that would "permit that stilling and slowing which turns the imagination in upon itself."[96]

In order to accomplish this goal, Yeats turns away from the busy stage movement and the "constant change" typical of bad plays and of the cinema. He substitutes "vivid words" for what he considers "irrelevant movement." Yeats adapts the classical ear/eye dichotomy to explain his position. "I have spent my life in clearing out of poetry every phrase written for the eye, and bringing all back to syntax that is for ear alone."[97]

Many of his essays are designed to educate the public about the new drama and its radical changes in staging. He defends innovative playwrights such as Synge, managers such as W. G. Fay, and set designers such as Gordon Craig. Often, Yeats tries to convince the public to end its addiction to pictorial representation of drama. He concedes that most people are "more easily moved through the eyes than through the ears. The emotion that comes with the music of words is exhausting, like all intellectual emotions, and few people like exhausting emotions." Despite the difficulty, Yeats urges his public to revive its interest in language because he believes that plays that rely on spectacle cause the imagination to atrophy.[98] These passages reveal the influence of the romantics and the influence of Lewes and other writers who sought to limit spectacle.

Yeats sees an irreconcilable conflict between poetic drama and overly realistic scenery or acting styles. The naturalistic set and acting jar the audience by highlighting the artificiality of having people speak in verse. Yeats argues that Shakespeare's plays are too full of metaphors, obscure motives, and improbable actions to accommodate overly realistic scenery. When "we set these cloudy actions among solid looking houses, and what we hope are solid looking trees, . . . illusion comes to an end, slain by our desire to increase it." The scenery should be "simple" and reflect the "make-believe" in the dramas.[99]

Yeats calls for a modern "theatre of art" with stylized gestures, scenery, and costumes. Such a theater will reconcile the poetic text and subdued spectacle. He views the Abbey Theatre as a model for this "theatre of art" because its productions emphasize language and integrate simple sets with the acting. The Abbey Theatre avoids pictorial excesses: "when we wish to give a remote poetical effect we throw away realism altogether, and are content with suggestion." Yeats points out that he has been influenced by Japanese drama in this view of spectacle.[100]

He recommends scenery that is "decorative, rather than naturalistic." Decorative scenery emphasizes patterns and colors, rather than verisimilitude, in order to evoke the audience's imagination.

A wood, for instance, should be little more than a pattern made with painted boughs. It should not try to make one believe that the actors are in a real wood, for the imagination will do that far better, but it should decorate the stage. It should be a mass of deep colour, in harmony with the colours in the costumes of the players.

Instead of elaborate properties, Yeats used subtle lighting, simple backdrops, music, and "pantomimic dance."[101]

This simple, evocative form of art transcends the external and the superficial to enable the public "to pass for a few moments into a deep of the mind that had hitherto been too subtle for our habitation."[102] Thus, dramatic art can put us in touch with our inner life.

Conclusion

Although the mid and late nineteenth-century critics of drama share their predecessors' ambivalence toward spectacle, writers like Lewes, Shaw, Wilde, and Yeats have more faith in the ability of "beautiful" and well-designed scenery and properties to stimulate the audience's aesthetic taste and receptivity to literature. These later critics argue that literature must involve the whole man or woman, and that spectacle is useful in achieving this total engagement.

Victorian and early twentieth-century critics abandon the neoclassical distinction between tragedy, which should only be read, and comedy, which can be staged effectively. Unlike Coleridge, Lamb, and Hazlitt, they believe that even the plays of Shakespeare benefit from performance. However, writers from Lewes to Yeats debate the usefulness of pictorial staging and the relevance of historical research applied to costumes and sets. Most agree with the romantics that the text should be at the core of any dramatic production. Some, like Yeats, advocate a radical simplification of the set in order to highlight dramatic language.

The twentieth century has witnessed the gradual abandonment of elaborate spectacle in the theater, with the exception of musicals and operas. For example, in Peter Brook's version of *A Midsummer Night's Dream* as performed by the Royal Shakespeare Company, one tree represented a woods. Of course, simplicity of decor is cost effective, but directors and producers are responding to a shift in taste forecast by many nineteenth-century critics and anticipated by experimental managers like William Poel.

Some twentieth-century writers have been influenced by the romantics' view of spectacle and by their terminology. Discussing Shakespeare's plays in 1904, A. C. Bradley argues that the "immense scope" and the imaginative and emotional intensity of *King Lear* make the tragedy "too huge for the stage." Bradley revives the romantics' critique of the senses when he insists that *King Lear*, unlike Shakespeare's other tragedies, has "something in its very essence which is at war with the senses, and demands a purely imaginative realisation." Similarly, George Saintsbury's works reveal the influence of Coleridge, Lamb, and Byron. In *A History of English Criticism* (1911), Saintsbury praises Lamb's essay "On the Tragedies of Shakspeare" and admits that he himself prefers to read drama. Byron's image of the mental theater appears in the following passage, taken from *A History of the French Novel* (1919): "The better the play is as literature, the more I wish that I might be left to read in comfort and see it acted with my mind's eye only." Like Coleridge, Saintsbury argues that "dresses and *décor*, scenery and music, and 'spectacle' generally . . . interfere with pure literary enjoyment."[1]

Likewise, Benedetto Croce contends in his *Aesthetic* (1922) that technical aspects of art, like spectacle, limit expression because they are "externals." Only some dramas need actors and scenery: "We can obtain the effect of certain plays by simply reading them; others need declamation and scenic display." In *Conversazioni critiche* (1918), Croce portrays performance as a "translation" of a drama, not as an equivalent in meaning to the text. A performance conveys a play "to those who cannot or do not know how to read it."[2] This last statement is close to Lamb's analysis in "On the Tragedies of Shakspeare."

T. S. Eliot considers Shakespeare a playwright whose dramas should be "read rather than seen" because only an actor of genius can interpret them adequately on stage. Furthermore, Eliot finds that performances disrupt the reader's close imaginative relationship to Shakespeare's plays: "I rebel against most performances of Shakespeare's plays because I want a direct relationship between the work of art and myself." After reading such a comment, one is not surprised to find that Eliot praises Coleridge as "the greatest of English critics."[3]

Critics like Wolfgang Iser, Siegfried Kracauer, and Seymour Chatman transfer the romantics' objections to spectacle in the theater to the medium of film. They find that the plethora of visual details in movie adaptations of novels and short stories overwhelms the viewer. Iser argues that by restricting the possibilities suggested by literature, films limit the viewer's imaginative response.

Recent books about the influence of television on culture make similar statements. In *Amusing Ourselves to Death: Public Discourse in the Age of Show Business,* Neil Postman contends that pictorial images are displacing language and making the viewers passive.[4]

Although twentieth-century critics seem unaware of their predecessors, critical concern with readers' responses to texts goes back at least as far as the Renaissance prefaces to published dramas. Eighteenth- and nineteenth-century drama critics are quite conscious of the distinction between readers and spectators, and these writers are well aware of their own readers' expectations and limitations.

More research needs to be done on pre-twentieth-century versions of reader-response theory. Although the earlier critics based their work on faculty psychology instead of depth psychology, their conclusions are as instructive as the more recent books of Harold Bloom, Norman Holland, Fish, and Iser. My analysis indicates that, in any century, concern with readers is related to the writer's view of the purpose of literature and his or her approach to education.

Many scholars have stressed the *distinctions* between the aesthetics of different eras and different countries. However, my research on the historical development of drama criticism has led me to believe that the *continuities* are equally significant. When this latter approach is taken, one sees that, for example, both eighteenth- and nineteenth-century European drama critics emphasize the reader's and the writer's imagination: there is no cataclysmic shift of emphasis. More work could be done on the interrelations of different literary circles.

Twentieth-century critics must stop treating Lamb and Hazlitt as "minor" or eccentric writers. Instead, the books and essays of these two men should be reread and acknowledged as sources for many current ideas about readers, plays, and spectacle. Even the directors of theaters can benefit from the insights of Lamb and Hazlitt regarding the production of Shakespeare's plays.

Similarly, critics need to pay more attention to Coleridge's prose. Even though his aesthetic observations are often scattered and rambling, his fragments reveal a consistent emphasis on the use of literature to educate and liberate the mind. Furthermore, an examination of his lectures and essays illuminates his poems, which also concern the act of communicating an insight to a sympathetic reader.

Because the opposition to spectacle has such a long history, stretching back at least to Horace, one must take the romantics' position seriously. To blame their bias on bad contemporary productions, on eccentricity, or on ignorance of the theater is an act of critical amnesia. It is more helpful to see the romantics as crusaders against the timeless problems of the idolatry of actors, the tendency to compensate for bad scripts with spectacle, and the elevation of the senses over the imagination.

Notes

Notes for Introduction

1. Samuel Taylor Coleridge, *Shakespearean Criticism*, 2:278–79; Charles Lamb, "On the Tragedies of Shakspeare, Considered with Reference to their Fitness for Stage Representation," *The Works of Charles and Mary Lamb*, 1:107; William Hazlitt, "Mr. Kean's Richard II," *A View of the English Stage*, in *The Complete Works of William Hazlitt*, 5:222.

2. J. R. de J. Jackson, "Coleridge on Dramatic Illusion and Spectacle in the Performance of Shakespeare's Plays," 13; Joan Coldwell, "The Playgoer as Critic: Charles Lamb on Shakespeare's Characters," 194; Jonas Barish, *The Antitheatrical Prejudice*, 318. See also René Wellek, *A History of Modern Criticism, 1750–1950*, 2:192; John Kinnaird, *William Hazlitt: Critic of Power*, 167; Sylvan Barnet, "Charles Lamb's Contribution to the Theory of Dramatic Illusion," 1158; and John I. Ades, "Charles Lamb, Shakespeare, and Early Nineteenth-Century Theater," *PMLA* 85, 3 (May 1970): 517 and elsewhere.

Notes for Chapter 1:
The Bias against Spectacle in Tragedy

1. Joseph Warton, *An Essay on the Genius and Writings of Pope*, 2 vols. (1782; rpt. New York: Garland Publishing, 1970), 2:381. Some university instructors taught Aristotle's *Poetics*, too. See M. L. Clarke, *Greek Studies in England, 1700–1830* (Cambridge: Cambridge University Press, 1945), 43. Other instructors published editions of the *Poetics* and may have taught it in their classes; this group includes Thomas Winstanley of Manchester and Brasenose College in Oxford and William Cooke of Eton and King's College in Cambridge. Some of the era's best Greek scholars flourished outside of the universities. Thomas Twining was a country parson. The eighteenth-century reading public was also interested in the classics. According to M. L. Clarke, Aristotle's *Poetics* and the *Rhetoric* were "widely read" in the 1700s (p. 114).

2. Plato, *Phaedo*, in *The Works of Plato*, 4:265–66, 293, 295, 316.

3. Marcus Tullius Cicero, "Pro Archia," *The Orations of Marcus Tullius Cicero*, trans. William Guthrie (London: Thomas Chaplin, 1819), 119, 122; John Dennis, "The Characters and Conduct of Sir John Edgar, Call'd by Himself Sole Monarch of the Stage in Drury-Lane; and his Three Deputy-Governors. In Two Letters to Sir John Edgar," *The Critical Works of John Dennis*, 2:183, 186.

4. Aristotle, *Aristotle's Treatise on Poetry*, ed. and trans. Thomas Twining, 78, 89, 133. All italics in these quotations are Twining's.

5. Aristotle, *Treatise on Poetry*, 133.

6. Samuel Johnson, Preface to *The Plays of William Shakespeare*, in *Samuel Johnson's Literary Criticism*, ed. R. D. Stock (Lincoln: University of Nebraska Press, 1974), 154. Johnson appears to have had mixed feelings about the effectiveness of the stage. He complained to Boswell in 1769, "Many of Shakespeare's plays are the worse for being acted: Macbeth, for instance." See James

Boswell, *Boswell's Life of Johnson*, ed. George Birkbeck Hill, rev. L. F. Powell, 6 vols. (Oxford: Clarendon Press, 1934), 2:92. However, in other written and oral comments, Johnson equates the acts of reading a drama and viewing a performance. He follows his distinction between the theater and the page, which I have cited above, with a contradictory statement in the next paragraph of the Preface: "A play read, affects the mind like a play acted" (p. 154). R. D. Stock cites other examples of Johnson's inconsistency on this subject in *Samuel Johnson and Neoclassical Dramatic Theory: The Intellectual Context of the Preface to Shakespeare*, 210–12.

7. Horace, "To Augustus," *The Epistles*, in *The Works of Horace*, 2:2.1.184–87, 202–7, 214.

8. John Webster, Preface to *The White Divel* (1612), in *An Anthology of Elizabethan Dedications and Prefaces*, ed. Clara Gebert (Philadelphia: University of Pennsylvania Press, 1933), 211.

9. Ben Jonson, Preface to *The Alchemist* (1616 folio), in *Ben Jonson's Literary Criticism*, 182. Though Ben Jonson was famed for his court masques, which featured elaborate spectacles, he criticized spectacular effects in ordinary dramas. According to Stephen Orgel, Jonson viewed plays as rational and persuasive rhetorical structures. See Steven Orgel, "The Poetics of Spectacle," *New Literary History* 2, 3 (Spring 1971): 380, 383.

10. Jonson, "The Prologue for the Court," *The Staple of News* (1631 folio), in *Ben Jonson's Literary Criticism*, 121. Jonas Barish contends that Jonson's comedies derive much of their appeal from the tension between the author's distrust of disguise and illusion and his equally strong fascination with these aspects of spectacle. This is manifested in characters like Face, Subtle, and Volpone. See Jonas Barish, *The Antitheatrical Prejudice*, 153–54.

11. Marvin Theodore Herrick, *The Poetics of Aristotle in England*, Cornell Studies in English, 17 (New Haven: Yale University Press, 1930), 64; John Dryden, *Essays of John Dryden*, 1:245, 248. See also Dryden's "Dedication of the Aeneas" (1697), *Essays of John Dryden*, 2:161, 165–66.

12. Jeremy Collier, *A Short View of the Immorality and Profaneness of the English Stage: Together with The Sense of Antiquity Upon this Argument*, 3d ed. (London, 1698; rpt. Munich: Wilhelm Fink Verlag, 1967), 5.

13. For a detailed discussion of the religious bias against performance, see Jonas Barish's *The Antitheatrical Prejudice* (1981).

14. Allardyce Nicoll, *The Garrick Stage: Theatres and Audience in the Eighteenth Century*, 37, 40, 117–18, 126–27, 130; Charles Beecher Hogan, *The London Stage, 1776–1800: A Critical Introduction*, vol. 5 of *The London Stage*, ed. Emmett L. Avery and Arthur H. Scouten, xliii–iv, lxvi; Allardyce Nicoll, *The English Theatre: A Short History* (New York: Thomas Nelson, 1936), 61, 80, 82, 115–17, 125–27; Allardyce Nicoll, *A History of English Drama, 1660–1900*, 3:23–27, 34, 39, and 4:38, 42, 46–47; Leo Hughes, *The Drama's Patrons: A Study of the Eighteenth-Century London Audience*, 116–17, 186–87.

15. James Roose-Evans, *London Theatre from the Globe to the National* (Oxford: Phaidon Press, 1977), 24; Stephen Orgel, *The Illusion of Power: Political Theater in the English Renaissance*, 7, 34–40, 58, 88.

16. Nicoll, *History of English Drama*, 3:24–28, 105–6.

17. Richard Flecknoe, "A Short Discourse of the English Stage," in *Critical Essays of the Seventeenth Century,* ed. J. E. Spingarn, 2:95–96.

18. Richard Steele, Prologue for *The Funeral, or Grief A-la-Mode,* in *The Plays of Richard Steele,* 23, ll. 1–13.

19. Joseph Addison, *The Spectator,* nos. 5, 42, 44, 1:23, 191, 177–78.

20. Henry Fielding, *The Champion,* 24 May 1740 and 1 April 1740, in *The Complete Works of Henry Fielding, Esq.,* 15:316, 265.

21. Oliver Goldsmith, letter 79, *The Citizen of the World* (1762), in *The Collected Works of Oliver Goldsmith,* 2:323–26. See also letters 21 and 97 (2:92–94, 389).

22. Richard Brinsley Sheridan, *The Critic, or A Tragedy Rehearsed* 3.1, in *The Dramatic Works of Richard Brinsley Sheridan,* 2:543–44, 548–49.

23. Adam Smith, "Of the Nature of that Imitation which takes place in what are called the Imitative Arts," *Essays on Philosophical Subjects,* 228–29.

24. Emmett L. Avery, *The London Stage, 1700–1729: A Critical Introduction,* vol. 2 of *The London Stage,* cx–cxi. In an article published in *ELH,* Avery examines the account books of Lincoln's Inn Fields Theatre and proves that receipts increased on most evenings when a pantomime was added to the standard repertory. New pantomimes could double or triple a theater's receipts. Avery concludes, "After 1720 . . . supplementary entertainments came close to dominating the evening's offerings. In fact, what might be considered the normal relation of play and entertainment became reversed: the pantomime began to have extended runs, evening after evening, with the play often changed nightly." See Emmett L. Avery, "The Defense and Criticism of Pantomimic Entertainments in the Early Eighteenth Century," *ELH* 5, 2 (June 1938): 129, 132–33.

25. Giacomo Oreglia, *The Commedia dell'Arte,* 3–4, 56–58; Evert Sprinchorn, Introduction to *The Commedia dell'Arte,* xii; Mel Gordon, *Lazzi: The Comic Routines of the Commedia dell'Arte,* 3, 9, 14, 21, 32–35, 41–42, 47, 51–53, 55–59; Allardyce Nicoll, *The World of Harlequin: A Critical Study of the Commedia dell'Arte,* 12, 70, 148; Richard Southern, *The Victorian Theatre: A Pictorial Survey,* 34.

26. Gordon, *Lazzi,* 29–31; Nicoll, *The World of Harlequin,* 177–81, 202; Oreglia, *Commedia dell'Arte,* 12.

27. Nicholas Rowe, Epilogue for *The Ambitious Step-Mother,* in *Plays,* 2d ed., rev., 2 vols. (London: J. & R. Tonson & H. Lintot, 1736), 1:ix, 27–28. Scaramouch was a cowardly braggart who loved eating and having affairs with women. He played musical instruments, danced, sang, and performed magic tricks (see Oreglia, *Commedia dell'Arte,* 105, 113–14).

28. Richard Bevis, *The Laughing Tradition: Stage Comedy in Garrick's Day,* 100; Hughes, *The Drama's Patrons,* 98.

29. Hogan, *The London Stage,* lxxxii–viii; George Winchester Stone, Jr., *The London Stage, 1747–1776: A Critical Introduction,* vol. 4 of *The London Stage,* cxvii, cxxiii–iv.

30. John Rich, "To Thomas Chamber, Esq.," in *Rape of Proserpine: with the Birth and Adventures of Harlequin,* by Lewis Theobald, 3d ed. (London: T. Wood, 1727), iv–vi; David Garrick, "Occasional Prologue, Spoken by Mr. Garrick at the Opening of Drury-Lane Theatre, 8 September 1750," in *The*

Poetical Works of David Garrick, ed. George Kearsley, 2 vols. (London, 1795; rpt. New York: Benjamin Blom, 1968), 1:102–3, ll. 25–36.

31. John Dryden, "Epilogue to the University of Oxford," in *The Poetical Works of Dryden,* ed. George R. Noyes, The Cambridge Poets (Boston: Houghton Mifflin, 1950), 73; Alexander Pope, *The Dunciad* (1729), in *The Poems of Alexander Pope,* 5:book 3, ll. 229–36, 244–60, 299–307; book 2, ll. 214–22; see also Malcolm Goldstein, *Pope and the Augustan Stage* (Stanford: Stanford University Press, 1958), 82–113. Fielding, who managed the Little Theatre in the Haymarket from 1736 to 1737, also satirized pantomime, rope dancing, and tumbling in *Pasquin, or a Dramatic Satire on the Times* (1736) and *Tumble-Down Dick, or Phaeton in the Suds* (1736).

32. William Hogarth, *A Just View of the British Stage,* in *Engravings by Hogarth,* ed. Sean Shesgreen (New York: Dover Publications, 1973), pl. 4.

33. Goldsmith, "On the present State of our Theatres," *Weekly Magazine,* no. 3 (12 January 1760), in *The Collected Works,* 3:54–55.

34. Twining, Notes to *Treatise on Poetry,* 317–18, n. 101.

35. Bevis, *The Laughing Tradition,* 66, 73–74; Sheridan, *The Critic,* act 3, scene 1, p. 543. Bevis's research indicates that eighteenth-century writers perceived a clear distinction between "laughing" stage comedy and closet "sentimental" comedy. Sentimental dramas were easier to publish because they relied on witty dialogue, while laughing dramas emphasized visual effects that required staging. Many authors wrote two quite different versions of their dramas—one for the stage and one for the closet. See Bevis, *The Laughing Tradition,* 11, 30–31, 33–35.

36. Carlo Goldoni, *Pamela fanciulla* (1750), trans. into English with the Italian original (London: J. Nourse, 1756); reprinted in *Pamela: Four Versions, 1741–1746* (New York: Garland Publishing, 1975), act 1, scene 16, p. 57.

37. Alfred Lord Tennyson, "To W. C. Macready," in *The Poems of Tennyson,* ed. Christopher Ricks, Longmans' Annotated English Poets (London: Longmans, Green, 1969), p. 990, ll. 10–11.

38. Hogan, *The London Stage,* cxxxix; Matthew Gregory Lewis, Epilogue for *Knave or Not?,* by Thomas Holcroft (Drury Lane, 1798), cited in Nicoll, *History of English Drama,* 3:99.

39. Dennis, "An Essay on the Opera's after the Italian Manner," in *The Critical Works,* 1:385–86; Richard Steele, *Tatler,* no. 4, 18 April 1709, in *The Tatler,* 1:40; Pope, *The Dunciad* (1743), in *The Poems of Alexander Pope,* book 4, ll. 45–49 and nn.; Fielding, "The Pleasures of the Town," *The Author's Farce,* in *The Complete Works,* 8:249, and *The Author's Farce,* act 2, scene 6, p. 223.

40. Thomas Shadwell, Preface to *The Humorists, A Comedy* (1671), in *Critical Essays of the Seventeenth Century,* 2:115.

41. John Vanbrugh, *The Relapse,* act 2, p. 39.

42. See also Nicoll, *History of English Drama,* 3:9.

43. Hogan, *The London Stage,* lii.

44. Dennis, "A Large Account of the Taste in Poetry," in *The Critical Works,* 1:293, 286–87. French writers also complain about the public's taste. Voltaire attacks the plays of Shadwell as fit only for the "vulgar" theater audience, not for the more sophisticated readers. "His plays, enjoyed by the vulgar for a few

performances, were disdained by all people of taste, and resembled so many plays I have seen in France that attracted the crowd and repelled readers." See Voltaire, "On Comedy," letter 19 in *Philosophical Letters,* trans. and intro. Ernest Dilworth, The Library of Liberal Arts (New York: Bobbs-Merrill, 1961), 90.

45. Pope, *The First Epistle of the Second Book of Horace,* in *The Poems of Pope,* 4:221, 223, ll. 304–31. Similarly, Pope accuses Theobald in a note to *The Dunciad* (1729) of bringing spectacles that were "agreeable only to the Taste of the Rabble" to the London theaters, where such frothy works entertained "the Court and Town" (book 1, p. 60, l. 2, n. 2).

46. Richard D. Altick traces this expansion of the reading public in *The English Common Reader: A Social History of the Mass Reading Public, 1800–1900.* Despite its subtitle, this book actually surveys the British reading public's growth beginning with the Renaissance. The Vanbrugh quotation is from *The Relapse,* act 2, p. 38. Charles Lamb, "Detached Thoughts on Books and Reading," in *The Works of Charles and Mary Lamb,* 2:172.

47. Fielding, *The Author's Farce,* act 1, scene 7, p. 208; William Hodson, "Observations on Tragedy," in *Zoraida: A Tragedy* (London: W. Richardson for G. Kearsly, 1780), 69.

48. Francis Gentleman, *The Dramatic Censor* 1 (1770): 14, 113, 154; *The Monthly Review* 62 (March 1780): 186.

49. Steele, Preface to *The Conscious Lovers: A Comedy,* 7. Like Steele, Goldsmith was concerned about the impact of a play on an audience's morals. However, Goldsmith concludes that reading a good play, not seeing a performance, is more conducive to virtue because performances emphasize debauchery. "While we are readers, every moral sentiment strikes us in all its beauty, but the love scenes are frigid, tawdry, and disgusting. When we are spectators, all the persuasives to vice receive an additional lustre. . . . An actor is chiefly useful in introducing new performances upon the stage, since the reader receives more benefit by perusing a well written play in his closet, than by seeing it acted." See Goldsmith, "Of the Stage," *An Enquiry into the Present State of Polite Learning in Europe* (1759), in *The Collected Works,* 1:324–25. The Dennis quotation is from "Remarks on a Play, Call'd, The Conscious Lovers, a Comedy" (1723), in *The Critical Works,* 2:258.

50. Robert Witbeck Babcock, *The Genesis of Shakespeare Idolatry, 1766–1799: A Study in English Criticism of the Late Eighteenth Century,* 199ff.

51. Babcock, *Shakespeare Idolatry,* 89; Hogan, *The London Stage,* lxi, clxxvii; Avery and Scouten, *The London Stage, 1660–1700: A Critical Introduction,* vol. 1 of *The London Stage,* xxvii and also lxxxviii; Hazelton Spencer, *Shakespeare Improved: The Restoration Versions in Quarto and on the Stage,* 172, 332, 372. See also Dennis Bartholomeusz, *Macbeth and the Players* (Cambridge: Cambridge University Press, 1969), 16–18.

52. Spencer, *Shakespeare Improved,* 163, 182–83, 281, 369, 372.

53. William Hazlitt, *The Complete Works of William Hazlitt,* 5:234–35.

54. Steele, *Tatler,* no. 167, 2 May and 4 May 1710, 3:281.

55. Henry Fielding, *The History of Tom Jones, A Foundling* (New York: Random House, 1950), book 7, ch. 1, p. 267; book 16, ch. 5, pp. 761, 758–59; Gentleman, *The Dramatic Censor,* 1:107.

56. Aristotle, *The Rhetoric*, book 3, sec. 1, in *The Works of Aristotle*, ed. W. D. Ross et al., 2:1403b–1404a.

57. Thomas Rymer, "To Fleetwood Shepheard," in *The Tragedies of the Last Age*, 5–6.

58. Goldsmith, letter 79, *The Citizen of the World*, in *The Collected Works*, 2:325; see also Goldsmith, "Of the Stage" (1759), in *The Collected Works*, 1:325–26, 329.

59. Sheridan, *The Critic*, act 2, scene 2, pp. 530–32.

60. Henry James Pye, *A Commentary Illustrating the Poetic of Aristotle, By Examples Taken Chiefly from the Modern Poets To which is Prefixed a new and Corrected Edition of the Translation of the Poetic*, n. 1 on ch. 4 of the *Poetics*, p. 117; n. 1 on ch. 26 of the *Poetics*, p. 531.

61. Pye, *A Commentary Illustrating the Poetic of Aristotle*, n. 1 on ch. 26 of the *Poetics*, p. 533.

Notes for Chapter 2:
The Romantics' Critique of Appeals to the Senses in the Arts

1. Walter Jackson Bate, Introduction to the section on William Hazlitt, in *Criticism: The Major Texts* (1952; enlarged ed., New York: Harcourt Brace Jovanovich, 1970), 283, and see also 289; René Wellek, *A History of Modern Criticism*, 2:199; Roy Park, *Hazlitt and the Spirit of the Age*, 2, and also see 99, 105–6, 155, 161–62, 169, 210, 215, 217, 235–36; Park, Introduction to *Lamb as Critic*, 7, 9, and see also 8, 11, 13, 33, 35.

2. See my discussion of Plato's *Phaedo* in Chapter 1 of this book.

3. Aristotle, *De Anima*, in *The Works of Aristotle*, 3:429a–429b.

4. Francis Bacon, *The Advancement of Learning*, book 2, ch. 4, in *The Advancement of Learning and New Atlantis* (1906; rpt. London: Oxford University Press, 1969), 97; William Hazlitt, *Lectures on the English Poets*, in *The Complete Works of William Hazlitt*, 5:3 (hereafter cited as *Works of Hazlitt* in the text).

5. Dryden, "Of Dramatic Poesy: An Essay," in *Essays of John Dryden*, 1:62–63. During the many literary debates in "Of Dramatic Poesy," Lisideius does not always take positions that Dryden would support. However, Neander, who is closer than Lisideius to Dryden's view of drama, does agree with Lisideius that deaths should not occur onstage. Neander, however, is more tolerant of battles and duels that take place before the audience (see 1.74–75).

6. From *Spectator*, no. 416, 27 June 1712, 3:560–61.

7. Edmund Burke, *A Philosophical Enquiry into the Origin of our Ideas of the Sublime and Beautiful*, ed. J. T. Boulton (London: Routledge and Kegan Paul, 1958), 58–63, 172.

8. Edmund Burke, *A Philosophical Enquiry*, 170, 173.

9. Friedrich Schiller, *On the Aesthetic Education of Man*, 98–99, 108; Immanuel Kant, "Critique of Aesthetic Judgement," in *The Critique of Judgement*, 57–58, 74, 94, 98, 166, and see also 107, 149 (the italics are Kant's).

10. Schiller, *Aesthetic Education*, 101, 108–9, 114, 138; see also Reginald Snell, Introduction to Schiller's *Aesthetic Education*, 4.

11. Goethe and Schiller, "On Epic and Dramatic Poetry," in *Goethe's Literary Essays*, 102–3.

12. William Blake, Annotations to Berkeley's *Siris*, in *Complete Writings with Variant Readings*, ed. Geoffrey Keynes (Oxford: Oxford University Press, 1971), 775; Blake, *The Letters of William Blake with Related Documents*, ed. Geoffrey Keynes, 3d ed. (Oxford: Clarendon Press, 1980), 44, 57–58; Blake, "The Everlasting Gospel," in *Complete Writings*, d:105–6; Blake, Annotations to Sir Joshua Reynolds's *Discourses*, in *Complete Writings*, 459. Despite Blake's criticism of the senses, he illustrated his own poems, thus juxtaposing art and literature to create what W. J. T. Mitchell calls "visible language." "Blake deliberately violates the boundary between written and pictorial forms" as part of his radical political stance, according to Mitchell. See Mitchell, "Visible Language: Blake's Wond'rous Art of Writing," in *Romanticism and Contemporary Criticism*, ed. Morris Eaves and Michael Fischer (Ithaca: Cornell University Press, 1986), 51, 54, 83, 86.

13. Blake, *Complete Writings*, 782–83; William Wordsworth, Miscellaneous Sonnets 25, in *Poetical Works*, ll. 4–7; Wordsworth, *The Prelude* (1850), in *Poetical Works*, book 12:127–50; Wordsworth, "Illustrated Books and Newspapers," in *Poetical Works*, ll. 12–14.

14. Samuel Taylor Coleridge, "On the Principles of Genial Criticism Concerning the Fine Arts," in *Biographia Literaria*, 2:227, and see also 230; Coleridge, "On Poesy or Art," *Biographia Literaria*, 2:253–54 (hereafter cited as *BL* in the text).

15. Sir Joshua Reynolds, Discourse Three, in *Discourses on Art*, 43–50; S. T. Coleridge, *Shakespearean Criticism*, 2:134 (hereafter cited as *SC* in the text).

16. "Abstract," *Dictionary of Philosophy and Psychology*, ed. James Mark Baldwin, 3 vols. (1925; rpt. Gloucester, Mass.: Peter Smith, 1960), 1:5; Aristotle, *Metaphysica*, in *The Works of Aristotle*, 8:1061a. Similarly, Hazlitt contends in a note to *On the Principles of Human Action* (1805) that imagination is the opposite of "sensation, or memory" (*Works of Hazlitt*, 1:19, n. 1).

17. Coleridge, *Logic*, in *The Collected Works of Samuel Taylor Coleridge*, 13:12–15, 18–19, 230; see also Coleridge, *A Lay Sermon*, in *The Collected Works*, 6:173.

18. Charles Lamb, "On the Tragedies of Shakspeare," *The Works of Charles and Mary Lamb*, 1:106; August Wilhelm Schlegel, lecture 18, in *Lectures on Dramatic Art and Literature*, 256.

19. John Keats, "To Benjamin Bailey," 22 November 1817, *Selected Poems and Letters*, ed. Douglas Bush, Riverside Editions (Boston: Houghton Mifflin, 1959), 258; W. B. Yeats, "The Thinking of the Body," in *Essays and Introductions*, 292–93.

Notes for Chapter 3:
*Coleridge's Emphasis on the Importance of
"Abstraction" in Education,
Reading Drama, and Self-Realization*

1. Exceptions to this rule are Alice D. Snyder, *Coleridge on Logic and Learning;* William Walsh, *Coleridge: The Work and the Relevance;* and Laurence S. Lockridge, *Coleridge the Moralist.*

2. Thomas Middleton Raysor, ed., *Shakespearean Criticism*, 2 vols. (London: J. M. Dent, 1960), 2:206, n. 2. Raysor may have been under pressure from his publisher to limit the length of the reprinted volumes. However, his stated justification is indefensible, I believe. Because of these deletions, I will use the 1930 edition of Coleridge's *Shakespearean Criticism* for further reference and cite it as *SC* in the text.

3. Peter Gordon and John White, *Philosophers as Educational Reformers: The Influence of Idealism on British Educational Thought and Practice*, 3, 5, 21, 195, 198, 210, 214, 225; Northrop Frye, *A Study of English Romanticism*, 37, 46. Coleridge was influenced by German idealists like Hegel, Kant, Schelling, and Fichte. See Gordon and White, *Philosophers as Educational Reformers*, 5, 8, 17–18, 48–49, 180ff.; Lockridge, *Coleridge the Moralist*, 148–49; Samuel Taylor Coleridge, *Biographia Literaria*, 1:93–107 (hereafter cited as *BL* in the text). However, "the concrete content and expression of Coleridge's self-realization theories are, in the main, his own and cannot be wholly attributed to any intellectual tradition" (Lockridge, *Coleridge the Moralist*, 149).

4. Samuel Taylor Coleridge, "Frost at Midnight," in *Poetical Works*, ed. Ernest Hartley Coleridge (Oxford: Oxford University Press, 1969), ll. 37, 52 *et passim*. All citations of Coleridge's poetry will be from this text.

5. Jean Jacques Rousseau, *Émile*, 5, 10, 50, 56–58, 67, 69, 71, 83–84. Although Rousseau insists that the child is being educated naturally, the tutor is, in fact, manipulating the child's environment surreptitiously: "His work and play, his pleasure and pain, are they not, unknown to him, under your control? . . . He should never take a step you have not foreseen, nor utter a word you could not foretell" (pp. 84–85).

6. Samuel Taylor Coleridge, *Inquiring Spirit: A Coleridge Reader*, 90 (hereafter cited as *IS* in the text). Coleridge is extending Locke's idea here: "Give them first one simple Idea, and see that they take it right, and perfectly comprehend it before you go any farther, and then add some other simple Idea." See John Locke, *Some Thoughts Concerning Education*, in *The Educational Writings of John Locke*, 291. See also Coleridge, *The Friend*, in *The Collected Works of Samuel Taylor Coleridge*, vol. 4, pt. 1, 500 (hereafter cited as *Friend* in the text). According to Lockridge, the term "self-realization" was coined by Coleridge (see Lockridge, *Coleridge the Moralist*, 149). At times Coleridge appears to have an organic view of teaching, as in this definition of education: "to educe, to call forth, as the blossom is educed from the bud. The vital excellences are within; the acorn is but educed or brought forth from the bud" (*Shakespearean Criticism*, 2:290). See also Coleridge, *Logic*, in *The Collected Works*, 13:9–10 (hereafter cited as *Logic* in the text). Lockridge interprets the organic metaphor underlying many of Coleridge's comments on education. "Coleridge's is a theory of self-realization based on the idea that the self is an organism with the latent power of growth, growth that must be directed mostly by the organism itself." However, Coleridge's writings also reveal his awareness that the organic metaphor cannot apply perfectly to human beings because "powers can be both educed and newly created through active and deliberate human effort," and a person can "consciously direct" his or her own growth (Lockridge, *Coleridge the Moralist*, 194, 172).

7. Samuel Taylor Coleridge, *Collected Letters of Samuel Taylor Coleridge,* 6:629-31 (hereafter cited as *Letters of Coleridge* in the text). All italics in passages quoted from Coleridge are his emphasis, unless otherwise indicated. Schiller, *On the Aesthetic Education of Man,* 27, 96-99, 101, 108-09, 111-12, 120, 123-28, 134, 136-37, 140. Coleridge may also be influenced by Aristotle's emphasis on principles. "Intellect has to do with the first principles of things intelligible and real" (Aristotle, *Magna Moralia,* in *The Works of Aristotle,* 9:1196b).

8. Though Coleridge attacks schools which merely teach pupils to memorize facts, he also criticizes schools which teach children to be overly sceptical smart-alecks before they are ready for true analytic thinking (see *Biographia Literaria,* 1:7-8).

9. Coleridge, *A Lay Sermon,* Addressed to the Higher and Middle Classes on the Existing Distresses and Discontents (1817), in *The Collected Works,* 6:164-66. *Lay Sermons* includes both *A Lay Sermon* and *The Statesman's Manual.* These two works will be cited in the text as *LS* and *SM.* Though Coleridge was pleased with the increase in Bible reading, he wanted his contemporaries to approach the Bible as symbolic literature rather than as literal truth. In order to accomplish this, a reader needed to meditate analytically on the text. It was to further such an approach to the Bible that Coleridge published *Aids to Reflection* in 1825. See Walter Jackson Bate, *Coleridge,* 220, 222-23.

10. Samuel Taylor Coleridge, *On the Constitution of the Church and State,* in *The Collected Works,* 10:48, 52 (hereafter cited as *CCS* in the text); *Biographia Literaria,* 1:120; Coleridge, *Essays on His Times in The Morning Post and The Courier,* in *The Collected Works,* vol. 3, pt. 2, 397 (hereafter cited as *EOT* in the text); Samuel Taylor Coleridge and Robert Southey, *Omniana, or Horae Otiosiores,* intro. Robert Gittings, Centaur Classics (Carbondale: Southern Illinois University Press, 1969), 110. Though Coleridge and Pestalozzi advocated a public school system for children of all social classes, both saw the need to tailor the education somewhat to the future social position of the students. See *Shakespearean Criticism,* 2:295; see also Kate Silber, *Pestalozzi: The Man and His Work,* 156, 188-90.

11. John Lawson and Harold Silver, *A Social History of Education in England,* 179-80; see also Michael Heafford, *Pestalozzi: His Thought and Its Relevance Today,* 82-83; Nora Rea Sinclair, "Coleridge and Education," 413-14, 417. Another obstacle was the antagonism between different religious groups which sponsored schools. In England, the nonconformists were nervous that the Church of England would control a state-supported educational system, and the Church of England feared losing its dominance of education (see Lawson and Silver, *A Social History,* 249). However, the need for a comprehensive system of schools was critical. According to Lawson and Silver, "Early industrial England probably had a literacy rate of under two-thirds for men and nearly a half for women. . . . The first parliamentary committee to consider education, in 1816, estimated that 120,000 London children were entirely without educational facilities" (p. 237).

12. See Robert Southey, *The Origin, Nature, and Object, of the New System of Education,* 161-62; Lawson and Silver, *A Social History,* 242-43, 246; Silber, *Pestalozzi,* 281.

13. Henry Crabb Robinson, *Henry Crabb Robinson on Books and Their Writers*, ed. Edith J. Morley, 3 vols. (London: J. M. Dent, 1938), 1:59. Passages in which Coleridge praises Bell include *Friend*, 1:102–3, 238; *Shakespearean Criticism*, 2:14, 294; *Biographia Literaria*, 2:46.

14. Coleridge also read Southey's *The Origin, Nature, and Object of the New System of Education* (1812) when preparing a lecture on education in Bristol in November 1813 (see *Friend*, 2:29, n. 6). Coleridge praises Southey's book in *Biographia Literaria* (1:45, n.) and in *The Stateman's Manual* (40, n.). However, it is not clear that Coleridge borrowed any ideas, since he had given a lecture on education four years earlier than Southey's book was published. In a letter, Coleridge complains, "Southey's Book is a dilution of my Lecture at the R. I." (*Letters*, 3:474). In fact, Southey cites Coleridge's lecture on education at the Royal Institute (3 May 1808) in which Coleridge praised Bell's system and attacked Lancaster's methods of punishing students. See Southey, *Origin*, 95–96, 192; see also H. C. Robinson's description of the lecture in *Shakespearean Criticism*, 2:14, and the Collier report of a later Coleridge lecture that criticized Lancaster (*Shakespearean Criticism*, 2:111–12).

Like Coleridge, Southey believes that the government should establish a national system to educate all poor children (see *Origin*, 119, 169, 199–200). Southey praises Bell as the man "who has discovered the north-west passage in education" and considers Bell's "new system" to be scientific and "perfect" (169, 194–95). In contrast, Coleridge, as we have seen, is far more sceptical about the efficacy of Bell's method because it does not teach analytic thinking. Another difference is that Southey, unlike Coleridge, does not discuss the role of the imagination in learning.

15. Lawson and Silver, *A Social History*, 175–76, 211; Locke, *Some Thoughts Concerning Education*, 114, 137–38, 198, 204, 272–73, 307.

16. Locke, *Some Thoughts Concerning Education*, 256–58, 280–81, 291.

17. Gordon and White, *Philosophers as Educational Reformers*, 5; Bate, *Coleridge*, 224–25. In a note for *Aids to Reflection*, Coleridge defines a "learned order" similar to the clerisy. See Coleridge, *Aids to Reflection*, vol. 1 of *The Complete Works of Samuel Taylor Coleridge*, ed. W. G. T. Shedd, 7 vols. (New York: Harper, 1884), 293 (hereafter cited as *AR* in the text). According to Jerome McGann, Coleridge shifted from an early emphasis on poets as "the masters of culture" to a later confidence in the clerisy to accomplish this mission. See McGann, *The Romantic Ideology: A Critical Investigation*, 104.

18. Silber, *Pestalozzi*, 206, 131–32, 279–80, 238, 282–92. Andrew Bell visited Pestalozzi's institute at Yverdon in 1816 but was not impressed. Silber contends that allegations that Pestalozzi's method "was 'not properly Christian'" in an orthodox sense prevented its adaptation in many areas of Britain (pp. 282, 305).

19. Heafford, *Pestalozzi*, 40, 53–54, 57; Pestalozzi, "Über Geist und Herz in der Methode," trans. by Heafford, 51; see also Pestalozzi, "Bericht an die Eltern und an das Publikum über den Zustand und die Einrichtungen der Pestalozzischen Anstalt," trans. by Heafford, 53; Silber, *Pestalozzi*, 140.

20. Locke, *Some Thoughts Concerning Education*, 150–51, 156, 185, 276;

Silber, *Pestalozzi*, 162; Heafford, *Pestalozzi*, 46–47; Snyder, *Coleridge on Logic and Learning*, 60.

21. Silber, *Pestalozzi*, 152–53, 228; Lockridge, *Coleridge the Moralist*, 23–24 *et passim*; Coleridge, *The Notebooks of Samuel Taylor Coleridge*, vol. 3, no. 3673. Here Coleridge is translating Fichte's *Das System der Sittenlehre*. In some of Coleridge's later work, he repudiates the search for self-knowledge as too egocentric and recommends, "Ignore thyself, and strive to know thy God!" See "Self-knowledge" (1832), in *Poetical Works*, l. 10.

22. Samuel Taylor Coleridge, *The Watchman*, in *The Collected Works*, 2:132.

23. William Hazlitt, *The Complete Works of William Hazlitt*, 4:4–5 (hereafter cited as *Works of Hazlitt* in the text). See also Hazlitt's letter to his son in 1822, where Hazlitt contends that by studying Latin and Greek, one can overcome selfishness and "carry the mind out of its petty and local prejudices to the idea of a more general humanity." This passage is from "To William Hazlitt, Jr.," February or early March 1822, letter 99, *The Letters of William Hazlitt*, 224. However, Hazlitt reverses himself in the later essay, "On the Ignorance of the Learned" (1821), where he argues that a classical education stresses the lower mental faculties, like rote memorization, and discourages students with active minds from thinking for themselves. Hazlitt believes that many "learned" people rely too much on other people's opinions and have no practical knowledge. He concludes that people can know only matters related to "their daily affairs and experience." All other learning "is affectation and imposture" (*Table-Talk*, in *Works of Hazlitt*, 8:71–77).

24. Coleridge, "The Education of Children," in *Miscellaneous Criticism*, 194–95. This was part of the eleventh lecture of Coleridge's 1818 series (hereafter cited as *MC* in the text).

25. See the following chapter on Hazlitt. See also Bate, *Coleridge*, 163ff.; Lockridge, *Coleridge the Moralist*, 159.

26. Altick, *The English Common Reader*, 74–75, 109–12, 123, 132–33.

27. Wordsworth praises the same imaginative children's books that Coleridge does, including Jack the Giant-Killer, Robin Hood, and St. George, and concludes, "The child, whose love is here, at least, doth reap / One precious gain, that he forgets himself." See William Wordsworth, *The Prelude*, in *Poetical Works*, book 5, 327–28, 336–46. Wordsworth's and Coleridge's criticism of nineteenth-century books for children anticipates the criticism of school inspectors in the 1860s like Matthew Arnold who argue that schoolbooks fail to appeal to children's imaginations and emotions (see Altick, *The English Common Reader*, 154, 159–60).

28. Snyder, *Coleridge on Logic and Learning*, 45.

29. Coleridge was well aware of his tendency to digress. In a notebook entry in 1804, he criticizes himself for using "five hundred more ideas, images, reasons &c than there is any need of" and thus confusing his audience: "my illustrations swallow up my thesis." Coleridge attributes this fault to his tendency to stress "the likenesses" between things (*The Notebooks of Samuel Taylor Coleridge*, 2:no. 2372). Similarly, Coleridge accuses himself of writing "sentences dislocated and perplexed by the parenthetic *Tangle*" in *A Lay Sermon* (see *LS*, 182, n. 2).

30. Walter Pater, "Coleridge," from *Appreciations*, in *Selected Writings of Walter Pater*, ed. Harold Bloom (New York: New American Library, 1974), 147; René Wellek, *A History of Modern Criticism: 1750–1950*, 2:188. Currently, Coleridge's prose is undergoing a reappraisal. Critics like Peter Hoheisel argue that Coleridge *is* methodical: the *Shakespearean Criticism* is unified by Coleridge's examination of "how successfully each play incarnates the idea" that Shakespeare had in mind. This idea usually concerns the central characters' relationship to one another. See Hoheisel, "Coleridge on Shakespeare: Method Amid the Rhetoric," 16, 21. Other writers contend that Coleridge's tendency toward fragmentation is typical of the romantic perception of reality. According to Thomas McFarland, works like *Biographia Literaria* intentionally violate conventional structure. Coleridge's fragments are "momentary epiphanies of a mind continuously in the process of thought." Romanticism contains the "paradox whereby the perception of parts and fragments implies the hypothetical wholeness of infinity." See McFarland, *Romanticism and the Forms of Ruin: Wordsworth, Coleridge, and Modalities of Fragmentation*, 7, 10, 21–22, 25, 29–30ff. Huw Parry Owen analyzes Coleridge's style as an attempt to mirror the flux of reflection for the readers. Owen observes, "He is searching after truth at the same time as he is stating it. Moreover, he intends his readers to share his search, and so share also his experience of ever-increasing mental growth. His style reflects this growth; it registers infallibly each pulse of thought; it moves with the rhythm, not of rhetoric, but of the creative mind itself." See Owen, "The Theology of Coleridge," *Critical Quarterly* 4, 1 (Spring 1962): 59.

One of the best recent defenses of Coleridge's method of writing prose is Kathleen M. Wheeler's *Sources, Processes and Methods in Coleridge's Biographia Literaria*. She argues that all the romantics expect the reader to serve as a "co-creator" of textual meaning. The active and imaginative reader can fuse the apparent fragments of *Biographia Literaria* into a unified whole because Coleridge structures the book to enable the reader to cope with difficult metaphors, interpolated passages from works of other writers and philosophers, paradoxical observations, and unusual word choice and sentence patterns. Coleridge hopes that the reader will be spurred to engage in self-criticism and self-analysis. Wheeler insists, "The reader of the *Biographia* must at all times be aware that his intellectual activity is a primary subject of the text." In fact, she argues that Coleridge's book is "a meta-critique of the reading situation." The purpose of the *Biographia* is to stimulate the reader to continue the dialogue begun by the text: Coleridge prepares the reader to generate his or her own questions and to find possible answers. See Wheeler, *Sources, Processes and Methods in Coleridge's Biographia Literaria* (Cambridge: Cambridge University Press, 1980), 96, 105–9, 112–13, 116–17.

31. R. J. White traces Coleridge's linkage of knowledge and power to Bacon's *Novum Organum*, though Coleridge develops the idea in his own fashion (*Statesman's Manual*, 24, nn. 1 and 2).

32. J. B. Beer notes that Coleridge also associates light imagery with Shakespeare (see *Shakespearean Criticism*, 2:163), effective symbols, and the human imagination. See Beer, *Coleridge the Visionary*, 52, 92–93, 97, 123, 138,

322, n. 93. Reeve Parker observes, "With Coleridge more often than with any other major English critic, speculative insights characteristically veer off into figurative language." See Parker, *Coleridge's Meditative Art*, 71. John R. Nabholtz explains why this happens. Unlike classical rhetoric, which appeals primarily to logic, Coleridge's best essays also require an "intimate response from the reader," a "poetic" involvement. See Nabholtz, *"My Reader My Fellow-Labourer": A Study of English Romantic Prose*, 122–23.

33. Robert DeMaria, Jr., "The Ideal Reader: A Critical Fiction," *PMLA* 93, 3 (May 1978): 466.

34. David Bromwich differentiates between the statements that Coleridge and Hazlitt make about the goals of good literature. "*Coleridge views the mind of the poet, or the text of a poem, as the staging ground for a reconciliation of opposites. Hazlitt sees no reason why opposites should be reconciled, and never leads us to expect this as a formal property of great works*" (italics are Bromwich's). See Bromwich, *Hazlitt: The Mind of a Critic*, 233–34.

35. Bate notes that the events in "The Rime of the Ancient Mariner" are not given "clear-cut" explanations. "When things are left indistinct, as Coleridge understood so well, the mind is more likely to continue to return to them and to find further meanings" (Bate, *Coleridge*, 60). This is also true of Coleridge's prose: he tries to present the reader with hints and images rather than overly specific interpretations. *Shakespearean Criticism* is a good example.

36. This passage is based on the Mishnah, *Pirke Avot* (*Ethics of the Fathers*), ch. 5, no. 18. The Hebrew text describes four different types of scholars. See *Daily Prayer Book* (*Ha-Siddur Ha-Shalem*), ed. and trans. Philip Birnbaum (New York: Hebrew Publishing, 1949), 520.

37. See Lawson and Silver, *A Social History*, 218–19, 237–38, 259–61; Altick, *The English Common Reader*, 45–77, 123, 217–39, 318–47.

38. In *The Citizen of the World*, Goldsmith has his Chinese philosopher, Lien Chi Altangi, complain about the "literary nausea" that results from reading too many books in the same style and on the same subjects. Instead of new ideas, most books offer mere "gaudy images" that do not arouse the mind or the emotions (letter 97, in *Collected Works of Oliver Goldsmith*, 2:387–88).

39. Coleridge may have taken this metaphor from Locke. In the preface to *An Essay Concerning Human Understanding* (1690), Locke compares the mind's search after truth to hunting. In contrast, a person who cannot think for himself is like a beggar. "Thus he who has raised himself above the Alms-Basket, and not content to live lazily on scraps of begg'd Opinions, sets his own Thoughts on work, to find and follow Truth, will . . . not miss the Hunter's Satisfaction; every moment of his Pursuit, will reward his Pains with some Delight." Locke advises his reader to "make use of thy own Thoughts in reading" and to judge for himself, rather than to borrow opinions from others. See Locke, "The Epistle to the Reader," *An Essay Concerning Human Understanding*, ed. Peter H. Nidditch (Oxford: Clarendon Press, 1975), 6–7. Sheridan also condemns lazy readers. In *The Critic*, Puff tells Sneer and Dangle that most theatergoers are indolent and believe the exaggerated newspaper accounts of the success of plays: "the number of those who go thro' the fatigue of judging for themselves is very small indeed!" (1.2, p. 515).

40. Here I have used the more accurate wording and punctuation of Raysor's 1960 edition of *Shakespearean Criticism*, 1:219.

41. Of course, Coleridge's reaction to reviewers was not completely objective: most of his published writing had been roundly criticized by contemporary reviewers. See John O. Hayden, *The Romantic Reviewers, 1802–1824*, 104–11. See also *Biographia Literaria*, 1:2–3, 35–49; *Friend*, 1:20. However, even unfavorable reviews often recognized Coleridge's genius (Hayden, *The Romantic Reviewers*, 111).

42. Similarly, in the essay "Outlines of Taste," Hazlitt asks, "What are the majority of mankind, or even readers, but grown children?" He is especially hard on female readers, like "the milliners' girls in London," who prefer a trashy "Minerva-press novel" to the masterpieces of Sir Walter Scott (*Works of Hazlitt*, 20:386).

43. Quoted in Snyder, *Coleridge on Logic and Learning*, 130–31. Coleridge may have had in mind some passages in Locke's *An Essay Concerning Human Understanding*. Locke complains, "Laziness and Oscitancy in general, or a particular aversion for Books, Study, and Meditation" make most people incapable of "serious thoughts." Thus, men do not examine the reasonableness of their opinions. Locke observes that many men mistake prejudices or received hypotheses for basic principles. Other people allow their "*prevailing passions*" to dominate their minds. However, Locke considers the most prevalent error in evaluating ideas to be "*giving up our Assent to the common received Opinions*, either of our Friends, or Party; Neighbourhood, or Country." Because people are so prone to this mistake, they have never bothered to weigh ideas objectively. Locke insists, "They have no Thought, no Opinion at all" (book 4, ch. 20, 710–15, 718–19). Hazlitt cites this section in "What Is the People?" (*Works of Hazlitt*, 7:272). Coleridge may also have been influenced by the essays of Sir Francis Bacon. In "Of Studies," Bacon advises his public that the proper approach to reading is active: "Read not to contradict and confute, nor to believe and take for granted . . . but to weigh and consider." See Bacon, *Essays and New Atlantis* (Roslyn, N.Y.: Walter J. Black, 1942), 207.

44. Although Hazlitt denigrates Coleridge's attitude toward the common reader, Hazlitt takes a Coleridgean position in his essay "On Pedantry" (originally published in *The Examiner* in 1816 and reprinted in *The Round Table* in 1817). Hazlitt argues that some pedantry is necessary in good writing, because learned jargon prevents literature from being judged by the superficial, uneducated reader. While "universal suffrage" is appropriate in politics, a good writer must be "tried by his peers" (*Works of Hazlitt*, 4:83).

45. McGann, *The Romantic Ideology*, 5, 124.

46. See also Walsh, *Coleridge*, 169; Lockridge, *Coleridge the Moralist*, 164–67.

47. See also *Opus Maximum*, B_2, f. 77, cited in Lockridge, *Coleridge the Moralist*, 231.

48. According to Lockridge, "Coleridge may have in mind Spinoza's belief that in passing from confused to distinct conceptions we experience 'active pleasure' as the mind's vitality is increased" (*Coleridge the Moralist*, 231). Coleridge may also have been influenced by British aesthetic theorists like Archibald Alison, who contends, "There is a pleasure . . . annexed by the

constitution of our nature, to the exercise of imagination." See Alison, *Essays on the Nature and Principles of Taste*, 2 vols. (1790; 2d ed., Edinburgh: George Ramsay, 1811), vol. 1, essay 1, 163.

49. John L. Mahoney interprets the passage in *Biographia Literaria* (2.11–12) to mean that the good writer activates "the whole human psychological process . . . —intellect, imagination, emotion." See Mahoney, *The Whole Internal Universe: Imitation and the New Defense of Poetry in British Criticism, 1660–1830*, 139. Jackson observes, "Shakespeare and Wordsworth represent for Coleridge respectively the ideal poet and the nearest contemporary approach to one. More of his criticism is devoted to these two writers than to all others put together" (*Method and Imagination in Coleridge's Criticism*, 122). For another defense of Wordsworth's poetry, see Lamb's remarks on "The Excursion" in *The Works of Charles and Mary Lamb*, 1:170. Lamb describes a "contract" between readers and writers that is similar to Coleridge's discussion here. See Chapter 5 of this book.

50. K. M. Wheeler stresses that Coleridge views reading as a creative process similar to the poet's act of composition. "The exposure of the illusion of the reader that his reading is a passive receptivity of an already fixed and determined complex of meaning becomes one of Coleridge's prime objectives, as he exhorts his reader to join him, as author, in the shared labour of an imaginative response." See Wheeler, *The Creative Mind in Coleridge's Poetry*, vii–viii.

51. Samuel Johnson also argues that great writers can enable their readers to increase the creative powers. He praises a dialogue in Congreve's *The Mourning Bride* and comments, "He who reads those lines enjoys for a moment the powers of a poet; he feels what he remembers to have felt before, but he feels it with great increase of sensibility." See Johnson, "Congreve," from *Lives of the Poets*, in *Johnson as Critic*, ed. John Wain (London: Routledge & Kegan Paul, 1973), 389. Coleridge goes beyond Johnson to argue that reading activates the mind, not just the emotions.

52. William Shakespeare, *The Complete Works*, ed. G. B. Harrison (1948; rpt. New York: Harcourt, Brace & World, 1968), Prologue for *Henry V*, ll. 11–14, 17–18, 23. All further references to Shakespeare's works will be to this edition. A. W. Schlegel, who influenced the dramatic criticism of the British romantics, argues that the dramas of authors like Shakespeare presuppose spectators with "willing imaginations." Members of the audience "must . . . supply, from their own imaginations, the deficiencies of the representation" (lecture 26, *Lectures on Dramatic Art and Literature*, 430–31). Like Coleridge, Schlegel cites Shakespeare's prologues for *Henry V* as evidence. Note that Schlegel's lectures were originally delivered in 1808 and revised for publication in 1811.

53. Nicoll, *A History of English Drama, 1660–1900*, 3:223–24, 4:61–62; J. A. Appleyard, *Coleridge's Philosophy of Literature: The Development of a Concept of Poetry, 1791–1819* (Cambridge: Harvard University Press, 1965), 149–50, see also 146–47; Paul S. Conklin, *A History of Hamlet Criticism, 1601–1821*, 141, 143; DeMaria, "The Ideal Reader," 470.

54. Hanmer/Anonymous objects to comic material being inserted in a

tragedy: he believes that such a mixture lacks "dignity" and decorum. See Thomas Hanmer/Anonymous, *Some Remarks on the Tragedy of Hamlet Prince of Denmark, Written by Mr. William Shakespeare*, 23–24, 35, 37, 39, 40, 43–44, 47. This was a typical eighteenth-century criticism of Shakespeare. See R. D. Stock, "Shakespeare Criticism," in *Samuel Johnson's Literary Criticism*, 135–36; see also Samuel Johnson, Preface to *The Plays of William Shakespeare* (1765), in *Samuel Johnson's Literary Criticism*, 144–46.

55. E. K. Chambers, *Samuel Taylor Coleridge* (Oxford: Clarendon Press, 1938), 122; cited in Richard M. Fletcher, *English Romantic Drama, 1795–1843: A Critical History*, 62, n. 54.

56. J. R. de J. Jackson, ed., Introduction, *Coleridge: The Critical Heritage*, 7.

57. Fletcher, *English Romantic Drama*, 63–66.

58. Coleridge, *Osorio*, in *The Complete Poetical Works*, ed. Ernest Hartley Coleridge, 2 vols. (1912; rpt. Oxford: Clarendon Press, 1975), vol. 2, 1.247–50.

59. Alan Richardson, *A Mental Theater: Poetic Drama and Consciousness in the Romantic Age* (University Park: The Pennsylvania State University Press, 1988), 2–3, 6, 8, 14, 178.

60. See also Schlegel, lecture 27, *Lectures on Dramatic Art and Literature*, 453. Here Coleridge is developing the ear/eye dichotomy established by Horace and others. See Chapter 1 of this book.

61. Coleridge's remarks about *The Tempest* should be compared to John Holt's *An Attempte to Rescue that Auncient English Poet and Play-Wrighte, Master William Shakespere, From the Maney Errours, faulsely charged on him, by Certaine New-fangled Wittes* (London: Manby & Cox, 1749; rpt. New York: Augustus M. Kelley, 1971). Holt's book consists of disjunct notes on troublesome passages in the comedy. The two critics both discuss Shakespeare as a conscious crafts-man (see Holt, *An Attempte*, 78, 92). However, Coleridge stresses the imagina-tive dimensions of *The Tempest*, while Holt emphasizes its morality. "The Plot is single; the making bad Men penitent, and manifesting that Repentance by restoring a deposed Sovereign Duke to his Dominions: With the additional Lesson, that Patience under Afflictions meets in the End its Reward" (Holt, *An Attempte*, 13–14).

62. Johnson makes this statement in his Preface to *The Plays of William Shakespeare*, in *Samuel Johnson's Literary Criticism*, 152–55. The quotation here is Coleridge's paraphrase.

63. Coleridge may be influenced by John Dennis's analysis of dramatic illusion. In the Preface to *Liberty Asserted* (1704), Dennis describes "that agree-able Delusion into which the Reader willingly and gladly enters, for the sake of his Pleasure" (*The Critical Works of John Dennis*, 1:324). In *A Discourse Upon Comedy*, George Farquhar also portrays the audience as actively engaging in dramatic illusion. Spectators have "strength of supposition and force of fan-cy." See Farquhar, *A Discourse Upon Comedy* (1702), in *A Discourse Upon Com-edy, The Recruiting Officer, and The Beaux Stratagem*, ed. Louis A. Strauss, The Belles Lettres Series (Boston: D. C. Heath, 1914), 31.

64. Coleridge was probably influenced by A. W. Schlegel's analysis of dramatic illusion: "The theatrical as well as every other poetical illusion, is a waking dream, to which we voluntarily surrender ourselves" (lecture 17, in

Lectures on Dramatic Art and Literature, 246). Coleridge's and Schlegel's discussion of dramatic illusion is an advance over the theories of earlier commentators such as Archibald Alison. Unlike the romantics, Alison does not differentiate between the illusion produced by art and the illusion produced by dreams because he views the reader or spectator as passive, in a "powerless state of reverie" (*Essays on the Nature and Principles of Taste*, 1:6, 58). Earl Leslie Griggs defines Coleridge's "willing suspension of disbelief" or "dramatic illusion" as "a state of mind in which the reader or spectator voluntarily relinquishes his usual propensity to judge in terms of possibility or reality." See Griggs, "'The Willing Suspension of Disbelief,'" in *Elizabethan Studies and Other Essays in Honor of George F. Reynolds*, 279.

65. Richard Haven, *Patterns of Consciousness: An Essay on Coleridge*, 164–65, 169, 57, 64, 67, 72–73.

66. K. M. Wheeler demonstrates that "The Rime" merges the illusion of the poem with the reader's situation by "destabilizing reality." She contends, "The framework, the narrating of the tale to the Wedding Guest . . . mirrors the reading situation and breaks down the fixed boundary between art or illusion and reality." See Wheeler, *The Creative Mind*, 42–43.

67. Coleridge may have arrived at his analysis of the Greek chorus independently, but Schlegel is a probable influence (see Raysor, *Shakespearean Criticism*, 1:174, n. 1). Sir Walter Scott explains the effect of the chorus on the audience in similar terms: "In the strains of the Chorus, the actual audience had those feelings suggested to them as if by reflection in a mirror, which the events of the scene ought to produce in their own bosom." See Scott, "An Essay on the Drama" (1819), in *The Miscellaneous Prose Works*, 6:265.

68. Jerome J. McGann, "The Meaning of *The Ancient Mariner*," *Critical Inquiry* 8, 1 (Autumn 1981): 41, 52, 57.

69. Katharine Cooke, *Coleridge*, 79.

70. Patricia M. Ball, "The Waking Dream: Coleridge and the Drama," in *The Morality of Art: Essays Presented to G. Wilson Knight by His Colleagues and Friends*, 168. Coleridge may have been influenced by *Some Remarks on the Tragedy of Hamlet*. Hanmer/Anonymous argues that the audience must voluntarily suspend disbelief: "No Dramatick Piece can affect us but by the Delusion of our Imagination." The anonymous author also defends Shakespeare from attacks on his violation of the unities of time and place: "For this Delusion is never perform'd in direct Defiance of our Reason; on the contrary, our Reason helps on the Deceit" (pp. 53–54). In *Some Remarks on the Tragedy of Hamlet*, the term "delusion" is used when Johnson or Coleridge would use "illusion." See the Introduction by Clarence D. Thorpe, p. 6.

71. Patricia Ball observes that because the reader or spectator must exert his will to suspend disbelief, "if the poet fails to convince, disbelief is not suspended, the work is exposed to adverse criticism" ("The Waking Dream," 167).

72. Schlegel agrees: "To lie morosely on the watch to detect every circumstance that may violate an apparent reality which, strictly speaking, can never be attained, is in fact a proof of inertness of imagination and an incapacity for mental illusion" (lecture 27, *Lectures on Dramatic Art and Literature*, 453).

73. See Lamb's essay, "On the Artificial Comedy of the Last Century," in *Works of Lamb*, 2:142. See also Janet Ruth Heller, "The Breeze and Sunshine: A Study of Lamb's Essay 'On the Artificial Comedy of the Last Century,'" *The Charles Lamb Bulletin*, n.s. 16 (October 1976): 149–56.

74. Bate, *Coleridge*, 148; see also M. H. Abrams, *The Mirror and the Lamp: Romantic Theory and the Critical Tradition*, 213; Donohue, *Dramatic Character in the English Romantic Age* (Princeton: Princeton University Press, 1970), 311; Badawi, "Coleridge's Formal Criticism of Shakespeare's Plays," *Essays in Criticism* 10, 2 (April 1960): 150, 152.

75. Joseph Addison, in *The Spectator*, no. 44 (20 April 1711), 1:186. Coleridge may also have derived this idea from Hanmer/Anonymous, who argues that the opening scenes of dramas should be constructed "with the greatest Simplicity, that so our Passions may be work'd upon by Degrees." Though the anonymous author does not go into as much detail as Coleridge presents in discussing act 1 of *Hamlet*, he does anticipate Coleridge in emphasizing that the dialogue before the Ghost's entrance "creates an Awe and Attention in the Spectators" that prepares them for the supernatural visitor (*Some Remarks on the Tragedy of Hamlet*, 8–9). Like Coleridge, Hanmer/Anonymous emphasizes how each scene contributes to the organic whole. "There is not one Scene in this Play but what some way or other conduces towards the *Denoüement* of the Whole; and thus the Unity of Action is indisputably kept up by every Thing tending to what we may call the main Design, and it all hangs by Consequence so close together, that no Scene can be omitted, without Prejudice to the Whole" (p. 59).

76. In a 1980 production of *Hamlet* by the Royal Court Theatre in London, the opening scene was deleted. See Jack Kroll, "The Hamlet of Our Time," *Newsweek*, 2 June 1980, p. 92. Perhaps directors like Richard Eyre should read Coleridge's analysis of this important sequence.

77. Raysor notes that Schlegel is the source for this last remark about pacing (*Shakespearean Criticism*, 2:273, n. 1).

78. Thomas Whateley, *Remarks on Some of the Characters of Shakespere*, 99–100.

79. Alfred North Whitehead, "The Aims of Education," in *The Aims of Education and Other Essays*, 13–14.

80. William G. Perry, Jr., *Forms of Intellectual and Ethical Development in the College Years: A Scheme* (New York: Holt, Rinehart and Winston, 1970), 33, 35–36, 39, 58–59 and *passim*.

81. Perry, *Forms of Intellectual and Ethical Development*, 211–12.

82. John P. De Cecco, *The Psychology of Learning and Instruction: Educational Psychology* (Englewood Cliffs, N.J.: Prentice-Hall, 1968), 464; Lee J. Cronbach, "The Logic of Experiments on Discovery," in *Learning by Discovery*, ed. L. S. Shulman and E. R. Keislar (Chicago: Rand McNally, 1966), 90; Jerome S. Bruner, "The Act of Discovery," 21–32.

83. Bruner, "The Act of Discovery," 23, 26–30.

84. Jackson, "Coleridge on Dramatic Illusion and Spectacle in the Performance of Shakespeare's Plays," 14–16.

Notes for Chapter 4:
*Hazlitt's Appeal to Readers in
His Drama Criticism*

1. Irving Babbitt, *Rousseau and Romanticism*, 225; Babbitt, "On Being Creative," in *On Being Creative and Other Essays*, 18; M. H. Abrams, *The Mirror and the Lamp*, 7, 134, 140 *et passim*; René Wellek, *A History of Modern Criticism, 1750–1950*, 2:203–04; Frank Kermode, *Romantic Image* (London: Routledge & Kegan Paul, 1957), vii, 2, 7, 28, 160. The German writer, Friedrich Schlegel, was among the first to contrast his era's subjectivity with the ancient Greeks' objectivity. Unlike Babbitt et al., Schlegel felt that the modern romantic values were *superior* to those of the Greeks. Abrams and Wellek demonstrate some awareness that the romantics cannot be confined to completely subjective categories. Abrams concedes in the last chapter of *The Mirror and the Lamp* that most of the British romantics "den[y] that the judgment of poetic value ought to be severed from the consideration of the effects on the reader" (p. 328). While Wellek considers Coleridge "almost oblivious of his audience," he believes that Hazlitt's essays reveal "a constant awareness of the needs and limitations of the middle-class audience" (2:188, 198).

2. George Saintsbury, *A History of Criticism and Literary Taste in Europe*, 3:258; William K. Wimsatt, Jr., and Cleanth Brooks, *Literary Criticism: A Short History*, 493–94; Charles I. Patterson, Jr., "Hazlitt's Criticism in Retrospect," *Studies in English Literature 1500–1900* 21, 4 (Autumn 1981): 648, 650–51, 663.

3. Walter Jackson Bate, *From Classic to Romantic: Premises of Taste in Eighteenth-Century England*, 143, 165; Bate, ed., *Criticism: The Major Texts* (New York: Harcourt, Brace & World, 1952), 282 (Hazlitt attacks Rousseau's egotism in *The Complete Works of Hazlitt*, 4:88, 92–93); see also Bate, *Coleridge*, 165; Morris Eaves, "Romantic Expressive Theory and Blake's Idea of the Audience," *PMLA* 95, 5 (October 1980): 797–98; John L. Mahoney, *The Whole Internal Universe: Imitation and the New Defense of Poetry in British Criticism, 1660–1830*, 124; Peter Hoheisel, "Coleridge on Shakespeare: Method Amid the Rhetoric," 15–23; Richard Haven, "The Romantic Art of Charles Lamb," *ELH* 30, 2 (June 1963): 137–46; John Nabholtz, *"My Reader My Fellow-Labourer": A Study of English Romantic Prose*, 35–66. In *The Romantic Reviewers, 1802–1824*, John O. Hayden observes that many of the best works of Wordsworth, Lamb, Hunt, Byron, and Shelley received frequent and favorable reviews. Early nineteenth-century critics "overwhelmingly favored the new literature of their age." Coleridge and Hazlitt did not fare as well: most of Coleridge's publications were damned, and Hazlitt's essays were often condemned because of his freethinking. However, "*Characters of Shakespear's Plays* (1817), the *Lectures Chiefly on the Dramatic Literature of the Age of Elizabeth* (1820), *Table Talk* (1821–1822), and *Characteristics* (1823) . . . enjoyed generally favorable receptions" (pp. 2, 74, 111, 204, 215). Hayden's evidence indicates that the early nineteenth-century public did *not* feel alienated from its best writers. José Ortega y Gasset has even gone so far as to describe romantic art in general as "made for the masses inasmuch as it is not art but an extract from life." He

points out that the romantics' works were published in "large editions" and were easy for the public to understand, unlike twentieth-century art. See Ortega, "The Dehumanization of Art," in *The Dehumanization of Art and Other Essays on Art, Culture, and Literature*, trans. Helene Weyl (Princeton: Princeton University Press, 1948, 1968), 5–6, 12, *et passim*. While this analysis is also extreme, it provides a good counterweight to Kermode's claims. Note that Ortega is no more sympathetic than Babbitt to the romantic's "private upper-middle-class emotions, his major and minor sorrows, his yearnings, . . . and, in case he was English, his reveries behind his pipe" (Ortega, "The Dehumanization of Art," 30). Mahoney argues that late nineteenth-century writers like Wilde, Swinburne, and Pater are closer to a "purely expressive theory of art" than the romantics are (*The Whole Internal Universe*, 152–53).

4. William Hazlitt, *The Complete Works of William Hazlitt*, 1:1, 3; 20:170; 18:345 (hereafter cited as *Works of Hazlitt* in the text). Hazlitt may be influenced here by Pope's Preface to his translation of *The Iliad* (1715). Pope praises Homer's invention and the resulting "fire and rapture which is so forcible in Homer that no man of a true poetical spirit is master of himself while he reads him. . . . The reader is hurried out of himself by the force of the poet's imagination." See Pope, "Preface to the Translation of the *Iliad*," in *Literary Criticism of Alexander Pope*, ed. Bertrand A. Goldgar, Regents Critics Series (Lincoln: University of Nebraska, 1965), 108. Mahoney contrasts Hazlitt's view of the mind as active to the passive model of Hobbes and Locke. The latter viewed the mind "as a kind of receptacle of impressions received from the world outside." In contrast, Hazlitt's "emphasis is on the imagination's activity, on its ability to project itself into the future, to identify with another experience, another personality." See Mahoney, "The Futuristic Imagination: Hazlitt's Approach to *Romeo and Juliet*," 65.

5. Coleridge had also praised Shakespeare for this ability to project himself into other identities and referred to the bard as a "Proteus" (*Shakespearean Criticism*, 1:37, 218; 2:17, 81, 137, 333). Hazlitt was not the first to use the criteria of passion and sympathy in evaluating drama. Critics like Dryden, Rapin, and Dennis used the term "concernment" to refer to the audience's solicitude for the heroes' sufferings. See Eric Rothstein, "English Tragic Theory in the Late Seventeenth Century," 317–19. Earl R. Wasserman traces the evolution of drama criticism that departed from the position of writers like Hume, Johnson, Descartes, and Hobbes. While Hobbes stressed self-love and the spectators' need to feel themselves at a safe distance from the dangerous plights of tragic heroes, Shaftesbury and the members of the Scottish school emphasize the audience's sympathy for protagonists and its closeness to their suffering. Edmund Burke, an English author whom Hazlitt admired, took this position. See Wasserman, "The Pleasures of Tragedy," 293, 297–99, 303, 305–6. Walter Jackson Bate found that the romantics were influenced by the Scottish intuitional school of moralists, which included Alexander Gerard, John Ogilvie, James Beattie, and Hugh Blair. These men believed that humans have an innate "'sensibility of heart,' by means of which, in poetry and drama, 'we become interested for some of the persons represented, and sympathize with every change in their condition.'" See Bate, "The Sym-

pathetic Imagination in Eighteenth-Century English Criticism," *ELH* 12, 2 (June 1945): 153, and also 144-51. Bate is quoting Gerard's *Essay on Taste* (1759). Thus, the sensitive reader experiences emotions similar to those of the characters. See also Bate, *From Classic to Romantic*, 132ff.

6. Hazlitt may have been influenced by Schlegel's remarks about sympathy in *Lectures on Dramatic Art and Literature*. Schlegel also emphasizes the need to transcend one's egotism when experiencing a tragedy and uses this transcendance as a measure of good drama (lecture 5, p. 68). Like Hazlitt, Coleridge criticizes *Measure for Measure* because it thwarts the sympathy of the reader. In addition, Coleridge objects to the lack of poetic justice in the play's conclusion. He terms *Measure for Measure* "a hateful work," unlike the bard's other dramas, which Coleridge considers "delightful." He identifies "unamiable" Isabella and "detestable" Claudio as problematic characters and thinks that Angelo should be punished (*Shakespearean Criticism*, 2:352). Both Hazlitt and Coleridge also use the criterion of sympathy in evaluating and championing *Richard II*. Hazlitt contrasts this history play with *Richard III*: while Richard III alienates the audience by his bestial conduct, Richard II's vulnerability generates "pity." Because his anguish links Richard II to the distresses of ordinary people, "we sympathize with him accordingly." For this reason, Hazlitt prefers *Richard II* to the other play (*Works of Hazlitt*, 4:272-73). Similarly, Coleridge emphasizes that despite Richard II's flaws, the king wins "our pity; for we find him much beloved by those who knew him best," especially his wife and Bishop Carlisle (*Shakespearean Criticism*, 2:281). Although both critics stress that Richard II gains the reader's sympathy, they have different explanations for this identification: Hazlitt emphasizes the king's sufferings, but Coleridge emphasizes Richard's close relationships.

7. William Hazlitt, "Schlegel on the Drama" (a review of John Black's 1815 translation), *Edinburgh Review* 26 (February 1816): 98. The Howe edition of *Works of Hazlitt* incorrectly reads "ingenius" (16:90).

8. M. H. Abrams traces to Longinus Hazlitt's efforts "to formulate a verbal equivalent for the aesthetic effects of the work under consideration" (*The Mirror and the Lamp*, 135).

9. Herschel Baker, *William Hazlitt*, 308. Similarly, Joseph W. Donohue, Jr., praises Hazlitt's "total involvement in the passionate experience of art" (*Dramatic Character in the English Romantic Age* [Princeton: Princeton University Press, 1970], 324). According to Arthur M. Eastman, *Characters of Shakespear's Plays* "speaks with none of the dull anonymity of the modern handbook but vibrates with personal enthusiasm and conviction. It starts the reader very well on his way and leaves it to him—as a good teacher ought—to arrive on his own." See Eastman, *A Short History of Shakespearean Criticism*, 109.

10. Leigh Hunt, " 'Characters of Shakespear's Plays,' by William Hazlitt," *The Examiner*, 26 October 1817, in *Leigh Hunt's Dramatic Criticism: 1808-1831*, 169, 170. Goethe also recommends that literary criticism "be done from a certain one-sided enthusiasm, or from a loving interest in the person and the work. . . . Sympathy and enjoyment in what we see are in fact the only reality." See "On Criticism" (1821-1824), in *Goethe's Literary Essays*, 141-42.

11. Lamb, unpublished review of *Table Talk*, first printed in *Lamb as Critic*,

300–307. Lamb contrasts Addison to Johnson, Hazlitt, and others because Addison avoided the personal touch and substituted "cold generalities." As a result, his essays lack humor and unity. The reader cannot sympathize with such a secretive, faceless author (pp. 300–301). Similarly, Lamb praises the personal involvement of writers like Bishop Gilbert Burnet and contrasts this with the "indifference" of writers like David Hume. See Lamb, "C. L. to Manning," 1 March 1800, letter 60, in *The Letters of Charles and Mary Anne Lamb*, 1:187–88 (hereafter cited as *Letters* in the text). However, Lamb does have some mixed feelings about Hazlitt's subjectivity. On the one hand, he finds Hazlitt overly "partisan" as a critic, but, on the other hand, Lamb praises his friend's "fearless" development of original ideas (see the review of *Table Talk* in *Lamb as Critic*, 307). W. P. Albrecht lauds Hazlitt for successfully "identifying the reader with a tragic character" in his essays. See Albrecht, *Hazlitt and the Creative Imagination*, 105. Similarly, John Kinnaird finds Hazlitt's style "freshly readable; for it implicates the reader in the act of criticism more intimately than ever before" (*William Hazlitt: Critic of Power*, 370).

12. William Hazlitt, *The Letters of William Hazlitt*, letter 58, p. 158.

13. Park, *Hazlitt and the Spirit of the Age: Abstraction and Critical Theory*, 36, 38, 48, 74, 109, 145, 161–67, 170, 194, 196.

14. Schlegel had written in his *Lectures on Dramatic Art and Literature*, "So little is he [Shakespeare] disposed to caricature, that rather, it may be said, many of his traits are almost too nice and delicate for the stage, that they can only be made available by a great actor, and fully understood by an acute audience" (lecture 23, p. 371). Hazlitt quotes this passage in his 1816 review of Schlegel's *Lectures* (see *Works of Hazlitt*, 16:95). In a letter to Elizabeth Montagu, Dr. James Beattie wrote, "I have often seen Hamlet performed by the underlings of the theatre, but none of these seemed to understand what they were about. Hamlet's character, though perfectly natural, is so very uncommon, that few, even of our critics, can enter into it." See Paul S. Conklin, *A History of Hamlet Criticism, 1601–1821*, 65, which cites this passage. Similarly, Leigh Hunt points out that, from an actor's perspective, the Prince is a difficult role because it demands skill in both tragedy and comedy. See Leigh Hunt, "Mr. Elliston" from *Critical Essays* (1807), in *Dramatic Essays*, 87. See also Chapter 1 of this book for a brief history of objections to the performance of tragedy.

15. Whately, *Remarks on Some of the Characters of Shakespere*, 99–100.

16. Howe observes, "The concluding paragraph is added from *The Examiner*, January 21, 1816" (*Works of Hazlitt*, 4:399, n.).

17. Elisabeth Schneider, *The Aesthetics of William Hazlitt: A Study of the Philosophical Basis of His Criticism*, 137.

18. Here, Hazlitt is developing a concept already outlined by Coleridge in an 1811 lecture: "The ordinary reader . . . often feels that some real trait of his own has been caught, that some nerve has been touched; and he knows that it has been touched by the vibration he experiences—a thrill, which tells us that, by becoming better acquainted with the poet, we have become better acquainted with ourselves. In the plays of Shakespeare every man sees himself, without knowing that he does so" (*Shakespearean Criticism*, 2:163). Likewise,

Coleridge recommended to his audience at the Bristol lectures of 1813–1814 that in order to understand the complex character of Hamlet, "we should reflect on the constitution of our own minds" (2:272). The tragedy requires an introspective reader.

19. Mahoney argues that Hazlitt and other romantics viewed the borders of genres as more fluid than neoclassical or twentieth-century critics do. The romantics mixed the familiar essay with the literary treatise to expand their audience and convey their insights more informally ("William Hazlitt: The Essay as Vehicle for the Romantic Critic," Romanticism and the Borders of Genre, MLA Convention, Chicago, 30 December 1985).

20. Hanmer/Anonymous found the delay in Hamlet's vengeance ridiculous. By retaining Hamlet's madness from the source chronicles, where it is more clearly motivated and connected to the delay, Shakespeare "has fallen into an Absurdity; for there appears no Reason at all in Nature, why the young Prince did not put the Usurper to Death as soon as possible, especially as *Hamlet* [sic] is represented as a Youth so brave, and so careless of his own life" (*Some Remarks on the Tragedy of Hamlet Prince of Denmark, Written by Mr. William Shakespeare*, 33). William Richardson anticipates Hazlitt and the other romantics in defending Hamlet from charges of immorality and defending Shakespeare's portrayal of the prince's madness and delay in avenging his father's murder. Despite the hero's strange behavior, "every reader, and every audience, have hitherto taken part with Hamlet." Like the romantics, Richardson uses psychological analysis to explain Hamlet's conduct, arguing that the prince (1) is trapped in a difficult situation and (2) has a very sensitive soul. This combination produces hesitation and spurts of revenge, the outward manifestations of the character's inner struggle. Richardson justifies his subtle analysis by pointing out that Shakespeare's dramas are complex: "The lines and colours are, indeed, very fine; and not very obvious to cursory observation. The beauties of Shakespeare, like genuine beauty of every kind, are often veiled; they are not forward nor obtrusive." The reader must penetrate these veils in order to understand the bard's characters completely. See Richardson, "Additional Observations on Shakespeare's Dramatic Character of Hamlet; in a Letter to a Friend," in *Essays on Shakespeare's Dramatic Characters of Richard the Third, King Lear, and Timon of Athens. To Which Are Added, an Essay on the Faults of Shakespeare; and Additional Observations on the Character of Hamlet* (London: J. Murray, 1784; rpt. New York: AMS Press, 1974), 150–52, 157–58, 162.

21. Lamb, "Imperfect Sympathies" and "On the Artificial Comedy of the Last Century," *Essays of Elia* (1823), in *Works of Lamb*, 2:59–60, 63–64, 141–44, 146. These essays were first published in 1821 and 1822 in the *London Magazine*. Lamb revised them and gave them new titles for the first edition of *Elia*.

22. Stuart M. Tave argues that the "amiable misanthrope" was a conventional character in eighteenth-century novels and plays. See Tave, *The Amiable Humorist: A Study in the Comic Theory and Criticism of the Eighteenth and Early Nineteenth Centuries*, 165, 276, n. 2. However, Hazlitt is unique in applying this oxymoron to Hamlet.

23. According to Nabholtz, Hazlitt does not present readers with only

one side of an issue. Instead, "Hazlit apparently wants the reader to participate in the argumentative process by imaginatively living through the powerful opposing evidence." Furthermore, Hazlitt shows us how his own mind analyzes an issue. Thus, the reader becomes "the witness to or the participant in the process of arriving at a truth." While Hazlitt's early essays have relatively smooth expositions and conclude "with a sense of finality and completion," by 1820 he prefers to explore more than one possibility and experiments with irony and "contrasting perspectives." These later essays end with tension and lack firm resolutions in order to provoke the reader to think more about the subject. "By manipulations of style and a persistently paradoxical method of argument, Hazlitt left the reader unbalanced and unsettled in his ordinary 'logical' response to a topic and thus prepared for fresh confrontation" (*"My Reader, My Fellow-Labourer,"* 4, 44, 47, 54–55, 59).

24. In the essay "Of Tragedy" (1757), David Hume stresses the paradox "that the same object of distress which pleases in a tragedy, were it really set before us, would give the most unfeigned uneasiness." He analyzes how tragedy gives pleasure by means of its eloquence, portrayal of the passions, development of conflict and suspense, and convincing imitation of human life. However, the audience must be aware that the performance is fictitious; otherwise, our distress would outweigh our pleasure. Hume emphasizes this need for aesthetic distance. See Hume, "Of Tragedy," in *Four Dissertations* (New York: Garland Publishing, 1970), 188–89. Samuel Johnson goes even further in his Preface to *The Plays of William Shakespeare* (1765). He dismisses those who censure the bard for neglecting the unities and insists,

> It is false, that any representation is mistaken for reality; that any dramatick fable in its materiality was ever credible, or, for a single moment, was ever credited.
>
> . . .
>
> The truth is, that the spectators are always in their senses, and know, from the first act to the last, that the stage is only a stage, and that the players are only players. (In *Samuel Johnson's Literary Criticism,* 152–53)

This awareness of fiction allows the audience to distance itself from a play's action and characters.

In contrast to the eighteenth-century English critics, romantic writers such as Coleridge, Lamb, and Hazlitt insist that to fully appreciate a drama, especially tragedy, the audience must become as *involved* as possible with the protagonists. Instead of reminding themselves that a scene is fictitious, the readers or spectators must accept its imaginative reality and validity. The ideal audience actively cooperates with the playwright to produce a special state of illusion.

Notes for Chapter 5:
Lamb and Reader-Response Criticism

1. Wolfgang Iser has coined the term "the implied reader" to parallel Wayne Booth's concept of "the implied author" in *The Rhetoric of Fiction*. Booth

discusses the author's attempts to shape a reader but calls the projected audience the "image of his reader," the "mock reader" (Walker Gibson's term), or "the postulated reader." See Wayne C. Booth, *The Rhetoric of Fiction* (Chicago: University of Chicago Press, 1961), 138, 177; Wolfgang Iser, *The Implied Reader: Patterns of Communication in Prose Fiction from Bunyan to Beckett*.

2. Jack J. Jorgens, *Shakespeare on Film* (Bloomington: Indiana University Press, 1977), 12; Siegfried Kracauer, *Theory of Film: The Redemption of Physical Reality*, x-xi, 105–6, 229; Seymour Chatman, "What Novels Can Do That Films Can't (and Vice Versa)," *Critical Inquiry* 7, 1 (Autumn 1980): 126; Chatman, *Story and Discourse: Narrative Structure in Fiction and Film*, 106, 118–19; Iser, *The Implied Reader*, 283. This perspective on contemporary films is not limited to critics in academia. Movie reviewer David Denby laments in *The Atlantic Monthly* that "the word . . . has been banished from the cinema." Similarly, Jim Fergus, writing for *Newsweek*, argues that films are typical of our "Lite Age" of superficiality. While movies with profound ideas fail at the box office, crowds rush to see the "nonstop action" of *Indiana Jones and the Temple of Doom*. According to Fergus, the popularity of this kind of film results from "our seriously foreshortened attention span, our modern preference for action, adventure and special effects instead of the old heavy stuff of theme, plot and character development." Such frivolous works "anesthetize" the viewers, making them passive. See Denby, "Stranger in a Strange Land: A Moviegoer at the Theater," *The Atlantic Monthly*, January 1985, p. 50; Fergus, "When Litening Strikes," *Newsweek*, 24 December 1984, p. 10.

3. William K. Wimsatt and Cleanth Brooks, *Literary Criticism: A Short History*, 494.

4. Lamb adapted the contrast of the city and the country that he used in the letter to Lloyd in a later essay, "The Londoner," which was originally published in *The Reflector* in 1802 and revised in 1818. In both passages, he expresses a preference for the theater crowds over pastoral scenes. See *The Works of Charles and Mary Lamb*, 1:39 (hereafter cited as *Works of Lamb* in the text). According to Roy Park, two-thirds of Lamb's literary criticism concerns drama (*Lamb as Critic*, 17). For a discussion of Lamb's views on comedy of manners, see Janet Ruth Heller, "The Breeze and Sunshine: A Study of Lamb's Essay 'On the Artificial Comedy of the Last Century,'" *The Charles Lamb Bulletin*, n.s. 16 (October 1976): 149–56.

5. John I. Ades, "Charles Lamb, Shakespeare, and Early Nineteenth-Century Theater," *PMLA* 85, 3 (May 1970): 519. The passage referred to by Ades occurs in Lamb's essay "On Some of the Old Actors," in *Works of Lamb*, 2:133–34.

6. Lamb may have been influenced by Dryden's view of "mob readers" in "Dedication of the Aeneis" (1697). Here, Dryden defines "mob readers" as "such things as are our upper-gallery audience in a playhouse, who like nothing but the husk and rind of wit" (*Essays of John Dryden*, 2:223). See also Chapter 1 of this book for other deprecating remarks about the new readers and playgoers. Despite the condemnation of "readers against the grain," Lamb does not oppose literacy per se. Like Hazlitt, he believes that readers can better themselves by extending their sympathy to real and imaginary

people. In an 1801 essay, Lamb defends Sunday newspapers, which were designed for poor people, because the papers familiarize readers with events of national importance and, *"what is more valuable"* (italics are Lamb's), chronicle the affairs of ordinary people. The Sunday periodicals ennoble the public by expanding the readers' "sympathy with *strangers* and persons *unknown.*" See Lamb, "What Is Jacobinism?," *The Albion*, 30 June 1801, p. 3; rpt. in *Young Charles Lamb, 1775–1802*, by Winifred F. Courtney, The Gotham Library (New York: New York University Press, 1982), 345. Similarly, Lamb argues that the circulating libraries' copies of *Tom Jones* and *The Vicar of Wakefield* soothe care-worn poor people after a hard day. However, he dislikes hearing newspapers and action-packed novels read out loud (see *Works of Lamb*, 2:173, 175).

7. Lamb, unpublished review of *Table Talk*, first printed in *Lamb as Critic*, 302.

8. Despite Lamb's harsh words for Sterne here, there is evidence that the eighteenth-century novelist shared Lamb's commitment to leaving much to the reader's imagination. Sterne writes, "The truest respect which you can pay to the reader's understanding, is to halve this matter amicably, and leave him something to imagine, in his turn, as well as yourself. For my own part, I am eternally paying him compliments of this kind, and do all that lies in my power to keep his imagination as busy as my own." See Laurence Sterne, *The Life and Opinions of Tristram Shandy, Gentleman* (1759–1767), ed. Ian Watt, Riverside Editions (Boston: Houghton Mifflin, 1965), book 2, ch. 11, p. 83.

9. Stanley Eugene Fish, *Surprised by Sin: The Reader in Paradise Lost*, x, 31, 344; Walter J. Slatoff, *With Respect to Readers: Dimensions of Literary Response*, 7, 37, 66, 143; the quotation cited by Slatoff is from Coleridge, *Biographia Literaria*, 2:12; Iser, *The Implied Reader*, 43, 56. See also Fish, "Literature in the Reader: Affective Stylistics," in *Self-Consuming Artifacts: The Experience of Seventeenth-Century Literature*, 386, 389.

10. An examination of contemporary reviews reveals some specimens of the narrow-mindedness that Lamb berates. While some reviewers appreciate the originality of writers like Wordsworth and Coleridge, others, like William Roberts of *The British Review*, object to Romantic poetry because it departs from "common sense." Roberts probably speaks for a segment of the reading public when he argues that a good poet must shape his "chaotic originalities" until they "look like natives of our own minds, and easily . . . mix with the train of our own conceptions." See *The British Review*, August 1816, cited in J. R. de J. Jackson, ed., *Coleridge: The Critical Heritage*, 221–22. Clearly, such logic violates the author/reader contract by imposing too much control over the writer's imagination.

11. Lamb's own dramas emphasize the characters' minds, not external action. Wayne McKenna concludes, "Lamb sacrificed too much stage effect in favour of the exploration of the thoughts of his characters. He allowed them scant opportunity for action." See Wayne McKenna, *Charles Lamb and the Theatre* (Gerrards Cross, England: Colin Smythe, 1978), 60. The letter cited is Lamb's "Letter to Samuel Rogers," December 1833, *The Letters of Charles Lamb to which are added those of his sister Mary Lamb*, 3:394. Coleridge uses a similar vocabulary in a comparison of pictorial art and literature in his lectures. He

argues that Shakespeare's characters are not "the mere portrait of an individual" but rather represent a general class of people. Furthermore, Coleridge views painting as a more circumscribed form of imitation. Pictorial art is "narrow" and "limited," while poetry has "boundless power." Although painting is restricted as an imitation because its images have a "distinct form," poetry stirs the mind because literature "rejects all control, all confinement." Coleridge contrasts Milton's imaginative depiction of Death in *Paradise Lost* with the typical painter's rendition of a skeleton. Milton's poetry keeps the reader's mind active, while the painter's skeleton lowers the brain "to the merest passivity" (*Shakespearean Criticism*, 2:130, 138–39).

An examination of *The Boydell Shakespeare Prints* (1802–1803) and other paintings of the era confirms Lamb's objections. Except for pictures of Lady Macbeth, the heroines look too much alike: they are sweet, young, and pretty with long hair in ringlets and innocent facial expressions. Many of the paintings stress the women's beautiful long gowns and fancy hats more than their faces. In general, the illustrations fail to capture the individuality and psychological depth of Shakespeare's female characters. See *The Boydell Shakespeare Prints*, introd. A. E. Santaniello (1802–1803; rpt. New York: Benjamin Blom, 1968); see also *A Brush with Shakespeare: The Bard in Painting, 1780–1910* (Montgomery, Ala.: Montgomery Museum of Fine Arts, 1985).

John Boydell was an important publisher of engraved prints. He hoped to both make money and further British historical painting by establishing the Shakespeare Gallery on Pall Mall and by printing a newly illustrated edition of Shakespeare's works. However, Boydell did not turn a profit because the fighting with France (1793–1815) disrupted his European trade and imitators stole some of his business.

Lamb was not the only one to find the gallery disappointing. In the print *Shakespeare Sacrificed; or The Offering to Avarice,* James Gillray satirized the project. Despite the criticism, Richard D. Altick argues, Boydell's Shakespeare Gallery strongly influenced people's taste: "It determined their visual conception of Shakespeare's characters and scenes as fatefully as Bowdler's edition, published in 1818, formed their notion of what he wrote." See Altick, *The Shows of London*, 106–8.

Like Lamb and Gillray, Hazlitt disliked the paintings in the Shakespeare Gallery. In an 1815 essay, Hazlitt argues that these pictures "disturb and distort all the previous notions we had imbibed from reading Shakespear." He mentions this in conjunction with his attack on what he considered a "farcical" and distorted production of *The Tempest* at Covent Garden. (*The Complete Works of William Hazlitt*, 5:234–35).

12. John R. Nabholtz comments, "All of Lamb's Essays of the Imagination are 'dramatic' in their structure and procedure. . . . They are the working out before our eyes, in the rhetoric, syntax and structure of the Essays, of the experience of imaginative liberation itself, the dissolving and dissipating of one perspective on experience, and the creation of a new perspective." See Nabholtz, "Drama and Rhetoric in Lamb's Essays of the Imagination," *Studies in English Literature* 12, 4 (Autumn 1972): 685; see also Nabholtz, *"My Reader My Fellow-Labourer": A Study of English Romantic Prose*, 10–34.

13. Later in "On the Tragedies of Shakspeare," Lamb returns to Garrick, castigating him for his "miserable cravings after applause." The essayist's animosity seems excessive in these passages, and I think he loses some of the reader's sympathy. Lamb has a better point in the following paragraphs, where he scolds Garrick for interpolating inferior scenes written by Nahum Tate and Colley Cibber in the "matchless" tragedies of Shakespeare (*Works of Lamb*, 1:104–5, 107).

Like Lamb, Thomas Babington Macaulay believes that the actor cannot convey the essence of a dramatic text. "The painter, the sculptor, and the actor can exhibit no more of human passion and character than that small portion which overflows into the gesture and the face, always an imperfect, often a deceitful, sign of that which is within. The deeper and more complex parts of human nature can be exhibited by means of words alone." See Macaulay, *Critical and Historical Essays*, ed. A. J. Grieve, 2 vols. (1907; rpt. London: J. M. Dent; New York: E. P. Dutton, 1961), 2:628. The passage quoted is from Macaulay's review "Moore's Life of Lord Byron," which originally appeared in the *Edinburgh Review* in 1831. Clearly, Macaulay shares the romantics' interest in a character's psychology.

In addition to objecting to actors because they are superficial by definition, Lamb and Hazlitt contend that actors often obscure the playwright's words by inappropriate or inconsistent presentations that fail to elucidate a character's personality and motivation. Even the best actors have this flaw. For example, Lamb argues that Kemble's stiff and cold acting in William Godwin's *Antonio* obscured the tragic hero's "*words*" for the inattentive audience (*Works of Lamb*, 2:293–94). Similarly, Hazlitt faults Kean for not "concentrating all the lines of the character, as drawn by Shakespear." Hazlitt would prefer a more sustained and "impassioned" Richard III, "with fewer glancing lights, pointed transitions, and pantomimic evolutions" (*Works of Hazlitt*, 5:181). As usual, Hazlitt views pantomimic acting as the opposite of true drama.

14. Coleridge made a similar remark: "Mrs Siddons as Lady, and Kemble as Macbeth . . . might be the Macbeths of the Kembles, but they were not the Macbeths of Shakespeare" (*Shakespearean Criticism*, 2:278). Martin Meisel quotes Lamb's contrast of vision and substance and comments that Lamb identifies "the pleasures of realization with our original fall." See Meisel, *Realizations: Narrative, Pictorial, and Theatrical Arts in Nineteenth-Century England*, 30.

15. Lamb once sat next to a blind man at a performance of *Richard III*. The man was profoundly moved by various scenes, while the rest of the audience was distracted by the bad acting. Lamb uses this experience as evidence that the staging of Shakespearean tragedy is not desirable (see "Play-House Memoranda" [1813], in *Works of Lamb*, 1:158).

16. Despite Lamb's harsh words for taking passages out of context, he himself committed this literary sin in *Specimens of English Dramatic Poets* (1808). See *Works of Lamb*, 4.

17. Lamb's view of Hamlet is an outgrowth of late eighteenth-century descriptions of the prince as sensitive, melancholy, and intellectual. Earlier critics like Rowe, Dennis, and Addison viewed Hamlet as manly, active, and heroic. See Paul S. Conklin, *A History of Hamlet Criticism, 1601–1821*, 9, 26,

34–52. In an article attributed to Lamb by William Macdonald, the essayist portrays Hamlet as a man of "sensibility" who "lives in a world of imagination; his projects have little of the solid and consecutive architecture of the earth." See "Mr Kean as *Hamlet*" (1820), in *The Works of Charles Lamb*, ed. William Macdonald, 12 vols. (London: J. M. Dent, 1903), 3:61 and nn. on pp. 307–8. E. V. Lucas does not include this essay in his edition of Lamb's *Works*.

18. In fact, Lamb opposed the suppression of the theater in Sydney, Australia. See "Barron Field's Poems" (1820), in *Works of Lamb*, 1:198.

19. Lamb's reference to "the whole" of Hamlet's character recalls Maurice Morgann's contention that one must consider the "whole" character of Falstaff rather than isolated incidents. Lamb may also have been influenced by William Richardson, who referred to "the whole character of Hamlet" to determine the prince's motivation. See Morgann, *An Essay on the Dramatic Character of Sir John Falstaff* (1777), in *Shakespearean Criticism*, ed. Daniel A. Fineman (Oxford: Clarendon Press, 1972), 162; William Richardson, *Essays on Shakespeare's Dramatic Characters*, 159.

Lamb's discussion of the totality of Hamlet also resembles that of Schlegel. According to Schlegel, most actors "consider their parts as a sort of mosaic work of brilliant passages, and they rather endeavour to make the most of each separate passage, independently of the rest, than to go back to the invisible central point of the character, and to consider every expression of it as an emanation from that point. They are always afraid of underdoing their parts; and hence they are worse qualified for reserved action, for eloquent silence, where, under an appearance of outward tranquillity, the most hidden emotions of the mind are betrayed" (*Lectures on Dramatic Art and Literature*, lecture 21, p. 337). In general, Schlegel, Lamb, Coleridge, and Hazlitt insist that an actor should unify a performance around a major aspect of the character.

20. While Hazlitt agreed with Lamb that Shakespeare's tragedies could not benefit from staging, the younger critic exempted *Richard III* from this ban, probably because Hazlitt admired Edmund Kean's portrayal of the king (*Works of Hazlitt*, 4:298).

21. Lamb also identifies with the characters in Cyril Tourneur's *The Revenger's Tragedy*. Lamb remarks in *Specimens*, "The reality and life of this Dialogue passes any scenical illusion I ever felt. I never read it but my ears tingle, and I feel a hot blush spread my cheeks, as if I were presently about to 'proclaim' some such 'malefactions' of myself, as the Brothers here rebuke in their unnatural parent" (*Works of Lamb*, 4:160, n. 1).

22. Jonas Barish, *The Antitheatrical Prejudice*, 330; Joan Coldwell, "The Playgoer as Critic: Charles Lamb on Shakespeare's Characters," 194; see also Ades, "Charles Lamb, Shakespeare, and Early Nineteenth-Century Theater," 520, n. 19.

23. Lamb's concern about the portrayal of the supernatural was shared by some contemporary writers and stage managers. Henry James Pye points out that Shakespeare's supernatural characters lose their eeriness when portrayed in a theater: "What representation can give us such ideas of the ghost of Hamlet as we received from the terrible and pathetic dialogue between that aweful phantom and his son. Perhaps the effect is stronger in the closet than

on the stage. This is certainly the case with Macbeth." Pye concludes that the witches in *Macbeth* become "objects of ridicule" when they appear in a performance. See Pye, *A Commentary Illustrating the Poetic of Aristotle*, n. 1 on ch. 14 of the *Poetics*, 274–75. In 1794, John Philip Kemble broke with tradition by eliminating Banquo's Ghost from the cast of *Macbeth*. Kemble also restored dignity to the witches, who had been presented as comic characters in other eighteenth-century productions. Kemble wanted to emphasize the witches' supernatural powers. See Bartholomeusz, *Macbeth and the Players* (Cambridge: Cambridge University Press, 1969), 133, 135.

Notes for Chapter 6:
The Metamorphoses of Nineteenth-Century
Views of Spectacle

1. Martin Meisel, *Realizations: Narrative, Pictorial, and Theatrical Arts in Nineteenth-Century England*, 38–39 and *passim*.

2. For a thorough discussion of the drama criticism of Wordsworth, Hunt, Byron, and Scott, please see my Ph.D. dissertation, "Dramas, Readers, and Theaters: A Study of Early Nineteenth-Century British Drama Criticism" (University of Chicago, 1987), 250–67.

3. Johann Wolfgang von Goethe, "Shakespeare ad Infinitum," trans. Randolph S. Bourne, in *Goethe's Literary Essays*, 175–76, 185–87. While he finds the stage distracting for Shakespeare's plays, Goethe does enjoy *hearing* these dramas recited. In expressing this preference, Goethe recalls Horace, Aristotle's *Poetics*, and the classical ear/eye dichotomy (see "Shakespeare ad Infinitum," 176). Unlike the British romantics, Goethe does not oppose all performances of tragedy. In his essay "On the German Theatre" (1815), he praises Schiller's adaptation of earlier plays for the stage and offers suggestions for the casting and acting of various German plays (see *Goethe's Literary Essays*, 109–25).

4. Anne Louise Germaine Necker, The Baroness de Staël-Holstein, *Germany*, ed. and trans. O. W. Wight, 2 vols. (New York: Derby & Jackson, 1859), 1:ch. 15 ("Of the Dramatic Art"), 260–61.

5. Maurice Maeterlinck, quoted in *Resistible Theatres: Enterprise and Experiment in the Late Nineteenth Century*, by John Stokes (London: Paul Elek Books, 1972), 171.

6. Stéphane Mallarmé, "Richard Wagner, Revery of a French Poet" (1885), in *Mallarmé: Selected Prose Poems, Essays, & Letters*, 77; George Noel Gordon, Lord Byron, "To John Murray," 23 August 1821, in *Byron's Letters and Journals*, ed. Leslie A. Marchand, 11 vols. (London: John Murray, 1973–1981), 8:186–87, see also 8:59; Mallarmé, "Hamlet" (1886) and "Solemnity" (1887), in *Mallarmé: Selected Poems, Essays, & Letters*, 58, 70–72. Similarly, Mallarmé writes Emile Verhaeren in 1898 that "the spiritual theater within ourselves" is the best place for dramatic productions (pp. 105–6).

In *The Antitheatrical Prejudice*, Jonas Barish discusses nineteenth-century British, French, and German objections to *acting*. He concludes that many writers who oppose acting believe that the human personality must be consistent and unified. From this point of view, the actor, in adapting to different roles, makes impermissible changes in his identity, which are "a form of metaphysical prostitution" (p. 323).

7. Michael R. Booth, *Victorian Spectacular Theatre, 1850–1910*, 3–4, 7–8, 10; see also Meisel, *Realizations*, 33–34.

8. Booth, *Victorian Spectacular Theatre*, 17–20, 22, 42, 44–45; see also Hogan, Introduction to *The London Stage, 1776–1800*, lxiv.

9. Booth, *Victorian Spectacular Theatre*, 14–15; see also Meisel, *Realizations*, 44–45.

10. Booth, *Victorian Spectacular Theatre*, 24–27; see also Charles Beecher Hogan, Introduction to *The London Stage, 1776–1800*, vol. 5 of *The London Stage, 1660–1800: A Critical Introduction*, gen. eds. Emmett L. Avery and Arthur H. Scouten, 5:lxvi; and Richard Southern, *The Victorian Theatre: A Pictorial Survey*, 61.

11. Southern, *The Victorian Theatre*, 7, 12; Booth, *Victorian Spectacular Theatre*, 6–7, 18–19, 42, 44–45; Meisel, *Realizations*, 33–34, 46–49, 91–246; Altick, *The Shows of London*, 128–62, 186. The frequent scene changes and transformations required complicated backstage equipment and a large crew. An 1839 patent application describes the area behind the scenes as "an indistinct chaos of ropes, frames, drums, blocks, windlasses, sheeves, &c. . . . and the number of men requisite for the performance of the varied operations are in proportion, varying from 20 to 50 and upwards, on especial occasions . . . who . . . scarcely ever complete a night's performance without blunders" (cited by Southern, *The Victorian Theatre*, 26–27).

12. Booth, *Victorian Spectacular Theatre*, 3, 10–11, 24, 27, 32–33, 39; Meisel, *Realizations*, 44.

13. Southern, *The Victorian Theatre*, 14, 47, 50; "Carpenter," *OED*; W. T. Moncrieff, "Advertisement" for *Zoroaster*, cited in Allardyce Nicoll, *A History of English Drama*, 4:26; Booth, *Victorian Spectacular Theatre*, 40, 31–32; William Charles Macready, *The Diaries of William Charles Macready*, ed. William Toynbee, 2 vols. (1912; rpt. New York: Benjamin Blom, 1969), 1:246.

14. Sir Edward Bulwer-Lytton, Preface to *Richelieu*, in *Dramas and Poems* (Boston: Roberts, 1898), 104, n.; see also *Richelieu*, act 3, p. 175, n.

15. Booth, *Victorian Spectacular Theatre*, 45–47; see also Southern, *The Victorian Theatre*, 48.

16. Booth, *Victorian Spectacular Theatre*, 16; Meisel, *Realizations*, 12, 36, 50–51.

17. William Bodham Donne, *Essays on the Drama*, 206, 74. Donne eventually became the Examiner of Plays.

18. Donne, *Essays on the Drama*, 76–77.

19. Donne, *Essays on the Drama*, 78.

20. G. H. Lewes, "Shakspeare's Critics: English and Foreign," 62.

21. Lewes, "Shakspeare's Critics," 40, 62, 66–69, 77. Lewes wrote plays and did some acting. His sympathetic portrayal of Shylock in March 1849 at the Manchester Theatre Royal prefigured the interpretation of Sir Henry Irving. See Alice R. Kaminsky, ed., *Literary Criticism of George Henry Lewes*, Regents Critics Series (Lincoln: University of Nebraska Press, 1964), 116, n. Henry James also wrote plays and had two produced in the 1890s, *Guy Domville* (which was booed) and a dramatization of his novel *The American*.

22. Lewes, "Shakspeare's Critics," 41.

23. Lewes, "Shakspeare's Critics," 42–43, 63.

24. Lewes, "Shakspeare's Critics," 46, 63, 76–77. Elsewhere, he emphasizes "the fascination to all minds of dramatic representation." See Lewes, "The Drama in Germany. 1867," in *On Actors and the Art of Acting* (1875), 183. Similarly, Lewes insists, "The stage may be in a deplorable condition at present, but the delight in mimic representation is primal and indestructible." See Lewes, "Foreign Actors on Our Stage," in *On Actors and the Art of Acting*, 114.

25. Lewes, "On the Decline of the Drama," Introduction to *Selections from the Modern British Dramatists*, 2 vols. (Leipzig: F. A. Brockhaus, 1867), 1:10; Lewes, "Charles Kean," in *On Actors and the Art of Acting*, 29; "Charles Kean and Sardanapalus," *The Leader*, 25 June 1853, in *Dramatic Essays*, 250–51. See also Lewes, "Sardanapalus," *The Leader*, 18 June 1853, in *Dramatic Essays*, 248–49. For Lewes's comments about Kean's *Macbeth*, see "Macbeth: and How the Keans Performed It," *The Leader*, 19 February 1853, in *Dramatic Essays*, 238–39.

26. Lewes, "Déjazet—The Corsican Brothers," *The Leader*, 28 February 1852, in *Dramatic Essays*, 187–88. The analogy between spectacle and bad meals had earlier been used by Steele (see Chapter 1 of this book).

27. Lewes, "The Old and Modern Dramatists," *The Leader*, 3 August 1850, in *Dramatic Essays*, 104; "King John," *The Leader*, 14 February 1852, in *Dramatic Essays*, 178–79; "On the Decline of the Drama," in *Selections from the Modern British Dramatists*, 1:8.

28. Lewes, "Epistle to Anthony Trollope," in *On Actors and the Art of Acting*, 9; "Art or Amusement?," *The Leader*, 28 June 1851, in *Dramatic Essays*, 152–54; "Valéria," *The Leader*, 12 July 1851, in *Dramatic Essays*, 160–61. By the eighteenth century, according to Lewes, drama in England and Europe "had become a mere amusement," on the level of rope-dancers and jugglers, instead of a genre in which "the poet instructed his nation . . . through their emotions." As an amusement, drama must provide spectacles to satisfy "the lower appetites of a miscellaneous public." Lewes attributes the problem to the lack of dramatic talent and the degeneration of dramatic subjects from the ideal to the prosaic. He queries, "What is the vital force of a drama which can be set aside by masques and pantomimes?" See Lewes, "The Rise and Fall of the European Drama," *Foreign Quarterly Review* 35 (1845): 303, 310, 324–26, 330–31.

29. Lewes, "The Drama in Germany. 1867," in *On Actors and the Art of Acting*, 183–84; "The Rise and Fall of the European Drama," 324–25.

30. Lewes, "Shakspeare's Critics," 57, 53; see also "The Drama in Germany. 1867," 193. Hazlitt anticipated Lewes in praising the long attention spans of the French theatergoers and the French public's appreciation for long speeches. Hazlitt contrasts the French people to British spectators, who reveal "ill-manners and want of taste." See Hazlitt, "Covent Garden Theatre," *The Atlas*, 4 October 1829, in *The Complete Works of William Hazlitt*, 20:284; see also *On the Principles of Human Action* (1805), in *Works of Hazlitt*, 1:25–26, n.

31. Henry James, "The London Theatres," *The Galaxy*, May 1877, in *The*

Scenic Art: Notes on Acting and the Drama, 1872–1901, 101–2. See also "The London Theatres," *Scribner's Monthly,* January 1881, where James also accuses the British of being simple-minded: "The English public . . . is not ironical, nor analytic; it takes things on the whole very simply" (in *The Scenic Art*, 153).

32. James, "Henry Irving as Louis XI; *Olivia* at the Court Theatre," *The Nation*, 13 June 1878, in *The Scenic Art*, 114; see also "The London Theatres," *The Nation*, 12 June 1879, in *The Scenic Art*, 122–23; "Tommaso Salvini," *Pall Mall Gazette*, 27 March 1884, in *The Scenic Art*, 188. James may have been influenced by Francisque Sarcey's letter to *Le Temps* from London, 16 June 1879. This letter was reprinted in Georges d'Heylli's *La Comédie française à Londres, 1871–1879*, ed. E. A. Poinsot (Paris, 1880), 111. Matthew Arnold summarizes Sarcey's letter in "The French Play in London": "M. Sarcey . . . says that we English are fatigued by the long speeches in *Hernani*, and that we do not appreciate what delights French people in it, the splendour of the verse, the wondrous beauty of the style, the poetry." See Matthew Arnold, *The Complete Prose Works of Matthew Arnold*, 9:75.

33. James, "John Gabriel Borkman," *Harper's Weekly,* 6 February 1897, in *The Scenic Art*, 291. Ibsen is James's exception to this rule.

34. James, "Coquelin," *Century Magazine,* January 1887, in *The Scenic Art,* 209; "The London Theatres," *Scribner's Monthly,* January 1881, in *The Scenic Art*, 137, 139, 140. Similarly, James condemns Henry Irving's portrayal of Shakespeare's heroes because the actor substitutes gestures and poses for declamation. "You cannot play Shakespeare by being simply picturesque. Above all, before all, for this purpose you must have the art of utterance; you must be able to give value to the divine Shakespearean line—to make it charm our ears as it charms our mind." See "The London Theatres," *The Galaxy,* May 1877, in *The Scenic Art*, 104–5. James may have been influenced by Percy Fitzgerald's *Principles of Comedy and Dramatic Effect* (1870). Fitzgerald revives Horace's ear/eye dichotomy and eighteenth-century comparisons of the stage to lower forms of public entertainment: "The rivalry in scenic shows, the introduction of objects of art and nature upon the stage, is still more desperate. All is material, scenes, construction, furniture, and, above all, the play, and the acting. We go not so much to hear as to look. It is like a gigantic peepshow, and we pay the showman, and put our eyes to the glass and stare" (p. 15). Because spectacles are so popular, more "intellectual enjoyments" do not receive the attention that they deserve. Like Lewes, Fitzgerald views the competition in scenery and costumes as a vicious circle: the elaborate spectacles simply whet the public's appetite for more costly accessories (p. 15). Fitzgerald blames "the decay of dramatic art" on the overemphasis on spectacle. Before, drama was based on "talent," but now anyone with enough money can mount an elaborate production, featuring "some mechanical prodigy" (pp. 16–18).

35. James, "After the Play," *New Review* 1, 1 (June 1889), in *The Scenic Art*, 230. A "supernumerary" or "super" is an actor who has a small walk-on role, often in a crowd scene. Today we call such an actor an "extra."

36. James, "London Plays," *The Atlantic Monthly,* August 1882, in *The Scenic Art*, 163–64; "After the Play," 232–33.

37. James, "Henrik Ibsen: On the Occasion of *Hedda Gabler*," *New Review* 3 (June 1891), in *The Scenic Art*, 245–46; "Tommaso Salvini," *The Atlantic Monthly*, March 1883, in *The Scenic Art*, 173, 176, 178; see also "Tommaso Salvini," *Pall Mall Gazette*, 27 March 1884, in *The Scenic Art*, 190; "Mr. Henry Irving's Production of *Cymbeline*," *Harper's Weekly*, 21 November 1896, in *The Scenic Art*, 282; "Irving's *Richard III.*; *Little Eyolf*," *Harper's Weekly*, 23 January 1897, in *The Scenic Art*, 288–89; "The London Theatres," *The Galaxy*, May 1877, in *The Scenic Art*, 107.

38. James, "The Acting in Mr. Irving's *Faust*," *Century Magazine*, December 1887, in *The Scenic Art*, 219–20, 222; "Edmond Rostand," *Cornhill Magazine*, November 1901, and *The Critic*, November 1901, in *The Scenic Art*, 315.

39. Max Beerbohm, "An Aside," *The Saturday Review* 87, no. 2,267 (8 April 1899): 428.

40. Beerbohm, "An Aside," 428.

41. Beerbohm, "At 'Her Majesty's,' " *The Saturday Review* 89, no. 2,308 (20 January 1900): 77.

42. Beerbohm, "At 'Her Majesty's,' " 78.

43. Arnold, "The French Play in London," *Nineteenth Century*, August, 1879, in *The Complete Prose Works*, 9:82.

44. Arnold, "The French Play in London," 9:80–81; Preface to *Essays in Criticism* (1865), in *The Complete Prose Works*, 3:287; *Culture and Anarchy* (1869), in *The Complete Prose Works*, 5:97–99, 105, 140, 207, and *passim*.

45. Arnold, "At the Princess's," *The Pall Mall Gazette*, 6 December 1882, in *The Complete Prose Works*, 10:94–95.

46. Arnold, "The French Play in London," in *The Complete Prose Works*, 9:77–78; "At the Princess's," in *The Complete Prose Works*, 10:95.

47. Arnold, "An Old Playgoer at the Lyceum," *The Pall Mall Gazette*, 30 May 1883, in *The Complete Prose Works*, 10:140–41.

48. Arnold, "An Old Playgoer at the Lyceum," 10:140.

49. Arnold, Preface to *Merope* (written December 1857, published 1858), in *The Complete Prose Works*, 1:61; see also "The French Play in London," 9:73. Despite Arnold's defense of the theater in his public essays, his private correspondence reveals more ambivalence. He writes to Arthur Clough on 6 March 1848 that a performance of *Othello* demonstrated "the unconquerable difficulty of the play" (quoted by R. H. Super in his notes for "At the Princess's," *The Complete Prose Works*, 10:480).

50. John Ruskin, "Of Queen's Gardens," *Sesame and Lilies* (given as lectures in 1864, published 1865), in *The Complete Works of John Ruskin*, 18:112–13; George Bernard Shaw, "[Prologue]," *The Daily News*, April 1905, in *Shaw on Shakespeare*, 5.

51. Ruskin, letter 34 (October 1873), *Fors Clavigera: Letters to the Workmen and Labourers of Great Britain*, vol. 3, in *Complete Works of Ruskin*, 27:627–28.

52. Ruskin, "Of Kings' Treasuries" (1865), *Sesame and Lilies*, in *Complete Works of Ruskin*, 18:64.

53. Ruskin, "Of Kings' Treasuries," 83; "Dramatic Reform," two letters, *Journal of Dramatic Reform*, November 1880, also in *Arrows of the Chace* (1880), in *Complete Works of Ruskin*, 34:549–50.

54. Ruskin, letter 34, *Fors Clavigera*, vol. 3, in *Complete Works of Ruskin*, 27:628; "The Mountain Gloom," *Modern Painters*, in *Complete Works of Ruskin*, 6:391–92, n.

55. Ruskin, "On the Present State of Modern Art, with Reference to the Advisable Arrangements of a National Gallery" (lecture delivered at the British Institution, 1867), in *Complete Works of Ruskin*, 19:212, 209–10; *Modern Painters*, in *Complete Works of Ruskin*, 3:81–82, n.; Margaret Lynne Ausfeld, "Catalogue of the Exhibition," in *A Brush with Shakespeare: The Bard in Painting, 1780–1910*, ed. Ross Anderson (Montgomery, Ala.: Montgomery Museum of Fine Arts, 1985), 71.

56. Ruskin, "Effect of Modern Entertainments on the Mind of Youth," *Time and Tide: Twenty-five Letters to a Working Man of Sunderland on the Laws of Work* (1867), in *Complete Works of Ruskin*, 17:468; see also "On the Present State of Modern Art," 19:212–14.

57. Shaw, "[Prologue]," *Shaw on Shakespeare*, 5; "A Void in the Elizabethan Drama," Preface to *Saint Joan* (1924), in *Nine Plays* (New York: Dodd, Mead, 1946), 1029–30; "The Moral Order in Writing," Preface to *The Irrational Knot*, in *Shaw on Shakespeare*, 230; "Better than Shakespear," *The Saturday Review*, 2 January 1897, in *Our Theatres in the Nineties*, 3 vols., in *The Works of Bernard Shaw*, 3:2; Shaw, in a symposium, *The Humanitarian* 6 (May 1895), in *Shaw on Theatre*, ed. E. J. West (New York: Hill & Wang, 1958), 63; "To Arthur Bingham Walkley," epistle dedicatory for *Man and Superman* (1903), in *Nine Plays*, 508–11. Samuel Johnson's remarks on Shakespeare's goals anticipate those of Shaw. Johnson argues in his Preface to *The Plays of William Shakespeare*, "He sacrifices virtue to convenience, and is so much more careful to please than to instruct, that he seems to write without any moral purpose." See Johnson, Preface to *The Plays of William Shakespeare*, in *Samuel Johnson's Literary Criticism*, 148.

Shaw later qualified his harshness toward Shakespeare. In a 1931 postscript to his preface to *Our Theatres in the Nineties*, Shaw cautions the reader that he was so excited by Ibsen's plays in the 1890s that he was not always "reasonable" enough in his criticism of Shakespeare and other playwrights. See Shaw, "The Author's Apology," in *Our Theatres in the Nineties*, 1:ix–x.

58. Shaw, *The Quintessence of Ibsenism*, in *Works of Shaw*, 19:150, 155–56.

59. Martin Meisel, *Shaw and the Nineteenth-Century Theater*, 128, 132, 135; Shaw, Preface to *Mrs. Warren's Profession*, in *Nine Plays*, 19.

60. Shaw, "Some Other Critics," *The Saturday Review*, 20 June 1896, in *Our Theatres in the Nineties*, 2:169–70 (this essay includes a review of *Dramatic Essays* by John Forster and G. H. Lewes as edited by William Archer and Robert Lowe); "Tolstoy: Tragedian or Comedian?," in *Shaw on Shakespeare*, 253; "The Religion of the Pianoforte," *The Fortnightly Review*, February 1894, in *Shaw on Shakespeare*, 257.

61. Shaw, *The Sanity of Art: An Exposure of the Current Nonsense About Artists Being Degenerate* (1895), in *Works of Shaw*, 19:328–29. This essay was first published in the American newspaper *Liberty* and then was revised and republished by Shaw in 1907. Note that *The Sanity of Art* has a title similar to Lamb's "Sanity of True Genius" in *The Last Essays of Elia*. Both authors are

defending creative writers and artists from the charge that they are disturbed and diseased.

62. Shaw, "The Heroic Actors," *Play Pictorial* 10 (October 1907), in *Theatrical Companion to Shaw; A Pictorial Record of the First Performances of the Plays of George Bernard Shaw*, ed. Raymond Mander and Joe Mitchenson (London: Rockliff, 1954), 63; Preface to *Great Catherine*, in *Shaw on Shakespeare*, 251.

63. Shaw, "Richard Himself Again," *The Saturday Review*, 26 December 1896, in *Our Theatres in the Nineties*, 2:305.

64. Shaw, "*King Arthur*," *The Saturday Review*, 19 January 1895, in *Our Theatres in the Nineties*, 1:13; "The Religion of the Pianoforte" (1894), in *Shaw on Shakespeare*, 256–57; "Toujours Daly," *The Saturday Review*, 13 July 1895, in *Our Theatres in the Nineties*, 1:188–89; "Poor Shakespear!," in *Our Theatres in the Nineties*, 1:25–27; "Shakespear and Mr Barrie," *The Saturday Review*, 13 November 1897, in *Our Theatres in the Nineties*, 2:254–55.

65. Shaw, Preface to *St. Joan*, in *Nine Plays*, 1032–33.

66. Shaw, "[Herbert Beerbohm Tree]," *Pen Portraits and Reviews* (1905), in *Shaw on Shakespeare*, 263.

67. Shaw, "Criticism on the Hustings," *The Saturday Review*, 20 July 1895, in *Our Theatres in the Nineties*, 1:198–99; see also "Poor Shakespear!," in *Our Theatres in the Nineties*, 1:26. Shaw's admiration for the simplicity of the platform stage should be compared to Coleridge's praise of the bare Elizabethan stage.

68. Shaw, Preface to *Plays Unpleasant* (1898), in *Shaw on Shakespeare*, 259.

69. Percy Bysshe Shelley, "A Defence of Poetry," in *Shelley's Critical Prose*, 6–8. While he favors art forms that appeal to more than one human faculty, Shelley elevates literature above the other arts because "language is arbitrarily produced by the imagination, and has relation to thoughts alone." Other forms of art convey thoughts less clearly because the other forms "limit and interpose between conception and expression." Thus, literature has the advantage that it stimulates the mind more directly than the other arts. Later in "A Defence of Poetry" Shelley again emphasizes the unique properties of literature/poetry: "it acts in a divine and unapprehended manner, beyond and above consciousness." The meaning of "unapprehended" here is "not derived from sense perception" (see the *OED*'s sixth definition for "apprehend"). Shelley denies that poetry is bound to reality and sense perception. In fact, he argues, literature can create a new world that is not "subjected to the accident of surrounding impressions." Shelley stresses that poetry alters "our inward sight" and puts us in touch with "the wonder of our being." See Shelley, "A Defence of Poetry," 8, 11, 32. These comments reveal Shelley's debt to Coleridge's analysis of the differences between literature and the other arts (see Chapter 2 and Chapter 3 of this book).

70. Shelley, "A Defence of Poetry," 14; Marvin Carlson, *Theories of the Theatre: A Historical and Critical Survey, from the Greeks to the Present*, 228.

71. Shelley, "A Defence of Poetry," 17.

72. Shelley, Preface to *The Cenci* (1819), in *Shelley's Critical Prose*, 58–59; see also "A Defence of Poetry," 16.

73. Shelley, Preface to *The Cenci*, 59. Alan Richardson points out that

Samson Agonistes also influenced Shelley and Byron because "Milton set the precedent for minimizing stage action . . . and concentrating instead on intense psychological portraiture." See Richardson, *A Mental Theater: Poetic Drama and Consciousness in the Romantic Age* (University Park: Pennsylvania State University Press, 1988), 15.

74. Shelley, "To Thomas Love Peacock," July 1819, *The Letters of Percy Bysshe Shelley,* in *Shelley's Critical Prose,* 122–23; "To Charles Ollier," 13 March 1820, in *The Letters of Percy Bysshe Shelley,* ed. Frederick L. Jones, 2 vols. (Oxford: Oxford University Press, 1964), 2:178; Stuart Curran, *Shelley's Cenci: Scorpions Ringed with Fire,* 168–72.

75. Shelley, Preface to *Prometheus Unbound* (1820), in *Shelley's Critical Prose,* 67; "To John Gisborne," 10 April 1822, in *Shelley's Critical Prose,* 140; Curran, *Shelley's Cenci,* 158, n. 2; Mary Shelley, Journal entry for 13 October 1814, *Mary Shelley's Journal,* ed. Frederick L. Jones (Norman: University of Oklahoma Press, 1947), 20. However, Curran documents Shelley's enthusiasm for operas, especially those by Mozart (p. 179 and n. 40).

Shelley consistently writes his friends and his publisher that he wants a small group of sophisticated readers, which he terms "the sūnetoi," "the esoteric few," or "the enlightened public" (*The Letters of Percy Bysshe Shelley,* 2:263, 330, 363). His remarks often resemble those of Coleridge, who was also attacked because of the difficulty of his works.

76. Shelley, Preface to *Prometheus Unbound,* in *Shelley's Critical Prose,* 65. Note that Byron also uses debates between characters in *Manfred.* All references to *The Cenci* and to *Prometheus Unbound* are based on the following edition: Shelley, *Prometheus Unbound* and *The Cenci,* in *Selected Poetry,* ed. Neville Rogers (Boston: Houghton Mifflin, 1968), 64–189. The "voluptuous joy" bribe occurs in *Prometheus Unbound,* 1.426.

77. Angela Leighton, *Shelley and the Sublime: An Interpretation of the Major Poems* (Cambridge: Cambridge University Press, 1984), 74; see also 76, 99.

78. Marlon B. Ross, "Shelley's Wayward Dream-Poem: The Apprehending Reader in *Prometheus Unbound,*" *Keats-Shelley Journal* 36 (1987): 119–21, 123, 125–26, 132–33.

79. Oscar Wilde, "The Truth of Masks" (1885, revised 1891), *Intentions,* in *Literary Criticism of Oscar Wilde,* 142; W. B. Yeats, "The Theatre" (February 1900), in *Essays and Introductions,* 167; Yeats, "Introduction" (1937), in *Essays and Introductions,* ix; Wilde, "*Twelfth Night* at Oxford," *Dramatic Review,* 20 February 1886, in *Literary Criticism of Oscar Wilde,* 131. I have found only two exceptions to the rule that Wilde enthusiastically supports the appropriate staging of good dramas. One passage occurs in "Puppets and Actors" (1892), a letter to the editor of the *Daily Telegraph.* Wilde insists, "I hold that the stage is to a play no more than a picture-frame is to a painting, and that the actable value of a play has nothing whatsoever to do with its value as a work of art." He argues that neither of the two best nineteenth-century British plays, Shelley's *Cenci* and Swinburne's *Atalanta in Calydon,* is "an actable play. Indeed, the mere suggestion that stage representation is any test of a work of art is quite ridiculous." See Wilde, "Puppets and Actors," *The Daily Telegraph,* 20 February 1892, in *The Letters of Oscar Wilde,* ed. Rupert Hart-Davis (London: Rupert

Hart-Davis, 1962), 310. Another passage that reveals remnants of the bias against spectacle is Wilde's review of the first production of *The Cenci* in 1886. He warmly praises the tragedy and Shelley's drama criticism. However, Wilde contends that staging *The Cenci* has not "added anything to its beauty, its pathos, or even its realism." The actors portrayed the major characters skillfully; nevertheless, "*The Cenci* needs for the production of its perfect effect no interpretation at all. It is, as we read it, a complete work of art—capable, indeed, of being acted, but not dependent on theatric presentation" ("*The Cenci*," *Dramatic Review*, 15 May 1886, in *Literary Criticism of Oscar Wilde*, 81–82).

80. René Wellek, *A History of Modern Criticism: 1750–1950*, 4:415; Wilde, "Shakespeare on Scenery," *Dramatic Review*, 14 March 1885, in *Literary Criticism of Oscar Wilde*, 117; Wilde, "Henry the Fourth at Oxford," *Dramatic Review*, 23 May 1885, in *Literary Criticism of Oscar Wilde*, 124.

81. Wilde, "Shakespeare on Scenery," 115.

82. Wilde, "The Truth of Masks," 150.

83. Wilde, "The Truth of Masks," 150, 155; Wilde, "Shakespeare on Scenery," 117–18.

84. Wilde, "The Truth of Masks," 132–34, 136–37.

85. Wilde, "The Truth of Masks," 148–52, 132; see also 157–58. Edward Bulwer-Lytton had written, "The attempt to archaeologise the Shakespearean drama is one of the stupidest pedantries of this age of prigs. Archaeology would not be more out of place in a fairy tale than it is in a play of Shakespeare." See Bulwer-Lytton, "Miss Anderson's Juliet," *The Nineteenth Century* 16 (December 1884): 886, n. 1.

86. Hazlitt's article had first appeared in *The Morning Chronicle* on 14 March 1814. Wilde, "Hamlet at the Lyceum," *Dramatic Review*, 9 May 1885, in *Literary Criticism of Oscar Wilde*, 120–21.

87. Wilde, "The Decay of Lying," *The Nineteenth Century* 25 (January 1889); rpt. in revised form in *Intentions* (1891), in *Literary Criticism of Oscar Wilde*, 174. Like Hazlitt, Yeats stresses the audience's identification with the tragic hero. However, Yeats considers the hero an undeveloped character who allows the spectators to fill in the outline with their own experiences. Because the tragic hero is not strongly defined, "it is always ourselves that we see upon the stage." Hazlitt had argued that Shakespeare's art helps the reader to experience Hamlet's life imaginatively as if it were the reader's own. According to Yeats, comedy relies on the barriers between people, but tragedy breaks down these barriers and moves toward universality. See Yeats, "The Tragic Theatre" (1910), in *Essays and Introductions*, 241. See also Yeats, "The Theatre of Beauty," *Harper's Weekly*, 11 November 1911, in *Uncollected Prose*, 2:398.

88. Fitzgerald, *Principles of Comedy and Dramatic Effect*, 14, 28–29, 33, 36. Fitzgerald edited Lamb's dramatic essays in *The Art of the Stage as set out in Lamb's Dramatic Essays* (London, 1885).

89. Stéphane Mallarmé, "Richard Wagner, Revery of a French Poet" (1885), in *Selected Prose Poems, Essays, & Letters*, 73–77.

90. Yeats, "The Return of Ulysses" (1896), in *Essays and Introductions*, 199. Yeats expresses his admiration for Shelley's work and argues that Shelley was

a major force in shaping Yeats's life (see Yeats, "Prometheus Unbound," in *Essays and Introductions*, 424).

91. Yeats, "Plans and Methods," *Beltaine*, May 1899, in *Uncollected Prose*, 2:160; "Irish Literary Theatre Lecture by Mr. W. B. Yeats," report in *The Irish Literary Society Gazette*, June 1899, in *Uncollected Prose*, 2:156.

92. Yeats, "The Theatre of Beauty," in *Uncollected Prose*, 2:399; "The Art of the Theatre," *The New Age*, 16 June 1910, in *Uncollected Prose*, 2:383–84. Yeats may have been influenced by Irving's experiments with hanging backcloths or "drop scenes" instead of pairs of flats, by Edward William Godwin's open staging, and by William Poel's simplified sets for Shakespeare's plays with platform stages and curtains.

93. Yeats, "Plans and Methods," *Beltaine*, February 1900, in *Uncollected Prose*, 2:203–4; "The Theatre" (February 1900), in *Essays and Introductions*, 165.

94. Yeats, "Ireland and the Arts," *United Irishman*, 31 August 1904, in *Essays and Introductions*, 203; "A Defence of the Abbey Theatre," *The Dublin Magazine*, April–June 1926, in *Uncollected Prose*, 2:469.

95. Yeats, "The Theatre" (February 1900), in *Essays and Introductions*, 166–67; "The Symbolism of Poetry," in *Essays and Introductions*, 155.

96. Yeats, "The Autumn of the Body" (1898), in *Essays and Introductions*, 189–93; "Aglavaine and Selysette," *The Bookman*, September 1897, in *Uncollected Prose*, 2:52; "An Introduction for my Plays" (1937), in *Essays and Introductions*, 529.

97. Yeats, "An Introduction for my Plays," 527–29.

98. Yeats, "The Theatre" (February 1900), in *Essays and Introductions*, 168–69.

99. Yeats, "The Theatre" (February 1900), 169; "At Stratford-on-Avon," *The Speaker*, 11 May 1901, in *Uncollected Prose*, 2:251. Other writers agreed with Yeats about the need for special theaters for dramatic masterpieces. William Archer and Granville Barker campaigned for a National Theatre as early as 1904. They wanted a theater in which the best dramas of the world, past and present, could be staged without financial pressures to make a profit. See George Rowell, Introduction to *Victorian Dramatic Criticism* (London: Methuen, 1971), xvii.

100. Yeats, "The Theatre," 170; "W. B. Yeats' Speech at the Matinee of the British Association, Friday September 4th, 1908," in *Uncollected Prose*, 2:367.

101. Yeats, "The Acting at St. Teresa's Hall," *United Irishman*, 26 April 1902, in *Uncollected Prose*, 2:292; "Certain Noble Plays of Japan" (April 1916), in *Essays and Introductions*, 221, 224.

102. Yeats, "Certain Noble Plays of Japan," 225. Yeats's mysticism differs from the more psychological perspective of Coleridge, Lamb, and Hazlitt, even though these romantic writers use much of the same terminology that Yeats did.

Notes for Conclusion

1. A. C. Bradley, *Shakespearean Tragedy: Lectures on Hamlet, Othello, King Lear, Macbeth*, 2d ed. (1905; rpt. London: Macmillan; New York: St. Martin's

Press, 1964), 247–48; George Saintsbury, *A History of English Criticism* (Edinburgh: William Blackwood, 1912), 351; Saintsbury, *A History of the French Novel*, 2 vols. (London: Macmillan, 1919), 2:297–98.

2. Benedetto Croce, *Aesthetic,* trans. Douglas Ainslie, rev. ed. (1922; rpt. New York: Noonday Press, 1960), 116; Croce, *Conversazioni critiche,* 5 vols. (Bari: Guis. Laterza, 1918), 3:72; trans. by Marvin Carlson, in *Theories of the Theatre: A Historical and Critical Survey from the Greeks to the Present,* 368–69.

3. T. S. Eliot, "Four Elizabethan Dramatists," in *Selected Essays,* 2d ed. (1950; rpt. New York: Harcourt, Brace & World, 1964), 95–96; T. S. Eliot, "The Perfect Critic," in *The Sacred Wood: Essays on Poetry and Criticism,* 7th ed. (1920; rpt. London: Methuen, 1972), 1.

4. Neil Postman, *Amusing Ourselves to Death: Public Discourse in the Age of Show Business* (New York: Viking Press, 1985).

Selected Bibliography

Primary Sources

Addison, Joseph, and Richard Steele. *The Spectator.* Edited by Donald F. Bond. 5 vols. Oxford: Clarendon Press, 1965.

Aristotle. *Aristotle's Treatise on Poetry.* Edited and translated by Thomas Twining. London: Payne and Son, 1789; rpt. New York: Garland Publishing, 1971.

———. *The Works of Aristotle.* Edited by W. D. Ross et al. 12 vols. 1908–1931; rpt. Oxford: Clarendon Press, 1963.

Arnold, Matthew. *The Complete Prose Works of Matthew Arnold.* Edited by R. H. Super. 11 vols. Ann Arbor: University of Michigan Press, 1960–1977.

Beerbohm, Max. "An Aside." *The Saturday Review* 87, 2267 (8 April 1899): 428.

———. "At 'Her Majesty's.'" *The Saturday Review* 89, 2308 (20 January 1900): 77–78.

Bruner, Jerome S. "The Act of Discovery." *Harvard Educational Review* 31, 1 (Winter 1961): 21–32.

Byron, George Noel Gordon, Lord. *Byron's Letters and Journals.* Edited by Leslie A. Marchand. 11 vols. London: John Murray, 1973–1981.

Chatman, Seymour. *Story and Discourse: Narrative Structure in Fiction and Film.* Ithaca: Cornell University Press, 1978.

———. "What Novels Can Do That Films Can't (and Vice Versa)." *Critical Inquiry* 7, 1 (Autumn 1980): 121–40.

Coleridge, Samuel Taylor. *Biographia Literaria.* Edited by J. Shawcross. 2 vols. 1907; rpt. Oxford: Oxford University Press, 1965.

———. *Collected Letters of Samuel Taylor Coleridge.* Edited by Earl Leslie Griggs. 6 vols. Oxford: Clarendon Press, 1956–1971.

———. *The Collected Works of Samuel Taylor Coleridge.* Edited by Kathleen Coburn and Bart Winer. Bollingen Series 75. 16 vols. London: Routledge & Kegan Paul; Princeton: Princeton University Press, 1969–.

———. *The Complete Poetical Works.* Edited by Ernest Hartley Coleridge. 2 vols. 1912; rpt. Oxford: Clarendon Press, 1975.

———. *Inquiring Spirit: A Coleridge Reader.* Edited by Kathleen Coburn. London: Routledge & Paul, and New York: Pantheon Books, 1951; rpt. New York: Minerva Press, 1968.

———. *Miscellaneous Criticism.* Edited by Thomas Middleton Raysor. Cambridge: Harvard University Press, 1936.

———. *The Notebooks of Samuel Taylor Coleridge.* Edited by Kathleen Coburn. Bollingen Series 50. London: Routledge & Kegan Paul; Princeton: Princeton University Press, 1957–.

———. *Shakespearean Criticism.* Edited by Thomas Middleton Raysor. 2 vols. London: Constable, 1930.

Dennis, John. *The Critical Works of John Dennis.* Edited by Edward Niles Hooker. 2 vols. Baltimore: Johns Hopkins Press, 1939–1943.

Donne, William Bodham. *Essays on the Drama.* London: John W. Parker, 1858.

Dryden, John. *Essays of John Dryden.* Edited by W. P. Ker. 2 vols. Oxford: Clarendon Press, 1926.

Fielding, Henry. *The Complete Works of Henry Fielding, Esq.* 16 vols. London: William Heinemann, 1903.

Fish, Stanley E. *Self-Consuming Artifacts: The Experience of Seventeenth-Century Literature.* Berkeley: University of California Press, 1972.

————. *Surprised by Sin: The Reader in Paradise Lost.* 1967; rpt. Berkeley: University of California Press, 1971.

Fitzgerald, Percy. *Principles of Comedy and Dramatic Effect.* London: Tinsley Brothers, 1870.

Gebert, Clara, ed. *An Anthology of Elizabethan Dedications and Prefaces.* Philadelphia: University of Pennsylvania Press, 1933.

Goethe, Johann Wolfgang von. *Goethe's Literary Essays.* Edited by J. E. Spingarn. New York: Harcourt, Brace, 1921; rpt. New York: Frederick Ungar, 1964.

Goldsmith, Oliver. *Collected Works of Oliver Goldsmith.* Edited by Arthur Friedman. 5 vols. Oxford: Clarendon Press, 1966.

Hanmer, Thomas/Anonymous. *Some Remarks on the Tragedy of Hamlet Prince of Denmark, Written by Mr. William Shakespeare.* London: W. Wilkins, 1736; rpt. The Augustan Reprint Society, Series 3, No. 3. Ann Arbor, Mich.: Edwards Bros., 1947.

Hazlitt, William. *The Complete Works of William Hazlitt.* Edited by P. P. Howe. 21 vols. London: J. M. Dent, 1930–1934.

————. *The Letters of William Hazlitt.* Edited by Herschel Moreland Sikes, Willard Hallam Bonner, and Gerald Lahey. New York: New York University Press, 1978.

Horace. *The Works of Horace.* Translated by Christopher Smart. 2 vols. London: J. Newberry, 1756.

Hunt, Leigh. *Dramatic Essays.* Edited by William Archer and Robert W. Lowe. London: Walter Scott, 1894.

————. *Leigh Hunt's Dramatic Criticism, 1808–1831.* Edited by Lawrence Huston Houtchens and Carolyn Washburn Houtchens. New York: Columbia University Press, 1949.

Iser, Wolfgang. *The Implied Reader: Patterns of Communication in Prose Fiction from Bunyan to Beckett.* Baltimore: Johns Hopkins University Press, 1974.

James, Henry. *The Scenic Art: Notes on Acting & the Drama, 1872–1901.* Edited by Allan Wade. New York: Hill & Wang, 1957.

Johnson, Samuel. *Samuel Johnson's Literary Criticism.* Edited by R. D. Stock. Regents Critics Series. Lincoln: University of Nebraska Press, 1974.

————. *The Works of Samuel Johnson.* Gen. eds. Allen Hazen and John Middendorf. New Haven: Yale University Press, 1958–.

Jonson, Ben. *Ben Jonson's Literary Criticism.* Edited by James D. Redwine, Jr. Regents Critics Series. Lincoln: University of Nebraska Press, 1970.

Kant, Immanuel. *The Critique of Judgement.* Translated by James Creed Meredith. Oxford: Oxford University Press, 1952; rpt. Oxford: Clarendon Press, 1980.

Kracauer, Siegfried. *Theory of Film: The Redemption of Physical Reality.* New York: Oxford University Press, 1960.

Lamb, Charles. *Lamb as Critic.* Edited by Roy Park. Routledge Critics Series. Lincoln: University of Nebraska Press, 1980.

————. *The Letters of Charles and Mary Anne Lamb.* Edited by Edwin W. Marrs, Jr. Ithaca: Cornell University Press, 1975–.

————. *The Letters of Charles Lamb to which are added those of his sister Mary Lamb.* Edited by E. V. Lucas. 3 vols. London: J. M. Dent & Methuen, 1935.

————. *The Works of Charles and Mary Lamb.* Edited by E. V. Lucas. 7 vols. London: Methuen, 1903–1905.

Lewes, George Henry. *On Actors and the Art of Acting.* New York: Grove Press, 1957.

————. "Shakspeare's Critics: English and Foreign." *Edinburgh Review* 90, 181 (July 1849): 39–77.

Lewes, George Henry, and Forster, John. *Dramatic Essays.* Edited by William Archer and Robert W. Lowe. London: Walter Scott, 1896.

Locke, John. *The Educational Writings of John Locke.* Edited by James Axtell. Cambridge: Cambridge University Press, 1968.

Mallarmé, Stéphane. *Mallarmé: Selected Prose Poems, Essays, & Letters.* Translated and introduction by Bradford Cook. Baltimore: Johns Hopkins Press, 1956.

Medwin, Thomas. *Medwin's Conversations of Lord Byron.* Edited by Ernest J. Lovell, Jr. Princeton: Princeton University Press, 1966.

Morgann, Maurice. *Shakespearean Criticism.* Edited by Daniel A. Fineman. Oxford: Clarendon Press, 1972.

Perry, William G., Jr. *Forms of Intellectual and Ethical Development in the College Years: A Scheme.* New York: Holt, Rinehart & Winston, 1970.

Plato. *The Works of Plato.* Edited and translated by Floyer Sydenham and Thomas Taylor. 5 vols. London: Thomas Taylor, 1804.

Pope, Alexander. *The Poems of Alexander Pope.* Gen. ed. John Butt. 10 vols. London: Methuen; New Haven: Yale University Press, 1939–1967.

Pye, Henry James. *A Commentary Illustrating the Poetic of Aristotle, By Examples Taken Chiefly from the Modern Poets To which is Prefixed a new and Corrected Edition of the Translation of the Poetic.* London: John Stockdale, 1792; rpt. New York: Garland Publishing, 1971.

Reynolds, Sir Joshua. *Discourses on Art.* New York: Collier Books, 1966.

Richardson, William. *Essays on Shakespeare's Dramatic Characters of Richard the Third, King Lear, and Timon of Athens. To Which Are Added, an Essay on the Faults of Shakespeare; and Additional Observations on the Character of Hamlet.* London: J. Murray, 1784; rpt. New York: AMS Press, 1974.

Rousseau, Jean Jacques. *Émile.* Translated by Barbara Foxley. London: J. M. Dent, 1911; rpt. London: J. M. Dent, 1950; New York: E. P. Dutton, 1950.

Ruskin, John. *The Complete Works of John Ruskin.* Edited by E. T. Cook and Alexander Wedderburn. 39 vols. Library Edition by London: George Allen, 1903–1912.

Rymer, Thomas. *The Tragedies of the Last Age.* 2d ed. London: Richard Baldwin, 1692.

Schiller, Friedrich. *On the Aesthetic Education of Man.* Translated by and intro. Reginald Snell. New Haven: Yale University Press, 1954.

Schlegel, August Wilhelm. *Lectures on Dramatic Art and Literature.* Translated by John Black. Rev. ed. by Rev. A. J. W. Morrison. 2d ed. London: George Bell, 1889.

Scott, Sir Walter. *The Miscellaneous Prose Works.* 6 vols. Edinburgh: Ballantyne, 1827.

Shakespeare, William. *The Complete Works.* Edited by G. B. Harrison, 1948; rpt. New York: Harcourt, Brace & World, 1968.

Shaw, George Bernard. *The Works of Bernard Shaw.* 33 vols. London: Constable, 1930–38.

———. *Shaw on Shakespeare.* Edited by Edwin Wilson. New York: E. P. Dutton, 1961.

Shelley, Percy Bysshe. *Selected Poetry.* Edited by Neville Rogers. Boston: Houghton Mifflin, 1968.

———. *Shelley's Critical Prose.* Edited by Bruce R. McElderry, Jr. Regents Critics Series. Lincoln: University of Nebraska Press, 1967.

Sheridan, Richard Brinsley. *The Dramatic Works of Richard Brinsley Sheridan.* Edited by Cecil Price. 2 vols. Oxford: Clarendon Press, 1973.

Slatoff, Walter J. *With Respect to Readers: Dimensions of Literary Response.* Ithaca: Cornell University Press, 1970.

Smith, Adam. *Essays on Philosophical Subjects.* Dublin, 1795; rpt. New York: Garland Publishing, 1971.

Southey, Robert. *The Origin, Nature, and Object, of the New System of Education.* London: John Murray, 1812.

Spingarn, J. E., ed. *Critical Essays of the Seventeenth Century.* 3 vols. Oxford: Clarendon Press, 1908–1909.

Steele, Richard. *The Conscious Lovers: A Comedy.* London: J. and R. Tonson, 1741.

———. *The Plays of Richard Steele.* Edited by Shirley Strum Kenny. Oxford: Clarendon Press, 1971.

———. *The Tatler.* Edited by George A. Aitken. 4 vols. London: Duckworth, 1898–1899.

Vanbrugh, Sir John. *The Relapse.* Edited by Curt A. Zimansky. Regents Restoration Drama Series. Lincoln: University of Nebraska Press, 1970.

Whately, Thomas. *Remarks on Some of the Characters of Shakespere.* Edited by Richard Whately. 3d ed. London, 1785; rpt. Eighteenth Century Shakespeare, No. 17. New York: Augustus M. Kelley Publishers, 1970.

Whitehead, Alfred North. *The Aims of Education and Other Essays.* 1929; rpt. New York: New American Library, 1961.

Wilde, Oscar. *Literary Criticism of Oscar Wilde.* Edited by Stanley Weintraub. Regents Critics Series. Lincoln: University of Nebraska Press, 1968.

Wordsworth, William. *Literary Criticism of William Wordsworth.* Edited by Paul M. Zall. Regents Critics Series. Lincoln: University of Nebraska Press, 1966.

———. *Poetical Works.* Edited by Thomas Hutchinson and Ernest de Selincourt. Oxford: Oxford University Press, 1969.

Yeats, W. B. *Essays and Introductions.* New York: Macmillan, 1961.

————. *Uncollected Prose.* Edited by John P. Frayne and Colton Johnson. 2 vols. New York: Columbia University Press, 1975.

Secondary Sources

Abrams, M. H. *The Mirror and the Lamp: Romantic Theory and the Critical Tradition.* Oxford: Oxford University Press, 1953; rpt. Oxford University Press, 1976.

Albrecht, W. P. *Hazlitt and the Creative Imagination.* Lawrence: University of Kansas Press, 1965.

Altick, Richard D. *The English Common Reader: A Social History of the Mass Reading Public, 1800–1900.* Chicago: University of Chicago Press, 1957.

————. *The Shows of London.* Cambridge: Belknap Press of Harvard University Press, 1978.

Avery, Emmett L., and Arthur H. Scouten, gen. eds. *The London Stage, 1660–1800: A Critical Introduction.* 5 vols. Carbondale: Southern Illinois University Press, 1968.

Babbitt, Irving. *On Being Creative and Other Essays.* Boston: Houghton Mifflin, 1932.

————. *Rousseau and Romanticism.* Boston: Houghton Mifflin, 1919.

Babcock, Robert Witbeck. *The Genesis of Shakespeare Idolatry, 1766–1799: A Study in English Criticism of the Late Eighteenth Century.* Chapel Hill: University of North Carolina Press, 1931.

Baker, Herschel. *William Hazlitt.* Cambridge: Harvard University Press, 1962.

Ball, Patricia M. "The Waking Dream: Coleridge and the Drama." In *The Morality of Art: Essays Presented to G. Wilson Knight by His Colleagues and Friends.* Edited by D. W. Jefferson. London: Routledge & Kegan Paul, 1969, pp. 165–74.

Barish, Jonas. *The Antitheatrical Prejudice.* Berkeley: University of California Press, 1981.

Barnet, Sylvan. "Charles Lamb's Contribution to the Theory of Dramatic Illusion." *PMLA* 69, 5 (December 1954): 1150–59.

Bate, Walter Jackson. *Coleridge.* New York: Macmillan; London: Collier-Macmillan, 1968.

————. *From Classic to Romantic: Premises of Taste in Eighteenth-Century England.* Cambridge: Harvard University Press, 1946; rpt. Harvard University Press, 1949.

Beer, J. B. *Coleridge the Visionary.* London: Chatto & Windus, 1959.

Bevis, Richard. *The Laughing Tradition: Stage Comedy in Garrick's Day.* Athens: University of Georgia Press, 1980.

Booth, Michael R. *Victorian Spectacular Theatre, 1850–1910.* Theatre Production Studies. London: Routledge and Kegan Paul, 1981.

Brier, Peter. "Dramatic Characterization in the Essays of Charles Lamb." *Coranto* 8, 2 (1973): 3–23; 9, 1 (1974): 17–31.

Bromwich, David. *Hazlitt: The Mind of a Critic.* Oxford: Oxford University Press, 1983.

Bullitt, John M. "Hazlitt and the Romantic Conception of the Imagination." *Philological Quarterly* 24, 4 (October 1945): 343–61.

Carlson, Marvin. *Theories of the Theatre: A Historical and Critical Survey, from the Greeks to the Present.* Ithaca: Cornell University Press, 1984.

Coldwell, Joan. "The Playgoer as Critic: Charles Lamb on Shakespeare's Characters." *Shakespeare Quarterly* 26, 2 (Spring 1975): 184–95.

Conklin, Paul S. *A History of Hamlet Criticism, 1601–1821.* New York: Columbia University Press, 1947.

Cooke, Katharine. *Coleridge.* London: Routledge & Kegan Paul, 1979.

Courtney, Winifred F. *Young Charles Lamb, 1775–1802.* The Gotham Library. New York: New York University Press, 1982.

Curran, Stuart. *Shelley's Cenci: Scorpions Ringed with Fire.* Princeton: Princeton University Press, 1970.

Eastman, Arthur M. *A Short History of Shakespearean Criticism.* New York: Random House, 1968.

Fletcher, Richard M. *English Romantic Drama, 1795–1843: A Critical History.* New York: Exposition Press, 1966.

Frye, Northrop. *A Study of English Romanticism.* New York: Random House, 1968.

Gordon, Mel. *Lazzi: The Comic Routines of the Commedia dell'Arte.* New York: Performing Arts Journal Publications, 1983.

Gordon, Peter, and John White. *Philosophers as Educational Reformers: The Influence of Idealism on British Educational Thought and Practice.* London: Routledge & Kegan Paul, 1979.

Griggs, Earl Leslie. "'The Willing Suspension of Disbelief.'" In *Elizabethan Studies and Other Essays in Honor of George F. Reynolds.* Edited by E. J. West. Studies in the Humanities, 2, No. 4, Series B. Boulder, Colo., 1945, 272–85.

Haven, Richard. *Patterns of Consciousness: An Essay on Coleridge.* Amherst: University of Massachusetts Press, 1969.

Hayden, John O., ed. *The Romantic Reviewers, 1802–1824.* Chicago: University of Chicago Press, 1969.

Heafford, Michael. *Pestalozzi: His Thought and its Relevance Today.* The Library of Educational Thought. London: Methuen, 1967.

Hoheisel, Peter. "Coleridge on Shakespeare: Method Amid the Rhetoric." *Studies in Romanticism* 13, 1 (Winter 1974): 15–23.

Hughes, Leo. *The Drama's Patrons: A Study of the Eighteenth-Century London Audience.* Austin: University of Texas Press, 1971.

Jackson, J. R. de J. "Coleridge on Dramatic Illusion and Spectacle in the Performance of Shakespeare's Plays." *Modern Philology* 62, 1 (August 1964): 13–21.

———, ed. *Coleridge: The Critical Heritage.* London: Routledge & Kegan Paul, 1970.

———. *Method and Imagination in Coleridge's Criticism.* Cambridge: Harvard University Press, 1969.

Kinnaird, John. *William Hazlitt: Critic of Power.* New York: Columbia University Press, 1978.

Lawson, John, and Harold Silver. *A Social History of Education in England.* London: Methuen, 1973.

Leighton, Angela. *Shelley and the Sublime: An Interpretation of the Major Poems.* Cambridge: Cambridge University Press, 1984.

Lockridge, Laurence S. *Coleridge the Moralist.* Ithaca: Cornell University Press, 1977.

McFarland, Thomas. *Romanticism and the Forms of Ruin: Wordsworth, Coleridge, and Modalities of Fragmentation.* Princeton: Princeton University Press, 1981.

McGann, Jerome J. *The Romantic Ideology: A Critical Investigation.* Chicago: University of Chicago Press, 1983.

McKenna, Wayne. *Charles Lamb and the Theatre.* Gerrards Cross: Colin Smythe, 1978.

Mahoney, John L. "The Futuristic Imagination: Hazlitt's Approach to *Romeo and Juliet.*" *British Journal of Aesthetics* 14, 1 (Winter 1974): 65–67.

———. *The Logic of Passion: The Literary Criticism of William Hazlitt.* New York: Fordham University Press, 1981.

———. *The Whole Internal Universe: Imitation and the New Defense of Poetry in British Criticism, 1660–1830.* New York: Fordham University Press, 1985.

Meisel, Martin. *Realizations: Narrative, Pictorial, and Theatrical Arts in Nineteenth-Century England.* Princeton: Princeton University Press, 1983.

———. *Shaw and the Nineteenth-Century Theater.* Princeton: Princeton University Press, 1963.

Nabholtz, John R. *"My Reader My Fellow-Labourer": A Study of English Romantic Prose.* Columbia: University of Missouri Press, 1986.

Nicoll, Allardyce. *The Garrick Stage: Theatres and Audience in the Eighteenth Century.* Edited by Sybil Rosenfeld. Manchester: Manchester University Press, 1980.

———. *A History of English Drama, 1660–1900.* 2d ed. 6 vols. Cambridge: Cambridge University Press, 1952–1959.

———. *The World of Harlequin: A Critical Study of the Commedia dell'Arte.* Cambridge: Cambridge University Press, 1963.

Oreglia, Giacomo. *The Commedia dell'Arte.* Translated by Lovett F. Edwards. Introduction by Evert Sprinchorn. New York: Hill & Wang, 1968.

Orgel, Stephen. *The Illusion of Power: Political Theater in the English Renaissance.* Berkeley: University of California Press, 1975.

Park, Roy. *Hazlitt and the Spirit of the Age: Abstraction and Critical Theory.* Oxford: Clarendon Press, 1971.

Parker, Reeve. *Coleridge's Meditative Art.* Ithaca: Cornell University Press, 1975.

Richardson, Alan. *A Mental Theater: Poetic Drama and Consciousness in the Romantic Age.* University Park: The Pennsylvania State University Press, 1988.

Ross, Marlon B. "Shelley's Wayward Dream-Poem: The Apprehending Reader in *Prometheus Unbound,*" *Keats-Shelley Journal* 36 (1987): 110–33.

Rothstein, Eric. "English Tragic Theory in the Late Seventeenth Century." *ELH* 29, 3 (September 1962): 306–23.

Saintsbury, George. *A History of Criticism and Literary Taste in Europe.* 3 vols. Edinburgh: William Blackwood, 1900–1904; rpt. William Blackwood, 1949.

Schneider, Elisabeth. *The Aesthetics of William Hazlitt: A Study of the Philosophical Basis of his Criticism.* Philadelphia: University of Pennsylvania Press, 1933.

Shaffer, Elinor S. "Coleridge's Theory of Aesthetic Interest." *The Journal of Aesthetics and Art Criticism* 27, 4 (Summer 1969): 399–408.

Silber, Kate. *Pestalozzi: The Man and His Work.* 3d ed. New York: Schocken Books, 1973.

Sinclair, Nora Rea. "Coleridge and Education." *Queen's Quarterly* 74, 3 (Autumn 1967): 413–26.

Snyder, Alice D. *Coleridge on Logic and Learning.* New Haven: Yale University Press, 1929.

Southern, Richard. *The Victorian Theatre: A Pictorial Survey.* Newton Abbot: David & Charles, 1970.

Spencer, Hazelton. *Shakespeare Improved: The Restoration Versions in Quarto and on the Stage.* Cambridge: Harvard University Press, 1927.

Stock, R. D. *Samuel Johnson and Neoclassical Dramatic Theory: The Intellectual Context of the Preface to Shakespeare.* Lincoln: University of Nebraska Press, 1973.

Tave, Stuart M. *The Amiable Humorist: A Study in the Comic Theory and Criticism of the Eighteenth and Early Nineteenth Centuries.* Chicago: University of Chicago Press, 1960.

Walsh, William. *Coleridge: The Work and the Relevance.* New York: Barnes & Noble, 1967.

Wasserman, Earl R. "The Pleasures of Tragedy." *ELH* 14, 4 (December 1947): 283–307.

Wellek, René. *A History of Modern Criticism, 1750–1950.* 3 vols. New Haven: Yale University Press, 1955, 1965.

Wheeler, Kathleen M. *The Creative Mind in Coleridge's Poetry.* Cambridge: Harvard University Press, 1981.

————. *Sources, Processes and Methods in Coleridge's Biographia Literaria.* Cambridge: Cambridge University Press, 1980.

Wimsatt, William K., Jr., and Cleanth Brooks. *Literary Criticism: A Short History.* New York: Alfred A. Knopf, 1959.

Index

Abbey Theatre, 163
Abrams, M. H., 113, 189*n6*; "expressive" theory, 96; *The Mirror and the Lamp,* 95, 187*n1*
Abstraction: Coleridge and, 33, 40–41, 42, 61, 62, 65, 91; definition of, 40; departure from, 33; in education, 51; Hazlitt and, 33, 40, 41, 42, 51, 102, 105; Lamb and, 33, 41, 42, 118, 123, 124, 126; in reading plays, 4, 7; Schlegel and, 33, 41–42
Actors, 3, 30, 116, 131–32, 136, 147, 150, 166, 198*n6*; Aristotle and, 30; Coleridge and, 75, 81, 197*n19*; Goldsmith and, 3, 30; Hazlitt and, 100–101, 102, 103, 107, 111, 112–13, 196*n13,* 197*n19*; Lamb and, 117, 122–23, 124, 126, 150, 196*n13*; Ruskin and, 147; Wilde and, 157, 158; Yeats and, 161
Addison, Joseph, 2, 3, 59, 85, 151, 190*n11,* 196*n17*; "Pleasures of the Imagination," 34–35; and realism, 15–16; and sense perception, 35
Ades, John I., 118, 169*n2*
Albrecht, W. P., 100, 190*n11*
Alison, Archibald, 182*n48,* 185*n64*
Altick, Richard D., 57, 132, 195*n11*; *The English Common Reader,* 173*n46*
Appleyard, J. A., 70
Aristotle, 8–9, 10, 12, 34, 40; influence of, 31, 33, 34, 177*n7*; katharsis, 95, 105, 106; *Poetics,* 2, 7, 9, 16, 37, 169*n1,* 198*n3*; *Rhetoric,* 30
Arnold, Matthew, 6, 129, 144–45, 147, 153, 179*n27,* 201*n32,* 202*n49*; *Merope,* 145
Audience. *See* Film: audience; Theater audience

Babbitt, Irving, 95, 106, 113, 187*n1,* 188*n3*
Bacon, Sir Francis, 3; *The Advancement of Learning,* 34; *Novum Organum,* 180*n31*; "Of Studies," 182*n43*
Badawi, M. M., 85
Baker, Herschel, 99
Ball, Patricia, 82

Bancroft, Squire, 133
Bannister, John, 101
Barish, Jonas, 1, 170*n10,* 198*n6*
Bate, Walter Jackson, 84, 95–96, 181*n35,* 188*n5; Criticism: The Major Texts,* 33
Beattie, James, 101, 188*n5,* 190*n14*
Beauty: in art, 152, 157; audience's sensitivity to beauty, 143; in drama criticism, 128–29, 137, 143, 144, 147, 157, 159
Beerbohm, Max, 147; and spectacle, 129, 140, 143–44
Bell, Andrew, 178*nn14,18*; and the monitorial system, 47
Bensley, Robert, 118
Betterton, Thomas, 29
Bevis, Richard, 20–21, 172*n35*
Blair, Hugh, 188*n5*
Blake, William, 37–38, 96, 175*n12*
Bloom, Harold, 167
Booth, M. R., 132, 133, 135
Boydell, John, 195*n11*
Boydell's Shakespeare Gallery, 121, 195*n11*
Bradley, A. C., 165
Brook, Peter, 165
Bruner, Jerome S., 5, 93
Bulwer-Lytton, Edward Robert, 159, 206*n85; Richelieu,* 134
Bunyan, John, 148
Burbage, Richard, 150
Burke, Edmund, 39, 188*n5; A Philosophical Enquiry,* 35–36
Byron, George Gordon, 74–75, 97, 165–66, 187*n3,* 205*n73; Manfred,* 205*n76; Sardanapalus,* 132, 138; and spectacle, 129, 131

Capon, William, 132
Carlson, Marvin, 153
Chatman, Seymour, 5, 115, 116, 122, 127, 166; *Story and Discourse,* 116
Cibber, Colley, 28, 196*n13*
Cicero: *Pro Archia,* 7–8
Clint, George: *A New Way to Pay Old Debts,* 104
Closet dramas. *See* Poetic plays
Coldwell, Joan, 1, 125–26

217

Pestalozzi, Johann Heinrich, 46, 49–50, 51, 177*n*10, 178*n*18
Phelp, Samuel, 133
Piaget, Jean, 50
Pictorialism: in art, 121, 123; in drama, 5, 128, 131–36, 138, 142, 151, 161–62, 163, 165, 195*n*11; in film, 166; in poetry, 35
Plato, 33, 34, 40; *Phaedo*, 3, 7, 33; *The Republic*, 11–12
Poel, William, 165, 207*n*92; Elizabethan Stage Society, 152
Poetic Plays, 2, 25–26, 172*n*35, 173*n*49
Pope, Alexander, 22, 24–25, 91, 188*n*4; *The Dunciad*, 19–20, 22, 173*n*45
Postman, Neil: *Amusing Ourselves to Death*, 166
Prati, Gioacchino de', 50
Princess's Theatre, 138
Prynne, William, 12
Pye, Henry James, 30–31, 197*n*23

Raysor, Thomas Middleton, 43, 70, 176*n*2
Reader-Response Criticism, 100, 115, 167
Reading: Coleridge and, 57–60, 62, 66, 67, 92, 183*nn*50,51; of drama, 7, 8, 41; Dryden and, 11; Lamb and, 117, 118, 120, 122, 124–25; romantics and, 1, 33, 41, 42, 113, 118, 120, 129; rooms, 57
Realism: animals on stage, 9, 13, 15–16; Coleridge and, 39, 78–79, 82–83, 84, 85, 86, 90, 91; Hazlitt and, 105, 108; and imagination, 34–35; in nineteenth century, 128, 129, 132–36, 141–44, 150–52, 156, 157–58, 159, 160, 161–62, 163–64
Reinhardt, Max, 115
Renaissance, 2, 12, 15, 60, 173*n*46; Coleridge and, 60, 61, 62, 68, 77; prefaces, 10–11, 166
Restoration: prefaces, 10–11; theaters, 2, 15
Reynolds, John, 12
Reynolds, Sir Joshua, 38–39
Rich, John, 18, 19
Richardson, Alan, 74, 113, 204*n*73
Robertson, Forbes, 150
Robinson, Henry Crabb, 47, 53

Romantics, the, 26, 28, 30, 32, 35, 36, 37, 43; and abstraction, 33, 40, 42, 118; and drama, 74, 80, 130, 131, 136–39, 165; and katharsis, 95, 106; and reading, 1, 33, 41, 42, 113, 118, 120, 129; and senses, 33, 34, 38, 40, 128, 156, 167; and their audience, 95, 96, 113, 135, 136; and their critics, 1, 5, 6, 43, 53, 63–64, 69–70, 95–96, 136–39, 142–43, 144–45, 146–51, 155–57, 159–60, 161, 163
Ross, Marlon B., 156
Rousseau, Jean Jacques, 95, 176*n*5; *Émile*, 44
Rowe, Nicholas, 18, 78, 196*n*17; *Jane Shore*, 13
Royal Shakespeare Company, 165
Ruskin, John, 6, 129, 144, 145–48, 153; "Of Kings' Treasuries," 146
Rymer, Thomas, 3, 27, 30; *The Tragedies of the Last Age*, 30
Saintsbury, George, 95; *A History of English Criticism*, 165; *A History of the French Novel*, 166

Scenery. *See* Theater Scenery
Schiller, Friedrich, 3, 38, 45, 49; *On the Aesthetic Education of Man*, 36–37; "On Epic and Dramatic Poetry," 37; *Wallenstein*, 73
Schlegel, A. W., 84, 101, 183*n*52, 185*n*67, 197*n*19; and abstraction, 33, 41–42; and dramatic illusion, 184*n*64, 185*n*72; *Lectures on Dramatic Art and Literature*, 98, 189*n*6, 190*n*14; and spectacle, 130, 136
Schneider, Elisabeth, 105
Scott, Sir Walter, 97, 129, 185*n*67
Sense Perception, 3, 4, 33, 36; Aristotle and, 33–34; Coleridge and, 38, 48–49, 61, 62, 65, 68, 69, 128, 138; Hazlitt and, 102, 128; Lamb and, 118, 123, 126, 128; Lewes and, 137; Locke and, 48; Plato and, 7, 33; Ruskin and, 147, 148; Shaw and, 150; Shelley and, 156
Shadwell, Thomas, 172*n*44; *The History of Timon of Athens*, 28; *The Humorists, A Comedy*, 22–23
Shakespeare, William, 1, 4, 5, 6, 18, 19, 20, 27, 136, 137, 165, 166; Arnold